Mindfulness for Coaches

Mindfulness for Coaches accessibly presents theory and research on the benefits of mindfulness training and explores how mindfulness can feature in coaching work. Michael Chaskalson and Mark McMordie explain how coaches can use mindfulness to become more deeply attuned to themselves and to clients, and to create transformational resonance.

The authors present a systematic methodology to cultivate and embody a way of being that enables growth and transformation in oneself and in others. The first book of its kind, *Mindfulness for Coaches* provides an experiential guide, inviting and supporting coaches to engage with the programme included, sharing new qualitative research into the potential impact of mindfulness on coaching process and outcomes, and explicitly linking mindfulness practice to global standards of coaching mastery. Presented in two parts, the book first outlines a unique eight-week programme, Mindfulness for coaches, and goes on to clarify the links between mindfulness, coaching mastery and different coaching approaches, share insights from the fields of psychotherapy, leadership and organisation development, and provide guidance for further learning.

Mindfulness for Coaches will be insightful and inspiring reading for coaches in practice and in training, coaching psychologists and academics and students of all coaching modalities.

Michael Chaskalson is the CEO of Mindfulness Works Ltd., a leading provider of mindfulness training in the workplace. With over 40 years of personal mindfulness practice, he taught for many years at Bangor University's Centre for Mindfulness Research and Practice, UK and is a Professor of Practice, Adjunct at Ashridge Executive Education.

Mark McMordie is Director of Coaching for Coachmatch, a global organisational development consultancy. Mark is an ICF accredited executive coach and has been coaching for 15 years. He has also had a personal mindfulness practice for over 10 years and trained as a mindfulness teacher with Bangor University's Centre for Mindfulness Research and Practice, UK.

'As this book demonstrates, mindfulness can transform your coaching. It can punctuate, highlight and lift your attending to the other. It can lead to experiences of great value where you hold your own stillness and quiet observation, in the midst of engagement. It can lead to the near rapture of attending as fully as you can to the other.'

—**Erik de Haan**, *from the Foreword*

'The beating heart of coaching is generative attention. Silken. Serene. Seamless. Michael and Mark understand this. They embody it. And they are offering to us all, eloquently, the knowledge that inhabits it. This book is a coach's long-needed teacher.'

—**Nancy Kline**, *Founder and President of Time To Think*

'I believe mindfulness training should be a vital component of all coach training, and that all coaches would benefit from having a regular mindfulness practice. So this book is the equivalent of music to my ears. Not only very well researched, it's very practical, laying out a clear map to follow for any coach who wants to incorporate mindfulness into their coaching practice, and their lives. If you really want to make a difference, read this book!'

—**Liz Hall**, *Coach, Author of* Mindful Coaching *and Editor of* Coaching at Work

'A must read for any coach committed to personal mastery, *Mindfulness for Coaches* offers us a wonderful route to a truly embodied coaching presence. This is an important book, created with heart, soul and dedication. We – and all those we coach – will benefit from the gifts that it brings.'

—**Trudi Ryan**, *Executive Chair, Coachmatch*

'*Mindfulness for Coaches* weaves together the wisdom of reflection, the beauty of art and years of practical clinical application. The wealth of ideas and practice presented in this illuminating work will be of great benefit and has the power to change individual and collective lives.'

—**Shauna Shapiro, PhD**, *Professor, Santa Clara University, USA; author of* The Art and Science of Mindfulness and Mindful Discipline: Raising an Emotionally Intelligent Child

'The book dovetails beautifully into Gestalt practice with lots of exercises that I'll adopt for myself, my students and coachees. Their explanation brings mindfulness practice to life. It is ideal for coaches to develop self-awareness and inner presence, which deepen their relationship and attunement with their coachees.'

—**John Leary-Joyce**, *Founder, Academy of Executive Coaching and author of* Fertile Void: Gestalt Coaching at Work

'*Mindfulness for Coaches* is an excellent contribution to the coaching literature, offering coaches an *experiential* guide to develop their mindfulness practice, while underpinning the material with links to mindfulness research and examples from the wide experience of these two hugely experienced authors. The book is essential reading for those who want to enhance their presence, focus and ability to be with the client in the present moment.'

—**Professor Jonathan Passmore**, *University of Evora, Portugal and Henley Centre for Coaching and Behavioural Change*

Mindfulness for Coaches
An Experiential Guide

Michael Chaskalson
Mark McMordie

LONDON AND NEW YORK

First published 2018
by Routledge
2 Park Square, Milton Park, Abingdon, Oxon OX14 4RN

and by Routledge
711 Third Avenue, New York, NY 10017

Routledge is an imprint of the Taylor & Francis Group, an informa business

© 2018 Michael Chaskalson and Mark McMordie

The right of Michael Chaskalson and Mark McMordie to be identified as authors of this work has been asserted by them in accordance with sections 77 and 78 of the Copyright, Designs and Patents Act 1988.

All rights reserved. No part of this book may be reprinted or reproduced or utilised in any form or by any electronic, mechanical, or other means, now known or hereafter invented, including photocopying and recording, or in any information storage or retrieval system, without permission in writing from the publishers.

Trademark notice: Product or corporate names may be trademarks or registered trademarks, and are used only for identification and explanation without intent to infringe.

British Library Cataloguing-in-Publication Data
A catalogue record for this book is available from the British Library

Library of Congress Cataloging-in-Publication Data
Names: Chaskalson, Michael, author. | McMordie, Mark, author.
Title: Mindfulness for coaches : an experiential guide / Michael Chaskalson, Mark McMordie.
Description: Abingdon, Oxon ; New York, NY : Routledge, 2018. | Includes index.
Identifiers: LCCN 2017028481 (print) | LCCN 2017040283 (ebook) | ISBN 9781315697307 (Master e-book) | ISBN 9781138841055 (hardback) | ISBN 9781138902688 (pbk.)
Subjects: LCSH: Personal coaching. | Mindfulness (Psychology)
Classification: LCC BF637.P36 (ebook) | LCC BF637.P36 C43 2018 (print) | DDC 158.3 – dc23
LC record available at https://lccn.loc.gov/2017028481

ISBN: 978-1-138-84105-5 (hbk)
ISBN: 978-1-138-90268-8 (pbk)
ISBN: 978-1-315-69730-7 (ebk)

Typeset in Times New Roman
by Florence Production Ltd, Stoodleigh, Devon, UK

For Annette
Michael Chaskalson

For Thay, Kundun, Otis and Zachary
Mark McMordie

Contents

About the authors — xi
Foreword: an awareness of now by Erik de Haan — xiii
Acknowledgements — xviii

Introduction — xx

PART ONE
Mindfulness for coaches: The eight-week programme — 1

1 Session 1: Introducing mindfulness — 3
2 Session 2: Embodiment — 30
3 Session 3: Working with thoughts — 52
4 Session 4: Empathy — 68

PART TWO
Joining the dots — 81

5 Further development — 83
6 Mindfulness and coaching approaches — 107
7 Mindfulness and psychotherapy — 128
8 Mindfulness and coaching mastery — 145
9 Mindfulness, leadership and organisation development — 181

Appendix A: Research methodology — 209
Appendix B: Our mindful coaches — 211

Appendix C: Good practice guidelines for teaching
mindfulness-based courses 213

Further reading 215
Further resources and downloads 217
Index 219

About the authors

Michael is founder and CEO of Mindfulness Works Ltd., a leading provider of mindfulness and mindful leadership programmes to organisations. A pioneer in the application of mindfulness in the workplace and in organisational leadership, he is the author of the agenda-setting book *The Mindful Workplace* (published by Wiley-Blackwell, 2011) and the bestselling *Mindfulness in Eight Weeks* (published by Harper Collins, 2014).

Based on his 40 years of personal practice of mindfulness and related disciplines, Michael now shares his insights and research with audiences worldwide as a keynote speaker, coach, consultant, and teacher. He works with global corporations and public sector organisations, as well as individuals, so that they better understand mindful leadership practices.

Michael has also been a successful social entrepreneur, founding a fair-trade company that came to have annual sales of £10 million and 200 employees. He is a Professor of Practice at Ashridge Executive Education.

Based in Cambridge, UK, Michael can be contacted at michael@mindfulnessworks.com

Mark is Director of Coaching at Coachmatch, a world-class organisational development consultancy delivering sustained culture change, learning, and transformation through vertical leadership development and coaching.

He is an executive coach and mindfulness teacher. Mark has an Advanced Diploma in Executive Coaching and is an accredited executive coach with the International Coach Federation (ICF). He has had a personal mindfulness practice for over 10 years, has been facilitating mindfulness groups since 2009 and trained as a mindfulness teacher at the Centre for Mindfulness Research and Practice at Bangor University. Mark also has a master's degree in Human Resource Development.

As an executive coach Mark works with leaders in a range of well-known brands including Vodafone, Rolls-Royce, Lloyds Banking Group, Burberry and Marks & Spencer. He has also designed and delivered mindfulness interventions in the financial services, media, hospitality and retail sectors.

Mark's executive coaching and leadership development work is deeply informed by his own mindfulness practice, his knowledge of research into the impact of mindfulness, as well as vertical leadership development.

Mark is based in London, UK, and is married with two children. He can be contacted at mark.mcmordie@coachmatch.co.uk

Foreword
An awareness of now

While reading this important book, I've been following my nose – quite literally.

Novels and adventure books set out to take you away from the present moment. This book, on the contrary, invites you arrive in the present moment; to be aware of how you sit, how you read. I decided to enhance this effect by paying attention to my breath as it passed through my nose. I directed my awareness to my breath and then to the next sentence or thought, and then back again, page after page.

That helped me to live and to own one of the key messages of the book – the value of mindful awareness.

Being mindful of the present moment as you read will help you to ask some important questions. Is what you read chiming with what you understand from your own experience of mindfulness right now? Does your sense of self, in this moment, accord with the definition just given? How attentive do you feel in this moment? How kind are you right now? How judgmental, how present? Can I take in this next idea? Can I hold it up lightly to see if it works for me? Am I distracted, do I need a break from reading? Am I glancing over my glasses to others in the room where I sit? And what does that say about me, now? What does it say about my engagement with this book?

Time and time again my mind returned to the same question. Can I read *and* be mindful? Can I take in a new thought *and* stay with where I am? Can I follow how I respond to the message *and* notice how I jump ahead at the same time?

I really struggled to read with self-awareness. Then I noticed my struggle, and brought myself gently back to the task – reading and breathing.

As a result of this dual task, I've been moved by the ideas in the book, and I've practiced with some of them at the same time.

For me, the issue of reading while being mindful has resonance with the issue of coaching whilst being mindful. From one point of view, you might see this a contradiction in terms, even a paradox. Your coaching or reading might take you out of the present moment. Strictly speaking, you might think, you can't both be mindful and deeply attend to a new thought. In all our experiencing, surely we can really only attend to one thing at a time?

That is a profound truth in terms of how the mind works: attention moves serially from one object to another, attention is indivisible, an atom.

On the other hand, that is precisely what creates meaning in this book: your awareness of yourself in your response to the many rich prompts and ideas in the chapters before you.

The cycles of movement of your attention between book and self, as the book changes from quote to quote, interacting with the cycles of movement of attending to the self or self-experience as this changes from breath to breath, is what the task of reading really amounts to.

A captivating novel or drama takes you away from yourself and your current circumstances. It gives you a 'second life' in the story's protagonists. But a good book about mindfulness, business, or coaching, will take you into yourself and within yourself. It will move, inform and ultimately change something in your sense of yourself in your 'first life' as coach, business-person and human being.

If you have read this far in my Foreword, you may think that it's beside the point for me to describe *how* I read this book. Perhaps you think I should rather be commenting on *what* I read – the many intrinsic ideas, statements and qualities of the book. But, I feel strongly that, as the book emphasises again and again, mindfulness is a practice and a process, not a knowledge, tool or achievement.

There's an old Zen Buddhist saying: 'If you meet the Buddha on the road, kill him'. From that perspective, you could ignore all the contents of this book. The really important thing to do is simply to get on with deepening your practice of mindfulness.

I've struggled to integrate reading and mindfulness. It's not something that comes easy, and on many occasions this book has transported me into the rich world of Mark and Michael's experience, taking me out of my awareness of self.

In the same way, I struggle to integrate my own coaching and mindfulness. And that is where this book is very helpful.

Mindfulness meditation is a practice one first of all does by oneself – carving out space and time for it. You assume a 'mindfulness posture', minimise distractions and allow your attention to go fully into yourself – a world away from the busy café where I am now reading this book.

You set the clock, switch your devices off, close your eyes, turn inwards and trust that no-one will come into the room and disturb you. If they do, ideally you would happily but determinedly keep turning inwards, to be with the discomfort of not attending to the other, not responding to the distraction; gently reverting to an almost imperceptible sense of the breath.

Coaching on the other hand is a rare, meaningful, critical, contracted conversation with an 'other', focusing on the other's agenda, goals and actions. Coaching takes attention away from the self and into the other's world. Not just that, coaching sets off a world of response within yourself, and the need to attend to that, as well as actively attending to the person who is putting their trust in you.

Foreword xv

Coaching is not mindfulness meditation. Like reading a gripping book, attending a moving drama performance, or dancing an enthralling, all-consuming dance, coaching involves placing all your attention away from the self and into the care of another and their 'learning objectives', even at times merging your attention with theirs in a co-created relationship that occupies the centre of all your attending.

And yet, as this book demonstrates, mindfulness can transform your coaching. It can punctuate, highlight and lift your attending to the other. It can lead to experiences of great value where you hold your own stillness and quiet observation, in the midst of engagement. It can lead to the near rapture of attending as fully as you can to the other.

I will give two examples from my own coaching conversations earlier today.

The first was a second interview with a senior executive who may choose to work with me as his coach. The arrangement that was in place stipulated that he would speak for half an hour with three coaches, and then make up his mind. A few days ago, the half-hour proved not to be enough. This executive appeared to be very rigorous, conscientious and detailed. He told me about his particular responsibilities in the greatest detail, and then started asking me questions about how I work.

Am I European in outlook, or rather American in terms of my coaching approach? How will I conduct my sessions, what kind of interventions would I employ? And he had questions about confidentiality as well, particularly as someone had suggested that I might write some kind of report about our sessions.

I responded as well as I could, but even the second half-hour today appeared too short for a full understanding to emerge between us.

I tried to be mindful, to notice myself and my breath as I was speaking with him, checking my experience of myself and how I was moved by what was happening. I did not feel I could do anything with what I noticed – and often I did not notice much at all, as I had to answer so many questions. You might say there was very little 'mindfulness' for me.

At the very end of our conversation, he turned to his direct-reports' observations of him, saying 'I think they want someone who jokes with them and practices small-talk. But that is just not me'.

This provided me with an opportunity. Finally, I could give back something I had noticed. Somewhat clumsily, I said, 'You do strike me as a very serious man. Mind you, if I had to select a coach for myself, I would be very serious as well, so I have every understanding . . .'

He confirmed that that was what he was like. People said he was thorough, rigorous, and extremely serious. I think for the first time in the two interviews he felt seen by me, as a human being. And I felt good because here, at the very end, and through an opening that he provided me with, I could bring at least one tiny fruit of mindfulness to my conversation with him.

Another example was earlier in the day, with a female client. She spoke about a conflict she recently had with a colleague, where her colleague referred to a big project they had championed together several years before. My client was extremely emotional, as the remarks of her close colleague had been so unexpected and so scathing. She had not been able to give any sort of response and had left the conversation with a polite excuse. But her legs had been trembling and she had felt that she might faint. She missed out on sleep for many nights following that feedback.

Again, I was following her, listening, captivated and using summaries to stay present in the session. She had already done so much of the thinking, what could I possibly add?

A good hour went by and she seemed grateful and positive about sharing the painful event with another person. It helped her to disentangle her myriad responses and the cocktail of emotions she experienced. I doubted if I was of any help, but I stayed present: listening, and attending to my breath, to my own self-awareness.

Suddenly, perhaps as suddenly as the colleague who had spoken to her, she turned to me and said, 'Please don't tell anyone. The project was business-critical and confidential. Nobody should know about this.'

I looked up and then she caught herself: 'How could I doubt you?' she asked. This made me sit up, even more alert and present – what was that about? I would call this a shared mindful moment. Finally, I said 'What happened there, just now, between us? What made it feel unsafe? . . . And is it similar to how you felt suddenly so unsafe with your trusted colleague?'

After that, new insights emerged.

She sent me an email later to thank me, reassuring me that she did trust me and that the session was a powerful learning for her in her struggles to trust others.

As a coach and mindfulness practitioner, I see myself often more as a goalie than as a monk, sussing out a rare moment in the ninety minutes where the here and now might enter my coaching relationship. Mindfulness and free association are similar: one is the conscious complement of the largely unconscious other – and they are both in a permanent state of recovery in coaching conversations.

Clients, cases, relationships: they all overwhelm us and take us away from our own associations. By being attentive to this, by never giving up the struggle to notice, we can occasionally, but only occasionally, recover our own awareness and as a result have something to offer in our coaching work.

The ancient Eastern practices of Buddhism, and similarly the ancient Greek practices of Skepticism,[1] can help us to stay aware, to keep coming back to fresh, mindful, associative inquiry.

As I write this Foreword now, looking back, I resist the temptation to re-read and I just ponder; catching my breath one more time. I have been rather lost in my rapid writing . . . Coming back to the breath – yes, it is still going past my nostrils, it hasn't lost any of its rhythm. In, out; in, out . . . in the same way as before. I had forgotten about it as I was lost in words, sniffing out words, rather than my own state of mind.

I have been lost in thought and suddenly I notice a mild headache has formed. I don't stay with that, but I return to my breath. In, out; in, out.

There is a temptation, again, to re-read. Was it any good? Can it stand on its own? Is it not too long? Feeling, yearning, almost rushing to go back – can I stop myself, can I just breathe, mindfully?

I notice the sounds around me: the distant barking of dogs, my wife singing, the soft rustling of the wind. And breathing. In, out; in, out.

I feel my defences crumbling, my temples mildly drumming. Soon I will give in to this desire to re-read, to judge, tweak, optimise, and to dread the responses of my readers. Once more the cycles of suffering will take over. But not yet – I will stay with this a little longer . . . in, out; in, out; in, out, in, . . .

Erik de Haan, Director of Ashridge Centre for Coaching and
Professor of Coaching, VU University Amsterdam

Note

1 Read, for example, Sextus Empiricus. See Empiricus, S. (2000) *Sextus Empiricus: Outlines of Scepticism*, Cambridge: Cambridge University Press.

Acknowledgements

This book would not have come together if it were not for the help and support of many people. We are enormously grateful to Susannah Frearson at Routledge for her interest in and patience with this project. We are also indebted to the many teachers who have informed and inspired us over the years and in the current secular context, to the significant influence of Jon Kabat-Zinn, Mark Williams and John Teasdale.

Michael:
To Annette for her love and support while I was writing this and for the past so many years – I am so thankful for that. To Megan Reitz – a wonderful co-researcher on our Mindful Leader programme; to John Teasdale and Ciaran Saunders for endlessly interesting conversations; to Dominic Houlder and Ann Scoular, who encouraged me to work with executive coaches; and to Sally Woodward, Debbie Percy, Gina Hayden, Linda Woolston, Daniel Burke, Des O'Connell and Ruth Sack – innovative pioneers from the first two cohorts of the Mindfulness for Coaches course back in 2006. Who'd have thought it would all turn out like this?

Mark:
Thanks go to my mum and my dad for providing a safe and loving home and an education that has made this book possible. Thank you to my wife Liz for your love and patience through the writing process and for supporting my other dearest love – thank you my darling. I am eternally grateful to Trudi Ryan, Angela Rutterford-Adams, Ben Thomas and the rest of the Coachmatch team – this book is testimony to our purpose of increasing *Success & Happiness* in individuals, organisations and society. I would also like to acknowledge Martin Ryan – I suspect that without him this book would not exist.

Many thanks go to Rosie Hyam for the hours she spent patiently transcribing interview recordings and the twenty-four coaches who gave their precious time to contribute to this book. As with all group inquiry, it was a humbling experience and this book is a reflection of us all. My heartfelt thanks go to three particular coaches who, at different stages, have supported me with this project – to Nancy Kline and your exquisite presence for surfacing my desire to connect with Michael in the first place; to Lisa Pettit for supporting me in the early collaborations with Michael on the Mindfulness for Coaches programmes; and to Lindsay Wittenberg for *being* my Thinking Partner during the writing phase. My thanks also go to Graham Lee for his mindful coaching supervision and the unique support he offers me in my professional work.

My deep gratitude goes to Jane Brendgen and Michael. Thank you Jane for supporting my growth as a mindfulness teacher, for your teaching supervision and your insight about interpersonal mindfulness. Michael – I will be forever grateful for this opportunity and the embodiment of mindfulness that you are. Finally, I wish to express my gratitude to the Heart of London Sangha – you have been the bedrock that has supported the growth of my practice and understanding.

Introduction

Mindfulness is everywhere. Books and apps abound, and news and magazine pieces suggest quick and easy routes to becoming more mindful in just a few moments.

If only it were that easy.

The aim of this book is to help its readers become more mindful coaches. We know from our own experience, and from reports from the coaches and leaders we've worked with over more than 10 years, that mindfulness training and practice can be deeply transformative – for coaches and for their clients. It can powerfully change the way you relate to yourself, to others and to the world you move in.

But the popular journalism which can create the impression that this is a quick and easy win is deeply misleading.

The rapid absorption of the idea of mindfulness into our culture over the past few years has been driven by science. By the close of 2015, over 4,000 scholarly papers had been written on the subject.[1] But what we rarely see in the more popular discussion around mindfulness, is the fact that the very large bulk of the research showing the benefits of mindfulness derives from trials conducted by experienced mindfulness trainers who teach it in a structured way, over usually eight weeks, to participants who engage in home practice of daily formal mindfulness meditation over that period.

So when, for example, Michael is approached by a magazine and asked for his 'six easy tips for having a more mindful Christmas' or when Mark is asked by a client to deliver a 30 minute session that will help to create a more mindful organisation, we sometimes struggle to find an appropriate response.

Mindfulness training can have significant implications for your own development, as a coach and as a person, as well as for development of the leaders you work with and hence the organisations that shape our society. But just as you can't learn to swim by reading all about the physics and dynamics of water, so the only way to really learn about mindfulness is actually to practice it.

For that reason, we begin our book in Part One with an actual eight-week Mindfulness for Coaches course, and we encourage you to get stuck in and to practice – every day for eight weeks. This course is a written-up variant of a course initially developed by Michael in 2006 and which he and Mark between them have delivered to hundreds of coaches since.

Based on what our course participants have told us over the years, we believe that formal mindfulness training and practice makes for more effective coaches – and we include several of our participants' stories later in the book.

Research from the field of psychotherapy suggests that rather than the therapist's preferred process or methodology, the biggest variance in client outcomes results from their way of being with clients.[2,3] In the coaching context, mindfulness training offers the possibility of greater transformational coaching as a result of affecting how we *are*, first of all with ourselves and then in turn with others.

As we hope you will discover through practice – when you bring mindful attention to any system it changes that system. So having explored the theme of mindfulness through intrapersonal practice, in Part Two we go on to explore what it means to bring mindful attention into the coaching relationship. We will share theory and research on the benefits of mindfulness training and explore how mindfulness might feature in coaching work.

But this book is *not* primarily about theory, tools or techniques. It's about how you show up as a coach, how you hold space for your clients to do the work they need to do. It's about your way of being with your clients – how you can more deeply attune to yourself and to them and how that can create transformational resonance.

Fundamentally this book is about how to cultivate and embody a way of being that enables growth and transformation in yourself and others.

Why this book now?

As we've said, mindfulness is everywhere. The UK's National Institute for Health and Clinical Excellence (NICE) recommends mindfulness as a front line intervention for certain conditions[4] and the US Marines have built it into training to support performance in high stress environments.[5] Congressmen Tim Ryan has long been lobbying about its benefits in the US[6] and more recently the UK's Mindfulness All-Party Parliamentary Group published *Mindful Nation UK*, making clear recommendations for health, education, the workplace and the criminal justice systems.[7] Public courses are now widely available as are programmes for schoolchildren, bringing emotional intelligence onto the curriculum in a way that was never available for previous generations.[8]

Increasingly, organisations are also offering mindfulness training, enabling employees to deal better with workplace stress, improve focus and concentration and increase levels of emotional intelligence.[9,10]

In parallel, coaching has also grown significantly over the last 10–15 years, offering individuals and organisations a way to increase resilience, enable growth and maximise performance and potential. As the coaching profession has grown, we have seen professional bodies like the ICF, EMCC and the Association for Coaching establish clear standards and ethics, and guide the development of increasing numbers of coaches in the marketplace. With an increasing supply of well-trained coaches, coaching is no longer simply available to a small number of privileged executives and high potential employees – the idea of coaching for everyone is now a distinct possibility.

Both mindfulness and coaching represent significant forces in optimising human functioning and in releasing human potential. Today, it's not uncommon to hear executives or sportspeople cite their coach as a significant factor in their success. Likewise, it's also not uncommon for executives or sportspeople such as Novak Djokovic[11] to cite mindfulness as a significant factor in their success. In sport and in the corporate world it's increasingly acknowledged that technical training and physical fitness will only take you so far. When you are more skilled at working with your mind and mental states things go better.

What's different about this book?

Mindfulness for Coaches is the first book of its kind to bring the two disciplines of mindfulness and coaching together in an *experiential* guide. What's presented here is a synthesis of over 10 years teaching experience, combined with the latest thinking from the fields of mindfulness, neuroscience, coaching and psychotherapy. Rather than simply discussing mindfulness at an intellectual level or focusing on 'coach interventions' the book provides guidance on the practicalities of developing and sustaining a mindfulness practice, and it shows how this can influence the coaching relationship and outcomes without explicit mindfulness interventions.

The book supports, and invites you, to develop your own personal practice and to notice how this begins to permeate your coaching work. By doing so, it offers you and your clients the opportunity for greater health, well-being and transformational change.

The structure of the book

Part one (Chapters 1 to 4) is based on the eight-week Mindfulness for Coaches programme, with each of the four chapters laying out a module of that course.

If you intend to practice that course, and we sincerely hope that you do, we suggest that you read each of the four chapters in turn at fortnightly intervals – not reading ahead – and that each week you undertake the home practice that we have set for that week. At the end of each of these chapters we have set two different weeks of home practice appropriate to the relevant module of the course.

Part two focuses on *joining the dots* between your own first-hand experience of regular mindfulness practice and other aspects of being a mindful coach.

Chapter 5 focuses on *further development* beyond the eight-week programme. We point to mindfulness and positive emotions as a means to cultivate unconditional positive regard, interpersonal mindfulness as a means to bring mindfulness into relationship, and we also discuss bringing mindful-

Introduction xxiii

ness explicitly into the coaching relationship by teaching it to others. Finally we explore self-compassion as a means of actively promoting mental and emotional well-being and self-care.

In **Chapter 6** we not only clarify overlaps and similarities between mindfulness and a range of coaching approaches, we also explore how mindfulness might support, enrich and deepen the application of these. Specifically, we highlight a Person Centred Approach, Time to Think, Relational Coaching, Gestalt, Cognitive Behavioural Coaching, Inner Game, Transactional Analysis, Psychodynamic and Somatic Coaching, as well as Focusing and Psychosynthesis.

In **Chapter 7** we explore mindfulness and psychotherapy. Since the coaching profession has always been informed by the therapeutic world we look beyond specific psychological approaches to the common factors that seem to matter most in terms of outcomes, and we share the emerging view of mindfulness as advanced therapeutic training. We also point to leading thinkers in the therapeutic field such as Shauna Shapiro, Dan Siegel and Paul Gilbert, who have relevance for the mindful coach.

In **Chapter 8** we orientate back to the world of coaching and propose a view of mindfulness training as advanced coach training. We draw specifically on professional coach competencies associated with coaching mastery and explore how mindfulness might support coach presence, establishing trust and intimacy with the client, active listening and creating awareness amongst others.

Finally, in **Chapter 9** we look at mindfulness within the wider context of leadership and organisation development. Specifically we explore the role mindfulness plays in developing emotional intelligence and vertical leadership development. We also consider a systems perspective, where conscious capitalism and resonant organisations secure long term competitive advantage through an increased capacity for agility, adaptation and change.

Using this book

In **Part one** each chapter includes instructions for a particular set of practices for you to engage in. The practices are cumulative and follow one another in a particular order, building from week to week. Details of downloadable audio materials are provided on p. 217 and if you want to look further into the research we mention there are references at the end of each chapter. If you're using the book as part of a teacher-led programme you'll get the most out of it if you leave any further reading until *after* you have participated in that week's session. Try to avoid reading ahead – it can undermine the effects of the work you'll be doing on the programme itself.

Home practice is essential

With regular mindfulness practice real changes are possible. What's on offer here are tangible changes in your well-being and the way you relate to yourself, others and the world around you and that holds the potential to permeate your coaching relationships and the outcomes you co-create. But like any new habit, establishing a regular practice isn't always a smooth journey. There can be ups and downs and we do tell people engaging in the programme that at first it can be stressful. After all, finding 15 to 20 minutes a day to fit in the practices might not be easy. But much like going to the gym, practice is essential and if you commit to it, real change can follow.

It's also worth bearing in mind that you don't have to try to change yourself. In fact, striving after results can inhibit the process. All you have to do is engage in the practices – again and again and again – and change will emerge. As best you can, put aside any idea of getting them right or doing them perfectly. That striving attitude is perfectly normal, but in this context it just gets in the way. So don't strive to get the practices right – just do them. You're also completely liberated from any obligation to enjoy the practices. Sometimes you might enjoy them, sometimes you might not. That's not the point. You don't need to enjoy them to get the benefit – but you do have to do them.

Become your own laboratory

Our aim here is not to sell you mindfulness or to 'prove the case' for mindfulness and coaching. With so much scientific research available we think it speaks for itself, so we will simply direct you to some of the most relevant pieces and encourage you to draw your own conclusions. However, ultimately you have to do so based on your own personal experience. After all, mindfulness has to be experienced to be truly known. This requires you to become your own laboratory – to test it out for yourself. Don't take our word for it. Be rigorous and become the subject of your own experiment – an eight-week experiment. In one of the earliest pieces of mindfulness research in a corporate environment, Michael Slater, a participant from a high-pressure biotech did just that:

> I doubt dogma and I test it. I do it at the laboratory bench. So this appealed to me because I could feel the reduction in stress. I could tell I was less irritable; I had more capacity to take on more stressors. My wife felt I was easier to be around. So there were tangible impacts. For an empiricist that was enough.[12]

So our invitation is simply to engage with the guided practices for eight weeks and to notice how you are relating to yourself, others and the world around you. Given our shared professional interest in coaching, our invitation also becomes more specific – to notice how you are relating to your coaching clients. To notice your way of being with them and the outcomes you co-create from this. Ultimately this is about how you can more deeply attune to yourself and your clients and how you can create transformational resonance.

By encouraging you to become your own laboratory we are also inviting you to trust your own experience more – to pay more attention to and trust your own felt sense. This represents a movement away from the head into the body – enabling you to trust your felt sense experience moment by moment. We know that within the executive coaching encounter we can often be seduced into 'intellectual sparring' with clients but we also know that this is unlikely to be where the transformation lies. So by encouraging you to become your own laboratory, our intention is to enable you to trust your felt sense experience moment by moment in the coaching encounter and by doing so, inviting your coaching clients to do the same.

Research methodology, inquiry and collective wisdom

Given our intention to produce an experiential guide, we have tried to capture the essence of a typical Mindfulness for Coaches programme – as best we can in written format. Mindfulness-based-programmes usually consist of three core components – psycho-educational input, guided practices and group inquiry.

Psycho-educational input lends itself reasonably well to the written word and we've provided downloads of guided practices for you to practice with at home. However, what is slightly more challenging to recreate is a sense of group inquiry. This is always unique to the participants and the moment by moment experience of each group. In guiding inquiry we simply seek to draw on the experience in the room as the group engages with regular mindfulness practice.

On the Mindfulness for Coaches programme we also invite participants to share their experience of what they are noticing interpersonally with clients as they engage in the eight-week programme. In order to re-create this sense of group inquiry we have sought to assemble a virtual group of mindful coaches to share their experience with you. So in later chapters you will hear from other professional coaches. Contributors had just two things in common – all were professional coaches and all had an established mindfulness practice of some kind, although experience varied. All had been practicing mindfulness regularly for over a year, and for some this stretched over more than 20 years. Likewise, frequency of practice varied – for most this consisted of regular daily practice ranging from 10 minutes to over an hour. All were invited to contribute to the inquiry process by completing a questionnaire and also taking part in an interview, from which we've selected useful quotations. Details of the questionnaire and interview can be found in Appendix A and details of our mindful coaches can be found in Appendix B.

Our intention

Intention is a core aspect of mindfulness. It's fundamental to any project, endeavour or journey.

So before moving into Part one we would like to clarify – our intention in writing this book is to enable you to:

- Develop and sustain your own daily mindfulness practice
- Begin making connections between your personal practice and how this might impact on the coaching relationship and the coaching outcomes you co-create with clients
- Explore further development once you have established a regular mindfulness practice

However, ultimately our intention is to:

- Enable more coaches to develop a personal mindfulness practice in support of their health, well-being, growth and transformation and that of their clients
- Stimulate debate within the coaching profession about the potential that mindfulness training offers as advanced coach training
- Encourage more evidence-based research linking mindfulness training for coaches to shifts in the performance and well-being of professional coaches and the outcomes they co-create with clients

Notes

1. Good, D. *et al.* (2016) 'Contemplating mindfulness at work: an integrative review' *Journal of Management*, 242(1): 114–142.
2. Wampold, B. (2001) *The Great Psychotherapy Debate: Models, Methods, and Findings*, London: Routledge.
3. Norcross, J. and Wampold, B. (2011) 'Evidence-based therapy relationships', *Psychotherapy*, 48(1): 98–102.
4. National Institute for Health and Clinical Excellence (2009) 'Depression in adults: recognition and management', www.nice.org.uk/guidance/cg90.
5. Jha, A. *et al.* (2010) 'Examining the protective effects of mindfulness on working memory capacity and affective experience', *Emotion*, 1: 54–64.
6. Ryan, T. (2013) *A Mindful Nation: How Simple Practice Can Help Us Reduce Stress, Improve Performance, and Recapture the American Spirit*, US: Hay House.
7. The Mindfulness All-Party Parliamentary Group (2015) 'Mindful nation UK', www.themindfulnessinitiative.org.uk/images/reports/Mindfulness-APPG-Report_Mindful-Nation-UK_Oct2015.pdf.
8. https://mindfulnessinschools.org/what-is-b/b-curriculum/
9. The Mindfulness Initiative (2016) 'Building the case for mindfulness in the workplace', http://themindfulnessinitiative.org.uk/images/reports/MI_Building-the-Case_v1.1_Oct16.pdf.
10. Tan, C-M. (2012) *Search Inside Yourself: The Unexpected Path to Achieving Success, Happiness (and World Peace)*, New York: HarperOne.
11. Technology Services Partner (2016) 'Djokovic & the power of mindfulness', www.atpworldtour.com/en/news/djokovicmedia-day-monte-carlo-2016.
12. Hall, S. (2003) 'Is Buddhism good for your health?', *New York Times Magazine* (14th September), www.nytimes.com/2003/09/14/magazine/is-buddhism-good-for-your-health.html.

Part one
Mindfulness for coaches
The eight-week programme

1 Session 1
Introducing mindfulness

What is mindfulness?

Definitions and history

So far as we know, the Buddha – who lived 2,600 years ago – was the first person in history to talk about mindfulness, and for thousands of years the practices associated with it were confined to small groups of elite monastics living in Asian Buddhist monasteries. Now, suddenly, it has erupted into the mainstream of life in Europe and North America.

How did mindfulness – a way of continuously paying attention to your immediate experience with care and discernment – make the journey from those Asian monasteries into the hospitals, consulting rooms, boardrooms, and barracks where we sometimes find it today?

A key figure in the story is Jon Kabat-Zinn who, in the late 1970s was working as a molecular biologist at a teaching hospital near Boston where he was preoccupied by two problems. The first of these was his concern for what the hospital system was offering those patients it couldn't fully cure. In conversation with physician colleagues, he concluded that perhaps only 20 per cent of patients were leaving the hospital *without* the suffering that had brought them there in the first place. What, he wondered, was the system doing for the other 80 per cent? Not much at all, he discovered, and this bothered him.

The second question that bothered him is a variant on one that often comes to the coaching room. 'What is my purpose in life? What can I do to earn my living that fires me up so much that I'd actually pay to do it?'

Kabat-Zinn was a meditator and both questions resolved themselves in an epiphany moment that occurred while on a meditation retreat. During a session of meditation, he suddenly realised that the way he was learning on that retreat to work with his mind and mental states would be profoundly valuable to those whom the hospital system was unable to cure. In the same moment, he realised that it would be possible to present the ideas and methods he was using to people in a way that was shorn of all the 'religious' ideas usually associated with it. One could develop a fully secular approach that was completely available to people of all religious beliefs, or none. He imagined hundreds of hospitals around the United States having specialist clinics where the ideas and practices of mindfulness could be taught. That was a vision that has more than come to pass.

After persuading the hospital authorities to give them some space in a basement, Kabat-Zinn and his colleagues set about devising what came in time to be known as the eight-week Mindfulness-Based Stress Reduction programme (MBSR). They researched the outcomes of their programme and it soon became clear that it was effective in helping patients to address issues like stress and chronic pain. What is more, biological changes started to show up in their research. They found that those patients with psoriasis who undertook the programme in conjunction with the high frequency UV light treatment that they were having at the hospital had rates of clear-up 50 per cent faster than those who didn't take the programme. The way in which they were training their minds was impacting on what was showing up in their bodies.

This was one of the starting points in a body of neurobiological research into the effects of mindfulness on the brain and the nervous system in general and compelling data has begun to emerge from that.

Studies have shown correlations between eight weeks of mindfulness training and increased cortical thickness[1] and between similar training and increased brain grey-matter density in areas associated with sustained attention, emotional regulation and perspective taking.[2] Other studies show decreased levels of amygdala activation after the training.[3] The amygdala is a key component in the brain's threat-detection system – when it is less active you feel more at ease with yourself and others. Another study correlates eight weeks of mindfulness training with increased activity in the left prefrontal cortex and reduced activity in the right prefrontal cortex.[4] The ratio of left to right prefrontal activation is a good predictor of overall happiness and well-being – if the left prefrontal is more active then you're likely to experience higher levels of well-being.

A study carried out with a cohort of US Marines showed that, compared to a control group, those Marines who participated in eight weeks of mindfulness training experienced an increase in their working-memory capacity.[5] Working memory is the system that actively holds information in the mind, to do tasks such as reasoning and comprehension, and to make that information available for further processing. Measures of working-memory capacity are strongly related to success in the performance of complex cognitive tasks. It is a key component in emotion regulation and it is reduced by acute or chronic stress.

We'll refer to these and other studies in more detail later in the book. For now, there is another turn in the story of the uptake of mindfulness that needs to be told.

In the late 1990s, a group of clinical psychologists – John Teasdale, Mark Williams and Zindel Segal – were commissioned to develop an economically affordable group-based treatment for relapsing depression.[6] Significant depression is hugely disabling. Besides the emotional pain they experience, people who are depressed also experience levels of functional impairment comparable to those found in major medical illnesses such as cancer and coronary heart disease. The World Health Organization suggests that of all diseases, depression will impose the second-largest burden of ill health worldwide by the year 2020.[7]

Roughly one in ten people in Europe and North America will experience serious depression at some point in their lives and in some parts of the population that is more like one in four. When people have had three or more serious episodes of depression there is a 67 per cent chance that their depression will relapse.[8]

In the early 1990s, the two treatments that evidence suggested were the most effective in treating people with relapsing depression were one-to-one cognitive behaviour therapy (CBT) or maintenance doses of antidepressants. Both are relatively expensive; not everyone is comfortable taking drugs and they can have unwanted side effects; and not everyone can have one-to-one CBT due to the limited availability of trained therapists.

One of the significant drivers of depression is a persistent pattern of negative ruminative thought that can become established in the mind in ways that can quickly tip people who are vulnerable to it from moments of sadness into deep troughs of disabling depression. The capacity to disengage from such thoughts, and to see them as 'just thoughts', can be a key component in helping people to stay well after depression.

While they were looking for a group-based way to help previously depressed patients to step away from that downward spiral, John Teasdale – who had long had a personal interest in meditation – was reminded of a Buddhist talk he had attended several years before where the speaker stressed that it is not your experience itself that makes you unhappy – it is your *relationship* to that experience. A central aspect of mindfulness meditation training is that you learn – among other things – to relate to your thoughts just as thoughts. In other words, you learn to see them just as mental events, rather than as 'the truth' or 'me'. John recognised that this way of 'decentering' from negative thoughts, standing ever so slightly apart from them and witnessing them as an *aspect* of experience rather than being completely immersed in them, as the whole of experience, might be a key.

Looking further into this, they came upon this piece from one of Kabat-Zinn's books:

> It is remarkable how liberating it feels to be able to see that your thoughts are just thoughts and that they are not 'you' or 'reality' ... The simple act of recognising your thoughts as *thoughts* can free you from the distorted reality they often create and allow for more clear-sightedness and a greater sense of manageability in your life.[9]

They contacted Kabat-Zinn and, based largely upon his MBSR programme, they formulated their own eight-week Mindfulness-Based Cognitive Therapy

(MBCT) programme. Although similar to MBSR in many ways, MBCT contains elements of cognitive therapy and theory that address the specific vulnerabilities and exacerbating factors that make depression recurrent.

Eight weeks of training in MBCT has been shown to be at least as effective as maintenance doses of anti-depressants in helping people to stay well after depression[10] and NICE – The UK's National Institute for Health and Clinical Excellence, which advises the country's National Health Service on appropriate treatments – recommends it as a frontline treatment for relapsing depression.

This growing body of evidence has driven the rapid spread of secular mindfulness training across a broad range of social sectors in Europe and North America.

One downside of the current enthusiasm for mindfulness is that the way the word is used can sometimes be blurred – at times quite literally. At the launch party for another book on mindful coaching, a coach who had dipped perhaps too deep into the wine that was freely on offer came up to us and slurred 'Oh yes, mindfulness, everyone wants mindfulness these days. I just keep doing what I've always done with my clients – but these days I call it mindfulness.' And that really won't do. At best, it is confused or self-deluded. At worst, it is plain deceitful.

So, what exactly is mindfulness? Perhaps the simplest description is that it's a way of being aware of yourself, others and the world around you. But maybe that doesn't convey quite enough and although scholars and researchers haven't yet settled on a single all-purpose definition of the term, and perhaps may never do so, a brief look at its early Buddhist usage might give a clearer sense of what it actually means.

The language that the Buddha spoke has died out but his teachings were preserved in two other ancient Indian languages – Pali and Sanskrit – and in Pali, the compound term *sati-sampajañña* describes much of what we mean when mindfulness is discussed in contemporary therapeutic and organisational contexts.

Sati – the first part of that compound, has connotations of remembering; 'it is due to the presence of *sati* that one is able to remember what is otherwise only too easily forgotten: the present moment.'[11] In the late nineteenth century the Pali translator and lexicographer T.W. Rhys Davids rendered *sati* as 'mindfulness' and the term has stuck ever since. But mindfulness, as we use the term in this book and as it's used in clinical and other contexts these days, means more than *sati* – more than just remembering to pay attention. Thus, the second part of the compound – *sampajañña* – which means something like 'clarity of consciousness' or 'clear comprehension'.[12] *Sati-sampajañña* has been spoken of as 'remembering to pay attention to what is occurring in your immediate experience with care and discernment'[13] and that seems to capture much of what is spoken about in the general literature around secular mindfulness training.

Another widely used description of mindfulness is Kabat-Zinn's,[14] who speaks of it as a quality of awareness that arises from paying attention: on purpose, in the present moment and non-judgmentally. By looking at some of the component parts of that description we may come to a deeper understanding of what mindfulness is all about.

To begin with, there is the area of intentionality. When you're mindful, you pay attention 'on purpose'. Much of the time our attention wanders. You set out to read a book and very soon you find your attention drawn away from it. You might hear a sound outside the window and that catches your attention for a time. Is that a fire-engine or an ambulance? For some reason, you need to find out. Or you suddenly feel an urge to check your email, and you reach for your smartphone. Or you wonder whether reading is really what you ought to be doing right now – wouldn't preparing for a client call that's coming up be more interesting . . . and so on. Our attention is much less stable and we use it much less purposively than we sometimes think.

When we're mindful, on the other hand, we *choose* to pay attention and we maintain that purpose – at least to some extent.

When we teach mindfulness to coaches, we often hear from our course participants early on in the first class that naturally they give their full and undivided attention to their clients. Of course, they think, it's what experienced coaches do. But by the time we come to the end of the class, and the participants have done some of the exercises we'll be describing later in this chapter, that story begins to change as the participants experience for themselves how unstable their attention really is. Minds wander, and the impression we have of maintaining a stable attention in a coaching, or any other context, usually comes about because we haven't paid sufficiently close attention to what our minds are actually doing in any given moment.

When we're mindful, we pay attention on purpose and we keep our attention in the present moment. Ordinarily, even when you're ostensibly listening to a client, your attention may skip for a moment – to thoughts about a meal you need to shop for, or to a comment that another client made last week, or to an intervention you might like to try in a few moments, or to something happening in your family tomorrow. We're rarely present-moment-centred for a continuous stretch of time.

We spend a lot of our time thinking about what is *not* going on around us: contemplating events that happened in the past, might happen in the future, or will never happen at all.

Killingsworth and Gilbert,[15] suggest that this 'stimulus-independent thought' may be the brain's default mode of operation – an evolutionary achievement that allows us to learn, reason and plan. But this can come at a high emotional cost. They conducted a study that used an iPhone app to randomly ask a sample of 2,250 adults in the United States a happiness question such as 'How are you feeling right now?' They were asked to rate that question on a scale of 0 (really bad) to 100 (very good). At the same time, they were asked an activity question 'What are you doing right now?' choosing from a list of twenty-two basic activities. They were also asked a mind-wandering question – 'Are you thinking about something other than what you're currently doing?' Their analyses of the answers revealed three facts –

Firstly, that people's minds wandered frequently, regardless of what they were doing. In fact, mind wandering occurred in nearly half the samples and in at least 30 per cent of the samples taken during every activity except making love. Then, they found that people were less happy when their minds were wandering than when they were not, and that was true for all activities – whether the activity itself was enjoyable or not. Finally, they found that what people were thinking was a better predictor of their happiness than what they were actually doing – irrespective of the activity.

'A human mind' they concluded 'is a wandering mind, and a wandering mind is an unhappy mind. The ability to think about what is not happening is a cognitive achievement that comes at an emotional cost' (p. 932).[16]

Mindfulness training helps people to pay attention on purpose and in the present moment – and that may go some way to increasing their happiness.

The final part of Kabat-Zinn's definition of mindfulness is that it is 'non-judgemental'. This is not to say that we don't make judgements when we're mindful, or that we stop discerning what is appropriate at any time from what is inappropriate. That would be foolish. But the built-in thesaurus in Microsoft Word gives these synonyms for 'judgemental': critical, hypercritical, condemnatory, negative, disapproving, disparaging, pejorative – and that points to what is meant here. The non-judgemental attitude of mindfulness is non-prejudicial. It is not disparaging, pejorative or condemnatory.

There is a wisdom dimension to this and there is a compassion dimension.

The wisdom dimension involves letting what *is* the case *be* the case.

'They shouldn't be like that!' 'It shouldn't be like this!' 'I ought to be somehow different' . . . We can put huge amounts of mental and emotional energy into refusing to allow things to be simply as they are. But things really only ever are as they actually are. Whether right or wrong, just or unjust, desirable or undesirable – things are as they are.

Counter-intuitively, it's only when we can accept that things are as they are that choice opens up for us. When we let what is the case, be the case, then we can begin to choose how to respond to it. What shall we do about what's showed up right now? What would be the most appropriate next step for us and for the situation as a whole? When we can't let what is the case, be the case, then we're stuck – rooted in a defensive posture of denial that closes down the possibility of a more creative engagement with whatever is going on. The wisdom element in the non-judgemental attitude of mindfulness, on the other hand, opens up the possibility for a more creative response to the situation, allowing for more creative choices.

With the compassion dimension to the non-judgemental attitude of mindfulness, to some extent at least, we still our inner critical voice. For much of the time many of us run an inner critical commentary on our experience. Sometimes that commentary can be directed at ourselves – 'I'm not good enough.' 'I don't measure up.'

We're not thin enough, good-looking enough, smart enough, fit enough, strong enough, witty enough, rich enough, clever enough, fast enough, enough enough . . .

Sometimes we turn that inner critical commentary on others – on their appearance, their intelligence, their emotional appropriateness and so on. Or we can run critical commentaries on our immediate environment – somehow or other, in one way or another, things just aren't what they should be. Nothing, ourselves included, is quite right.

The compassion dimension to the non-judgemental attitude of mindfulness allows us to rest simply with things as they are – at least to some extent. We allow ourselves to be ourselves, we allow others to be who they are, and we rest a little bit more at ease with life as it actually is – with a bit more kindness towards ourselves, others and the world around us.

The quality of acceptance that emerges from mindfulness training isn't simple passivity. You don't passively let the world roll over you and you don't stop making ethical judgements when you're more mindful – far from it. Mindfulness training may even enable you to be more appropriately assertive, sharpening your capacity for drawing ethical distinctions. But all of this can be done with wisdom and with kindness. With mindfulness training you begin to develop a greater capacity to allow what is the case to be the case and to respond skilfully and appropriately with a warm open-heartedness.

The benefits of mindfulness training

The UK's Mental Health Foundation published a report in 2010[17] that examined the health benefits of mindfulness training. The report noted that evidence coming from mindfulness and well-being research shows that mindfulness confers significant benefits on health, well-being and quality of life in general. According to the report, people who are more mindful are less likely to experience psychological distress, including depression and anxiety.

- They are less neurotic, more extroverted and report greater well-being and life satisfaction.
- They have greater awareness, understanding and acceptance of their emotions, and recover from bad moods more quickly.
- They have less frequent negative thoughts and are more able to let them go when they arise.
- They have higher, more stable self-esteem that is less dependent on external factors.
- They enjoy more satisfying relationships, are better at communicating and are less troubled by relationship conflict, as well as less likely to think negatively of their partners as a result of conflict.
- Mindfulness is correlated with emotional intelligence, which itself has been associated with good social skills, ability to cooperate and ability to see another person's perspective.

- People who are mindful are also less likely to react defensively or aggressively when they feel threatened. Mindfulness seems to increase self-awareness, and is associated with greater vitality.
- Being more mindful is linked with higher success in reaching academic and personal goals.
- Practising meditation has repeatedly been shown to improve people's attention, as well as improve job performance, productivity and satisfaction, and to enable better relationships with colleagues, resulting in a reduction of work-related stress.
- People who are mindful feel more in control of their behaviour and are more able to override, or change internal thoughts and feelings and resist acting on impulse.
- Meditation practices more generally have been shown to increase blood flow, reduce blood pressure and protect people at risk of developing hypertension; they have also been shown to reduce the risk of developing and dying from cardiovascular disease, and to reduce the severity of cardiovascular disease when it does arise.
- People who meditate have fewer hospital admissions for heart disease, cancer and infectious diseases, and visit their doctor half as often as people who don't meditate.
- Mindfulness can reduce addictive behaviour, and meditation practices generally have been found to help reduce use of illegal drugs, prescribed medication, alcohol and caffeine.

The foundations of practice

There are very good reasons for coaches to take up a mindfulness practice and this brings us to a crucial point – the idea of *practice*. Mindfulness emerges as a result of engaging in mindfulness practice. Just as we can talk about physical fitness as a set of capacities that emerge when you engage in physical activities over time, so mindfulness is a set of capacities that emerge when you engage in mental training over time. Just as no amount of reading about physical exercise and its benefits will increase your fitness, simply reading about mindfulness will do nothing to increase your level of it. You need to practice – regularly and over time.

We don't know exactly how much practice you need to do to get the positive benefits of mindfulness training. Individuals vary and the evidence from research isn't clear. But there is some evidence that the outcomes one might expect will depend on the extent of input.[18] There is evidence from the study done with a cohort of US Marines, referred to earlier, that those who did more than 12 minutes of formal practice per day over eight weeks had an increase in working memory capacity – even though they were doing the course under high stress conditions. Whereas those who did less than 12 minutes of practice a day found their working memory capacity degraded by that stress.[19]

Although the evidence itself is not yet unequivocal, our own lived experience of mindfulness leads us to assert that more practice over longer periods of time yields more significant outcomes – as one might intuitively expect.

For the purposes of the course laid out in this book we have chosen to set 20 minutes of home practice each day for 6 days of each week that the course runs.

Anecdotal evidence from the many coaches who have taken the course with us suggests that if you do that regularly you can expect meaningful outcomes in just eight weeks. But there's a caveat – and one that can seem counter to many of the approaches that the coaches who read this book will be used to. When it comes to mindfulness practice, goal-orientation can be self-defeating.

Mindfulness is an emergent capacity and how and when whatever emerges actually emerges is very much down to the individual and his or her history and circumstances. It's going to be different for everyone and the process of continually checking yourself for progress can be like continually digging up a young seedling to see whether the roots are developing as they should. It's easy to fall into a striving, slightly wilful attitude to practice that is counter-productive.

Our strong advice is that you put all thoughts of progress aside and, instead of setting yourself any goals and desired outcomes, just establish the intention to practice every day. When you slip away from that intention, as many people naturally do, just acknowledge that and come back to the intention once more.

Conscious choice – coming out of automatic pilot

The first meditation we'll do on this course is an eating meditation. But we're not going to eat very much – in fact we'll eat just one raisin. And we hope that by eating one raisin mindfully you'll get a much more experiential sense of what mindfulness is all about.

To do this exercise, get hold of a raisin or a small section of fruit or a piece of a vegetable that you'll be happy to eat, find somewhere quiet where you can sit uninterrupted for 10 or 15 minutes and follow the instructions below:

The raisin exercise

Our first meditation on the Mindfulness for Coaches course is always an eating meditation. We give everyone a single raisin and invite them to eat it mindfully – and we guide that in some detail. In some circles this meditation has become something of a cliché, but we continue to use it as it's so enormously helpful in illuminating much of what we mean when we talk about mindfulness.

You might want to do that exercise now. If so, get yourself a single raisin or a small piece of any fruit or vegetable that you'd be happy to eat; put aside 10 minutes or so and follow the audio guidance from Track 1 'The Raisin Exercise'.

There's no predicting what you will find when you do this exercise. We're all different and we all come to the process with our own unique histories and ways of seeing. What's important here is that you allow your experience of doing that exercise simply to be what it was – there is no right or wrong way of doing it. The key issue is to notice and reflect on what you actually experienced.

What was it like, in detail, for you?

Perhaps spend a few moments now turning the experience over in your mind. What did you notice as you went through the exercise? If nothing much comes to mind, here are some things you might want to consider:

- What struck you most about the exercise?
- How did the raisin feel on your palm?
- What did you notice as you examined its colour and shape?
- What did you notice when you explored it with your fingers?
- And when you looked at it more closely?
- Was there any aroma? What was that like?
- How did it feel in your mouth?
- Were you aware of any impulses as the raisin sat between your back teeth *before* you began to bite and chew?
- If there were, what was it like to sit with an impulse and not act on it?
- What was the first bite like?
- And the second?
- How did it sound as you chewed?
- How did it taste?
- What did it feel like, eating a raisin so slowly?
- Anything else?

This isn't an exercise in trying to *remember* the details of the exercise. It's more about just noticing what you noticed.

When we do this exercise with coaches on a group-based course we hear back all kinds of things that participants may have noticed as if for the first time. People tell us that they had never noticed before what a raisin felt like on the palm or between the fingers or in the mouth. That they'd forgotten what one smelled like (and often that it brought back Proustian memories of family Christmases or grandmother's baking) and that they'd never been aware before how the second bite tasted different to the first, or how noisy a raisin might seem.

Some people find the experience deeply enjoyable. 'I never knew what a raisin tasted like before!' Others find it unpleasant: 'I thought I enjoyed raisins, but actually I discovered that I really hate the taste of them – the skin was really bitter. I just never noticed that before.' Sometimes people say the opposite: 'I don't like raisins, and I wasn't looking forward to this at all, but that wasn't bad at all. In fact I quite liked it.'

Some people find that their mind just keeps wandering off to think of other things – maybe things sparked off by elements of the experience. Some people find that they don't experience very much at all.

We have such different experiences – some pleasant, some unpleasant. But whether it's pleasant or unpleasant, whether there's a lot of experience or very little, whether you stayed focused on the experience or your mind kept wandering off is neither here nor there in this context. This exercise is just about *noticing* what you experienced.

Over and again we hear back from people that their ordinary experience of eating raisins – sometimes by the handful – is that they do it automatically and most often while also doing other things: watching television, driving in their car, working at their desk.

We all have a hugely developed capacity to do things automatically and this is a great thing, although – as we'll see – there are downsides.

Have you ever driven 30 miles down a motorway and then asked yourself 'how did I get here?' Isn't that extraordinary? You drove 30 miles down a road, a highly complex and potentially lethal task, and all the time you were hardly conscious of doing that. Perhaps you were thinking of a client you saw last week and some of the details of her case, or maybe you were wondering about the holiday you need to book this week before the best places are taken, or maybe you were planning a shopping list for a meal you were going to cook that night and almost certainly you were reviewing your to-do list . . . and all the time there were powerful trucks thundering along right next to you, other cars hurtling past on the other side. The slightest twitch of your steering wheel in one direction or another and you'd cause carnage and mayhem – and it generally doesn't happen.

Human beings have an extraordinary capacity to do things on automatic pilot.

When you think back to the first few times you drove yourself in a car it's highly unlikely that you'd have had the ability to do that. Which is the brake, where is the accelerator, how do you use a clutch, where are the indicators? You certainly wouldn't have had the ability even to carry on a simple conversation about the weather while trying to turn a right-hand corner in traffic – let alone plan a coaching session. But soon you automated the process and now you can drive 30 miles down a busy motorway hardly conscious that you're there at all.

That capacity for automaticity is a great thing because we use far fewer brain resources when we do things automatically. It seems to be energy efficient. That's great. The trouble is that as we come to do more and more things automatically, it can also seem that we're hardly alive.

When we're on automatic we miss things.

Some of what we miss is inconsequential, of course, but some of it could give you a real boost to your day. The unique and surprising pattern of clouds in the sky as you're travelling between clients; the sense of well-being that comes from a healthy body walking on a warm day; the smile on a newspaper vendors face as he hands a paper to a customer . . . all of these are so easily missed and all can boost your mood. Some of what we miss is more crucial. That catch in your partner's voice that might have told you that they're struggling with something and can't articulate it yet – but you missed it as you were getting ready for your day. The tone of voice that your child uses over breakfast that might tell you they're being bullied at school and don't know how to talk about it at home. But you missed it because you were reviewing your to-do list while doing 'family breakfast on automatic pilot' – just as you have so many times before. That glance in a client's eye that might have revealed key information that you missed as the conversation unfolded as it has so many times before – and as you listened on automatic to a story you've heard so often . . .

What is more, when we're on automatic we're much more likely to find ourselves running one or another unhelpful automatic routine. Our lives, after all, consist of an enormous number of automatic routines. We all have hundreds – maybe thousands – of these. When I arrive at my desk in the morning, for example, I just sit down, boot my computer, navigate to my email and check my morning's mail, look at my appointments for the day, make my to-do list and so on – and it's all stuff I do pretty much automatically. I don't enter my office with a slight undertow of anxiety – 'It's a working day. How shall I handle that? Hmm . . . I know, I should switch on my computer. Good idea. Computer. Boot, password . . . Great! Now what? Hmmm . . . I know – email. That's a good idea. Email. Click on the mail icon. Great! Now what? Hmmm . . . Respond to mail . . . No. Better . . . to-do list. Yes, great, to-do list. No . . . calendar . . . First check calendar . . .etc. etc.'

Some of these automatic routines are connected with actions and behaviours, like the one above, and some are connected with patterns of thinking and feeling. Some of the latter can give us an unduly hard time.

In the course of our growing up we've all at some point taken on-board a mixture of helpful and unhelpful automatic routines. For example, some of us may be familiar with the 'I'm not really good enough' automatic routine. At some point in our upbringing this one somehow got embedded by teachers, friends, care-givers or whoever – perhaps even thinking that what they were offering was all in our best interests. But whatever the motive and whatever the means, there may be strong traces in our psyches that somehow or other we don't really come up to scratch. We're never quite good enough. So, you may be about to deliver a presentation to a group of thirty senior leaders in any organisation and somewhere in the back of your mind there's a routine running that whispers – or maybe even shouts – the message that this isn't going to go very well, that you've not put in enough preparation time, that they're not going to like it and so on. Routines like that can run with little bearing on the actual truth of the matter in hand. They're just legacy automatic routines.

The really great thing, however, is that you can't be mindful and automatic at the same time. When you're mindful, as people discover on our courses, especially when you're mindful of the body, you're *not* running on automatic – and that can change everything. Unhelpful, negative automatic routines seriously undermine one's well-being. Mindfulness can help to counter that.

Perhaps most of all, although it can be really valuable to do some things on automatic, like driving a car, a life lived fully automatically is barely a human life at all. After all, our life is finite. We have this moment, and the next moment and the next moment and the next. Moment after moment. But eventually, for all of us, those moments run out. Eventually we die. What a tragedy it will be to arrive at our last moment and to realise that we hardly showed up for the moments that went before – that we lived our lives on automatic, preoccupied over and again with our emails, to-do lists and smartphones, barely aware of the people and world around us, hardly aware of our own thoughts, feelings, sensations and impulses.

We can all come out of automatic more of the time. We all have the innate ability to step out of automatic more frequently and more at will. That is a capacity that can be trained and the whole aim of mindfulness training is to enhance that. One very effective way of doing that is by way of mindfulness meditation.

There's some confusion in our culture around these terms 'mindfulness' and 'meditation'. Their meanings tend to blur. People say things like – 'I'm going off to do my mindfulness' when what they mean is that they're going off to meditate. Or the term 'mindfulness' is used indiscriminately to describe a whole host of different approaches to meditation.

We've already discussed the word 'mindfulness'. It refers to a quality of awareness of yourself, others and the world around you that is present-centred, open, intentional, curious and kind. 'Mindfulness meditation', on the other hand, refers to those formal meditation practices that are consciously intended to develop and enhance the capacity for mindfulness.

Not all forms of meditation are mindfulness meditations. There are meditations that are designed to enhance your faith and devotion, for example, such as meditations on a Hindu deity or contemplations of the Madonna. There are meditations that are designed to develop particular emotional states such as loving-kindness, or compassion, or delight in the happiness of others, or equanimity. There are meditations that set out to dwell in the ultimate nature of reality. And no doubt there are many, many more. Each of these meditation practices has its own goals and intentions. The intention of mindfulness meditation is simply to enhance mindfulness – nothing more.

One of the simplest of these, and one which we'll return to over and again as the course unfolds, is the mindfulness of breathing meditation, to which we turn next.

Mindfulness of the breath

Our emotions change the way we breathe and the way we breathe can also change our emotions. You find yourself breathing quite short breaths, you realise that you're tense, pause – take a few more deliberate in-breaths and out-breaths – and you become a bit calmer.

The breath can be an emotional barometer. It can help you to read the quality of your inner weather and it can help you to regulate your emotions. Mindfulness practices often begin by tuning in to the breath. Practising in that way, you begin to notice how your breath changes in relation to your moods, emotions, thoughts and activity. This isn't about controlling the breath. It's just about being more aware of it, more interested in what it's up to, there in the background.

That can help you to relax tensions when you need to, or to focus more sharply when that's called for.

With the 'mindfulness of breathing' meditation, you settle into a comfortable meditation posture and after calming and tuning in to the body, you allow your attention to settle on the breath. With each in-breath and each out-breath.

What people find as they begin to practice is that their minds wander – it's just what minds do. So each time you become aware that your mind has wandered away from the breath, you simply notice where it went to and then gently and kindly return your attention to the breath.

The idea here is to cultivate a warm and friendly interest in the quality of each breath. Each breath is unique and, without forcing this in any way, begin to notice that and to allow your attention to rest with the breath.

That's all there is to it.

Before going into the practice in more detail, a word about posture. On our public courses and in the work we do teaching mindfulness in organisations, we meditate sitting in chairs. Nothing special is needed to do that. The main thing is to find a posture that works for you. One that is comfortable, alert and dignified – and which takes the limits of your body into account.

When meditating in a chair, it's best to choose one that is more or less upright. An office chair, which can be adjusted for height and seat angle, can be a good choice, as is a dining or kitchen chair.

Let your back become more or less upright. Not stiff or stretched – just gently rising up from the seat. You could come away from the support of the backrest, or use it if you prefer, but in any case allow the back to rise up, comfortably. Allow your hands to rest where they feel most comfortable – on your thighs or in your lap. It can be good to adopt a more or less symmetrical posture if that's comfortable for you. That can encourage an attitude of wakefulness and poise.

Take the time to experiment and make adjustments until you find the posture that works best for you. When it comes to human beings with human bodies, though, there's always a limit. There is no perfect posture that eliminates the discomforts that come from having a body in the first place. That's just how it is, so find a posture that's more or less workable, find what comfort you can, and see what it's like to rest in acceptance of whatever is left over.

'Mindfulness of breathing' meditation

If you're able to set aside another 10 or so minutes for practice right now, you might want to try the 'mindfulness of breathing' meditation – Track 4 of the audio guidance. Just find somewhere where you can adopt the posture discussed above, somewhere relatively quiet and where you'll be undisturbed, and follow the instruction on that track.

Remembering and forgetting

You set out to do a practice like the 'mindfulness of breathing' meditation with the intention of paying attention to the breath with an attitude of gentle kindliness towards whatever you experience.

There are three key terms here: intention, attention and attitude. We forget each of these and then we remember them. Then we forget. Then we remember. Over and over.

Here's how it goes.

We're given an instruction . . .

Follow the breath . . .

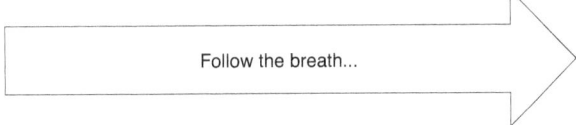

And because of how we've grown up, most of us will set out to 'get that right!'

Most of our learning to date has carried with it the implicit assumption that there is always a right way and a wrong way of doing things. There is a right way to spell and a right way to add figures. A right way to hold your knife and fork and a right way to taste wine. Right ways and wrong ways – thousands of them.

So, when you're given an instruction in meditation, such as 'follow the breath', it's only natural to think that there is a right way of doing this. If you can keep your attention with the breath – in the case of the illustration above, within the bandwidth indicated by the shading inside the arrow – then you're 'doing it right'. And whenever your attention wanders outside that bandwidth, then you're 'getting it wrong'.

But here's what actually happens to almost everyone when they first engage with this practice.

Your attention wanders off on a journey of its own . . .

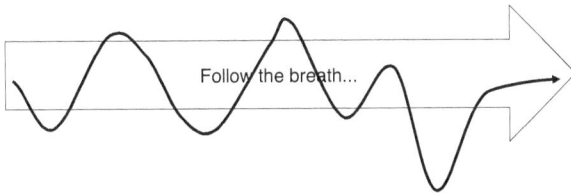

What happens to almost everyone who does this is that very quickly you forget to meditate. You forget, and you go off on another journey, and then you remember – and you come back to the meditation: over and over. This forgetting and remembering takes place over three domains:

1) You forget and remember your intention

You set out to meditate with the *intention* of paying attention to the breath for maybe 10 minutes. You stay with that intention for two or three breaths and then you forget it.

'Oh,' you might unconsciously think 'here's a bit of empty space. Why don't I do some planning?' So you plan and you plan and you plan . . . And then you remember your intention to meditate and you come back to the breath again.

Soon, though, you forget that intention again and instead you decide to give yourself a little treat and you start to dream: 'Hmmm . . . If I won the lottery . . . what would I spend the money on . . .?' So you dream and you dream and you dream . . . And then you remember your intention, you come out of the dream and come back to the meditation.

Then you forget your intention to meditate and begin to nod off. You settle into a half-doze and go with that for a while, and you doze and you doze and you doze . . . And then you remember your intention to meditate, you straighten up, perhaps, maybe half open your eyes, and come back to the meditation.

Over and over – you forget and remember your intention to meditate.

2) You forget and remember to pay attention

You set out to pay attention to the breath and you do that for two breaths, three breaths, maybe even four breaths . . . but very soon something else comes along and grabs your *attention*. Maybe there's a noise from outside the room where you're practising. That takes your attention right away and you begin to wonder what made the noise. What does it mean? Maybe it's a fire engine going by. You start to wonder where the fire is . . . Then you remember to pay attention to the breath and you bring your mind back. Then you become aware of a twinge in your lower back and you forget about the breath as your attention goes there. Maybe you start to think about it: 'Why is my back hurting right now? I wonder if it is because of the way I was carrying that heavy bag last week . . .' Then you remember the breath and draw your attention back.

Over and over – you forget and remember to attend to the breath.

3) You forget and remember the attitude

You set out with the intention of bringing your attention to the breath with an *attitude* of kindness and curiosity – and you do that for a few breaths. But very soon you forget that attitude. Your mind keeps wandering and you begin to get annoyed with yourself – 'Come on, it's not rocket science. Stay with the breath. Can't I even do something as simple as that?' Then you remember the attitude and you come back to a kinder approach. You stay with that for a bit until maybe there's another noise outside – perhaps a pneumatic drill starts up in the road a few blocks down. 'This city! It's so noisy! How is anyone supposed to meditate or even do anything! They're so inconsiderate, doing those road works at the weekend when we're trying to relax.' And then you remember the attitude – gentle, kindly, curious, allowing – so you soften around the noise, you stop trying to defend yourself against it and maybe the rhythm even becomes a soothing beat in the background.

Then something starts to niggle in the intonation of the meditation instruction you're listening to. You forget the attitude and you start to get a little irritated with the instruction. Then you remember the attitude, drop your irritation and settle back into the meditation.

Over and over – you forget and remember the attitude you're seeking to bring to the meditation.

None of this is wrong!

Here's the really great thing: each time you forget is another opportunity to remember, and each time you remember it's as if you're laying down tiny deposits in the neural pathways connected with sustained intention, sustained attention and an attitude of kindness and curiosity.

The idea that the brain is changed by our patterns of behaviour is well known these days. Many of us will have heard about the taxi drivers who have to memorise thousands of routes around London and so have significantly greater than average brain grey-matter volume in the parts of their brains that are specialised for navigation. This capacity of the brain to reshape and rewire itself in response to behaviour is called 'neuroplasticity', and the secret of neuroplasticity is repeated behaviour over time. If you do something just a few times, that might not have much impact. But if you do it thousands and thousands of times, you begin to restructure your brain.

Most people who undertake a mindfulness course such as this one and who keep up the home practice requirement over eight weeks will find their mind wandering thousands and thousands of times. That means thousands and thousands of opportunities to remember their *intention* to pay *attention* with an *attitude* of gentle and kind curiosity.

People often say 'Oh, I can't meditate – I tried it, but I can't empty my mind' or 'I just can't stop my thoughts.' We hope you'll see now that this really isn't the point. The point is simply to notice and come back, notice and come back – over and over and over. Each time you forget your intention, attention or attitude, is an opportunity to come back, and each time you come back, each time you remember, it's as if you're laying down those vital deposits in the neural pathways you want to develop. Each act of forgetting and then remembering is like moving weight in a gym. Tiny step by tiny step, over and over, you're building mental and emotional muscle.

Not only that. Each time you do this practice you're gradually cultivating your capacity for mindfulness. The practice isn't about stopping your thoughts. It's about becoming *aware* of them. When you're more aware of what's moving in your mind from moment to moment, more aware of your thoughts, feelings, sensations and impulses, you can gradually begin to exercise more choice around them.

Practising like this, you begin to develop four key skills.

1) The skill of seeing that your attention isn't where you want it to be

In daily life our minds often wander and we don't notice that they have. You may be sitting at your desk, for example, planning your week's work, but gradually your attention wanders off and you start thinking about the holiday you want to book when you get home that night. Then you begin to think about your dry-cleaning, you make a note to remember to pick up your clothes on the way home, then you start to plan what you're going to eat this evening . . . and so on.

With mindfulness training, you'll become more adept at noticing where your attention is, from moment to moment.

2) The skill of unpicking your attention from where you don't want it to be

Maybe you've noticed how your thoughts, dreams and mental wanderings often come to you with a kind of stickiness – maybe even a degree of compulsion. Your mind keeps going back to your to-do list, or to thoughts about events in the past or events yet to come. You may be anxious about what's coming and regretful about the past, or you may be pleased and delighted by what's to come and OK with what's been. But, however such things show up for you, they can often be quite hard to let go of.

With mindfulness training it gradually becomes easier to see these mechanisms at work and to let go of them, unpicking your attention from the past or future.

3) The skill of placing your attention where you want it to be

Over and over again on this course you'll find your mind has wandered. Over and over again you bring it back to your chosen focus. If you do the home practice regularly you'll gradually build the neural pathways associated with sustained attention.

4) The skill of keeping your attention where you want it to be

Gradually over time your attentional 'muscles' start to build. With mindfulness training you become better able to maintain some degree of sustained, present-moment attention, better able to place and maintain your attention where you want it to be. It just takes time, patience and a gentle persistence.

Be gentle with your wandering mind

Minds wander and it's easy to get irritated with yourself. But none of that helps. You just need to gently and kindly draw your attention back to where the practice guidance suggests. Just do the practices and be patient with yourself. In important ways, there's nothing to be achieved here. All you're doing is noticing what your mind gets up to. And the moment that you notice that, even if you're hundreds of miles away from where the meditation guidance was suggesting your attention might be, then you're mindful again. Mindfulness is simply about noticing what's actually going on – in each moment.

Sensing rather than analysing

Try this very brief exercise, right now, it will only take a minute or two.

Begin by looking at your hands for a few moments.

Now, spend a few moments *thinking* about your hands. Just let your thoughts go wherever they take you while you're thinking about your hands.

Now, put the book to one side and clap your hands together twice – quite forcefully.

Now, *feel* what is going on in your hands. What sensations do you find? Tingling? Stinging? Warmth? Anything else?

Notice the difference here between *thinking* about your hands and *feeling* your hands.

In the early stages of our public mindfulness classes, we often hear people describing their sensations in terms of thoughts. For example, in the mindfulness of breathing meditation, people say afterwards – 'I was thinking about my breath, as you instructed . . .' But in fact we didn't instruct people to *think* about their breath. We invited them to *feel* the breath, or to *sense* it. We asked them to pay attention to sensations, or to the quality of each breath.

But our culture these days seems to prioritise the business of thinking and analysing over feeling and sensing and that can lead to something of a loss.

To be clear: we really don't intend to denigrate or under-value the processes of thinking and logical analysis. In fact, we highly value these. But there are aspects to our shared humanity that are easily lost when we over-emphasise thought and analysis, losing touch with the crucial feeling and sensing part of our being.

From the perspective of mindfulness practice, we think of experience as dividing into four key aspects: thoughts, feelings, sensations and impulses. Most moments of experience will comprise a complex blend of each of these. When we pause, quieten and look within, we can begin to discern a kind of interacting weather system in our minds. Sometimes the weather may be calm and clear, sometimes dark and stormy. At times it can be relatively placid, at other times a vigorous swirl of events.

22 The eight-week programme

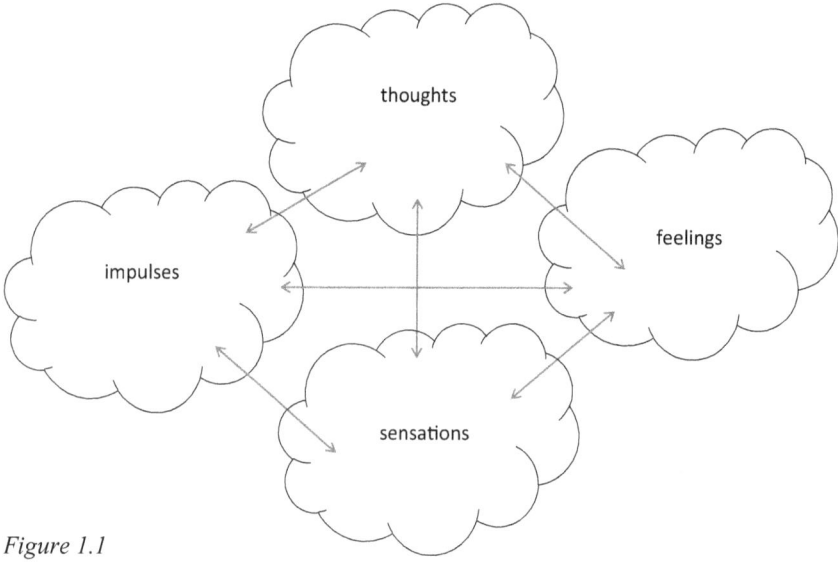

Figure 1.1

Let's take a simple example, one that several of us may be familiar with: the experience of being shoved and squashed on an over-crowded train on the London Underground in rush hour.

Thoughts: People are so rude! This city is un-liveable. I don't know how much more of this I can take . . . In the mornings they stink of aftershave, in the evenings it's body odour . . . If one more person shoves their backpack into my face I swear I'll scream!
Feelings: irritability, agitation, tension.
Sensations: Hot face and chest, churning stomach, tight jaw, sore shoulders.
Impulses: Shout . . . Stamp . . . Push back!

What we've described here is a state of considerable irritability. When you're caught up in such a state, unmindfully immersed in it, going through automatic pilot reactions to it, it can be as if the whole world is coloured by it. It can be as if your life is marked by those irritable characteristics – at least that's how it can seem.

But notice what happens when you make a tiny shift into mindfulness – when you give even a tiny moment of mindful attention to your thoughts, feelings, sensations or impulses *as* thoughts, feelings, sensations, or impulses. 'Oh yes – I'm having irritable thoughts. Uh huh.' Can you sense the shift that enables?

The move from being simply immersed in irritation to the recognition that you're just having irritable thoughts is tiny but it can change everything. You step ever so slightly away from the state of immersive irritation. One moment you're lost in irritation as an experiencing *subject*. The next moment you're acknowledging and observing your irritable thoughts as an *object* of your experience – and the irritable thoughts lose their power to shape your experience, at least to some extent.

You can make that move with any of the four elements described.

With the case above, you might take your attention to the area of physical sensations. You might explore the sensations that come along with tightness in your jaw, for example. Where do they start? Where do they stop? Do they change or pulse? What happens if you soften that? What happens if you tighten it further?

When you engage in an exploration like that, your whole inner setup subtly shifts and several things happen. For a few moments you come away from the patterns of thinking that are driving your irritability and that allows new configurations to emerge. 'Ah yes – irritability! Only a few more stops though.' You also engage your curiosity – and you may find that you can't be curious and irritable at one and the same time.

We'll return to this discussion in more depth in future chapters. For now, it's just important to note this idea that paying attention to your thoughts, feelings, sensations and impulses separately and as *objects* of attention can allow a bit more choice and a bit more freedom than when you're immersed in the tumbled spin of them all together.

The next practice we teach on the course is the body scan meditation. It can really help with the process of learning to track and to bring mindful curiosity to body sensations from moment to moment.

As we discussed earlier, there is a powerful tendency in our culture for us to be overly immersed in the thinking part of our minds. With the body scan, we learn to make a shift from thinking and analysing to simple sensing. We discover from moment to moment what's actually happening in our bodies (and you may discover that what you're *actually* sensing is rather different from what you *think* you'll sense when you move your attention around your body).

The body scan

When we do the body scan on our public Mindfulness for Coaches courses, as when we do it in other organisational contexts, we do it, like our other meditations, sitting in chairs. But when you do it at home you might prefer to do it lying down. It doesn't really matter.

The practice is simple. For around 15 minutes we invite you to close your eyes and to move your attention systematically through your body, noticing sensations at your toes to begin with and then moving from there to your feet, your shins, calves and lower legs, and onwards throughout the whole body, ending up by paying attention to the sensations at your head.

Remember – what you're doing here is paying attention to sensations. Earlier in this chapter we asked you to clap your hands vigorously, so creating an obvious sensation that you could pay attention to. Most of us don't find that extent of sensation in every part of our bodies when we do the body scan. That's fine. The aim of the practice is simply to feel whatever sensations you feel, from moment to moment, even if it's not very much at all. You might even find that there are parts of the body where it seems there is almost no sensation at all. That's fine, it's perfectly normal and the intention is just to notice whatever is there.

Many of us today suffer from some degree of sleep deprivation, and when you do the body scan it can be very easy to fall asleep. Although that might be refreshing, it's not the intention of the practice. Instead, the intention is to remain as awake and as aware as you can be. If you *do* fall asleep for a few moments you can always just pick the practice up again. If sleepiness becomes a problem, you might find it helps to change your posture.

When you're ready to try the practice, find the posture that's right for you and follow the instructions on Track 3 'The Body Scan (Shorter Version)'.

These are some of the kinds of comments we hear from people when they try the body scan for the first time:

I hardly felt anything at all in legs and toes. That was really strange and uncomfortable because I thought I ought to be feeling something there.

That can be a little disconcerting. But what we're doing here is discovering what we *actually* sense in the body, not what we *think* about it – and the two can be different. In some parts of the body you might sense a lot, in some parts hardly anything at all. That's not right, it's not wrong, it's just how you find it. But notice how quickly we can move to judgement here. We're set up to think that there's a right way of doing this, and we want to do it right – we want to feel sensations wherever the guidance takes us. If we don't we can feel we're not doing it right or it's not the way it *should* be. And notice any tendency now to judge that judgement! It's what we do. Instead, you might just gently notice any tendency to judge. You could even say to yourself, in a friendly kind of way: 'Oh yes, there I go, judging my experience again', and then, as best you can, come back to what you're actually experiencing.

I fell asleep!

That's not uncommon. Many of us are a little sleep-deprived and it's not a problem to fall asleep for a few minutes. It might even be quite refreshing. If it happens, just carry on with wherever the instruction has got to when you wake up again.

If you keep falling asleep and so miss large parts of the practice, you might try do the practice sitting upright in a chair, or with your eyes open. Experiment and see what works best for you.

I was really fidgety. It was so uncomfortable. I wanted to move around, but I gritted my teeth and hung on –resisting the urge to move.

See what's going on here. It's easy to fall into a striving attitude, 'I need to do this right'. Perhaps try seeing what it's like for a few moments just to acknowledge 'Oh yes, there's restlessness', or whatever. Then, if you find you keep wanting to move, just move mindfully. Or maybe try staying with it for a bit longer, exploring your experience in each moment. There's no right way or wrong way of handling restlessness – or any other experience. Experiment. See what you find.

I thought this was supposed to help me relax!

Of course many of us would love to relax a bit more. Practices like the body scan may help you to relax or they may not. That's not the main thing here. The aim of the exercise is to enable you to be more mindful, finding out what goes on for you in each moment and to bring a kindly awareness to whatever you discover.

I kept getting itches in different parts of my body and I really wanted to scratch. At one point I just opened my eyes to see what time it was. Then I thought 'I'm not supposed to do that'.

Itches can be really uncomfortable, of course, but maybe there's another way of being with that kind of experience. With an itch, you might even see if you can allow it to be there and explore it. Where is it most intense? Where is it least intense? Is it changing . . . moving . . . pulsing? Can you open to it and explore it? In the end, there's no problem with gently and mindfully scratching. Just as there's no problem with opening your eyes for a few moments. There's no right way, or no wrong way, to do this exercise. There's just what you find, what you mindfully experience.

My mind kept wandering.

That's what minds do, they wander. So when your mind wanders just notice where it went and gently bring it back. You could say to yourself 'Oh yes, there I was planning again' and then gently and kindly bring your mind back. If your mind wanders off a hundred times, just bring it back a hundred times. It's all great practice.

Coaching exercise for session 1

Working relationally with present moment attention

We have adapted this exercise from Nancy Kline's *Time to Think*.

Pair up with a practice buddy at some point in the next two weeks and try this exercise. It will take a minimum of 15 to 20 minutes to complete, although you could take quite a bit more time over it if you want to.

In this exercise one person listens, the other talks (about any subject). Then you swap around. To begin, the listener might say something like 'What would you like to talk about and what are your thoughts?' The listener then needs to listen to what the speaker wants to say, without interrupting, until they sense that the speaker has fully said what they wanted to say. At this point, they might say something like 'What more do you think, feel or want to say?' At a minimum, allow 5 minutes for this process.

While the speaker is speaking, the listener's task is to give them their attention, certainly, but they should also notice where their own attention goes.

How much is that attention present-moment focused and really centred on what the speaker is saying? To what extent are they perhaps already running forward to formulate a solution for the speaker? To what extent might they be anticipating what the speaker might be about to say next? To what extent might their attention be wandering into the past – triggered by what is said to remember associations from their own past? How might that trigger a desire to give advice based on their own past experience? To what extent might elements in the conversation be catching the listener's attention in such a way that they remain fixed on something that was said 10 seconds ago, 15 seconds ago, 2 minutes ago – so that they lose their attention to what is being said right now?

It's not that this movement forwards and backwards in time is wrong, it's just what minds do, but much of the time we don't notice the movement.

This exercise is designed to help the coach become aware of that.

As we will discuss in the section on 'Coaching presence' in Chapter 8, that is a crucial coaching skill.

When it's time to change over, drop into silence together for a few moments and then swap over and repeat the procedure with the person who was previously speaking now listening.

Once that has followed its course, drop into silence again for a few moments and then discuss – how did all of that go for each of you? What did you find?

Home practice for week one

- Practise the body scan meditation for at least 6 days of the coming week. Use 'The Body Scan (Shorter Version)' (Track 3) for guidance. Don't expect to feel anything in particular from doing the practice, rather – as much as possible – put aside all expectations about it. Just let your experience be your experience.
- If you would like to, maybe start a journal where you can make a brief note of the experiences that emerge for you each time you do the practice.
- Choose a routine activity in your daily life and make a deliberate effort to bring moment-to-moment awareness to that activity each time you do it, just as we did in the raisin exercise. Possibilities include things like your first cup of tea or coffee, brushing your teeth, showering, drying yourself or getting dressed; your walk to the bus, train or car; eating – anything that you do every day. Just make a point of knowing what you are doing as you are actually doing it.
- Note any times when you find yourself able to become more deeply aware of what you eat in the same way you noticed the raisin. Eat at least one meal mindfully (and that doesn't necessarily mean slowly) – in the way that you ate the raisin.

Home practice for week two

- Practise 'the body scan' meditation again for at least 6 days of the coming week. Use 'The Body Scan (Shorter Version)' (Track 3) for guidance. As before, don't expect to feel anything in particular from doing the practice, rather – as best you can – put aside all expectations about it. Just let your experience be your experience.
- At a different time, practise 5 minutes of 'mindfulness of breathing' meditation for 6 days. Use 'Mindfulness of Breathing (5 Minutes)' (Track 5) for guidance. Being with your breath in this way each day provides an opportunity to become aware of what it feels like to be connected and present in the moment without having to do anything.
- Complete the pleasant-events diary (*see page 28*). Make one entry per day. Use this as an opportunity to become more fully aware of the thoughts, feelings, sensations and impulses that come with one pleasant event each day. Notice these and record them as soon as you're comfortably able to. For example, you might try to record any words or images that occurred with your thoughts, or the precise nature and location of bodily sensations. But don't strain at this – it's just a guide to help you to notice.
- Choose a new routine activity to be especially mindful of – your first cup of tea or coffee; brushing your teeth; showering; drying yourself; getting dressed; your walk to the bus, train or car; eating – anything that you do every day. Again, just make a point of knowing what you are doing as you are actually doing it.

Notes

1 Lazar, S. *et al*. (2005) 'Meditation experience is associated with increased cortical thickness', *Neuroreport*, 16(17): 1893–1897.
2 Hölzel, B.K. *et al*. (2010) Mindfulness practice leads to increases in regional brain gray matter density, *Psychiatry Research: Neuroimaging*, 191(1): 36–43.
3 Hölzel, B.K. *et al*. (2010) 'Stress reduction correlates with structural changes in the amygdala', *Social Cognitive and Affective Neuroscience*, 5(1): 11–17.
4 Davidson, R.J. and Kabat-Zinn, J. (2003) 'Alterations in brain and immune function produced by mindfulness meditation', *Psychosomatic Medicine*, 65: 564–570.
5 Jha, A.P. *et al*. (2010) 'Examining the protective effects of mindfulness training on working memory capacity and affective experience', *Emotion*, 10(1): 54–64.
6 Segal, Z.V., Williams, J.M.G. and Teasdale, J.D. (2002) *Mindfulness-Based Cognitive Therapy for Depression*. London: Guildford Press.
7 Murray, C.L., Lopez A.D. (1998) *The global burden of disease: A comprehensive assessment of mortality and disability from disease, injuries and risk factors in 1990 projected to 2020*, Boston, MA: Harvard University Press.
8 Kessler, R.C., McGonagle K.A., Zhao S., et al. (1994) 'Lifetime and twelve-month prevalence of DSM-III-R psychiatric disorders in the United States: results from the National Co-morbidity Study', *Archive of General Psychiatry*, 51, 8–19.
9 Kabat-Zinn, J. (1991) *Full Catastrophe Living: Using the Wisdom of Your Body and Mind to Face Stress, Pain and Illness*. New York: Delta.

Table 1.1 Pleasant-events diary

Day	What was the experience?	How did your body feel – in detail – during the experience?	What feelings came along with the event?	What thoughts went through your mind at the time?	What impulses came along with the event?	What are you thinking right now, as you write this?
Example	On the way to work, stopping to catch the scent of a shrub.	Shoulders dropped, chest opened. Feeling of a smile.	A small feeling of joy and optimism.	Oh at last – spring is on its way.	Just to stop for a moment and enjoy it.	Yes – spring is on its way. How good.
Monday						
Tuesday						
Wednesday						
Thursday						
Friday						
Saturday						
Sunday						

10 Kuyken, W, Hayes, R, Barrett, B., Byng, R, *et al*. (2015) 'Effectiveness and cost-effectiveness of mindfulness-based cognitive therapy compared with maintenance antidepressant treatment in the prevention of depressive relapse or recurrence (PREVENT): a randomised controlled trial', *The Lancet*, 386(9988): 63–73.
11 Anālayo (2003) *Satipaṭṭhāna: The Direct Path to Realization*. Birmingham, UK: Windhorse.
12 Nyanatiloka (1972) *Buddhist Dictionary: Manual of Buddhist Terms and Doctrines*, Kandy, Sri Lanka: Buddhist Publication Society.
13 Shapiro, S.L. and Carlson, L.E. (2009) *The Art and Science of Mindfulness: Integrating Mindfulness into Psychology and the Helping Professions*, Washington DC: American Psychological Association.
14 Kabat-Zinn, J. (1994) *Wherever You Go, There You Are: Mindfulness Meditation in Everyday Life*, New York: Hyperion.
15 Killingsworth, M.A. and Gilbert, D.T. (2010) 'A wandering mind is an unhappy mind'. *Science*, 330(6006): 932.
16 Ibid.
17 Mental Health Foundation (2010) 'Mindfulness report', www.mentalhealth.org.uk/sites/default/files/Mindfulness_report_2010.pdf.
18 Carmody, J. and Baer, R.A. (2008) 'Relationships between mindfulness practice and levels of mindfulness, medical and psychological symptoms and well-being in a mindfulness-based stress reduction program' *Journal of Behavioural Medicine*, 31: 23–33.

Rosenzweig, S. *et al*. (2010) 'Mindfulness-based stress reduction for chronic pain conditions: variation in treatment outcomes and role of home meditation practice' *Journal of Psychosomatic Research*, 68: 29–36.

Britton, W.B. *et al*. (2010) 'The contribution of mindfulness practice to a multicomponent behavioral sleep intervention following substance abuse treatment in adolescents: a treatment-development study', *Substance Abuse*, 31: 86–97.
19 Jha, A.P. *et al*. (2010) 'Examining the protective effects of mindfulness training on working memory capacity and affective experience', *Emotion*, 10(1): 54–64.

2 Session 2
Embodiment

Evolution hasn't fully prepared us for the lives we live today.

Detailed opinions on this vary, but many evolutionary theorists seem to think that it took evolution around 6 million years to produce humans from our ancient ape-like ancestors, and that beings who are anatomically like us have only been around for about 200,000 years. The agricultural revolution that kicked off farming and enabled us to live in settled societies took place just 12,000 years ago. We've had widespread access to the internet since about 1995 and smartphones have been with us since about 2007.

Evolution hasn't had time to catch up with the lives we live today, where our attention is so scattered and fragmented.

There are ceaseless demands on our attention from email, texts, instant messaging, social media, the internet, phone calls and virtual meetings. Some of us give more of our attention to our digital devices than we do to the human beings in our immediate environment, and that affects us – profoundly.

Instead of living as embodied people, we can go about as if we are digital clouds loosely tethered to sticks. But those 'sticks' – our human bodies – are a precious resource of information, and potential well-being, that we ignore at our peril.

We don't yet know the lasting physical and emotional consequences of the advent of smartphones and the digital revolution. There are many upsides. The devices most of us have within easy reach enable us to access an extraordinary range of knowledge and they have hugely increased the breadth of our connectedness. But there is a downside. On the mindfulness courses we run, we've noticed over the years a dramatic increase in the number of people reporting experiences of sleeplessness and feelings of being overwhelmed by the sheer volume of input they struggle somehow to manage. More and more people speak of the way their various devices fracture their attention and how they're unable to stay undividedly focused on any given task for very long.

Consumer Insights, a division of Microsoft Canada, reported research in Spring 2015[1] which suggested that the average adult attention span in 2013 was 8 seconds. That was a significant reduction from the already scant 12 seconds it was when they measured it in 2000.

From the perspective of mindfulness in the coaching context, one of the biggest downsides of the way we're impacted by the digital revolution is that it causes so many of us to lose touch with our bodies. This can cut us off from hugely important sources of knowledge about what is happening – in the coach, the coachee and in the coaching relationship between them – from moment to moment. An increased capacity to be aware of what is going on in your body in each present moment is a significant outcome of the Mindfulness for Coaches course.

The importance of bodily awareness – for coaches and other human beings

As we saw in the previous chapter, we can think of our experience as a mix of thoughts, feelings, body sensations and impulses. In the next chapter, we're going to focus on working with thoughts. In this chapter, we will focus on the body and on the information we take in from our bodies via the senses. We will see how being more mindful of our bodies enables us to stay more present: for ourselves, for our coaching clients, for the people we love and the people we work with – and for everyone we meet.

Reading ourselves

Our bodies are exquisitely designed to present us with rich information from moment to moment about what is happening inside us and around us. As our internal, physical ecosystem changes, we register those changes as changing body sensations – the twinge of indigestion, the tightness of a strained muscle, the ease and pleasure of a hot, relaxing bath. But it's not just our physical ecosystem that the body is reading. We also read our changing emotional ecology by way of the body. Think of the way almost unconscious anxiety in the presence of another person can be read as a slight tightening in the stomach or a faint clenching in the jaw. The way ease and pleasure in good company can show up as a minute dropping of the shoulders.

We discover much of what is going on in our inner climate by reading our bodies. Unfortunately though, we seem to be becoming increasingly adept in our culture at ignoring those bodily signals. As we become more and more preoccupied with the digital aspect of our lives and overwhelmed by inputs of one sort or another, we can come to lose touch with some of the subtler signals from our bodies, and so become clumsier at reading ourselves.

Mindfulness training can help you more easily to stay tuned to the constantly changing sense of your own body.

The physical barometer

Trish Bartley at the Centre for Mindfulness Research and Practice at Bangor University has developed a practice called the 'physical barometer' which is designed to bring a heightened awareness of feelings into your everyday life.[2]

When you read an old air-pressure barometer, designed to indicate whether the local air pressure is rising or falling, you first tap gently on the glass that covers its dial and then look to see which way the needle inside the glass moves. If the needle moves up, the air pressure is rising and the weather will very likely improve. If the needle goes down, it may be going to rain. Things vary according to seasons, and it's quite complicated to predict the weather, but a barometer can help.

You can use your body in a similar way to get very sensitive information about how things are for you at any given moment.

Here is how you can do that:

1. Determine some part of the body – such as the chest area or the abdomen or somewhere in between the two – that for you is especially sensitive to your inner climate. Often, we find that this is where stress or difficulty shows up for us.
2. Once you have located this place it can become your 'physical barometer', and you can tune in to it, paying attention to sensations there regularly, at different moments, every day. If you are stressed, you may notice sensations of tension or discomfort. Depending on the intensity of the difficulty, these sensations may be strong or not so strong and may change as you pay attention to them. When you tune in to the experience of ease and pleasure, you may notice quite different sensations.
3. As you become more practiced at reading your physical barometer, you may find that you start to notice subtle variations that offer you detailed and early information about how you are feeling moment by moment, long before you are aware of this in your mind.
4. Any time you tune in to your physical barometer, if you wish, you can move to doing the 'three-step breathing space' (which we'll outline later in the chapter) to help you stay present with whatever it is you're experiencing. Alternately, you may choose just to monitor the sensations in your physical barometer moment by moment and be with them just as they are, allowing things to be, accepting as best you can how things are and being with your experience moment by moment.

Reading others

It's not just our own inner weather that we're adapted to read so well. Evolution has also gifted us with an astonishing capacity to swiftly and wordlessly read others.

Imagine a group of monkeys, foraging in a clump of trees. Then a predator shows up – perhaps a leopard. As soon as one of the monkeys sees the leopard she will freeze. She doesn't want to make a sound or allow her movement to be spotted by the leopard. As soon as she freezes, the monkeys who see that also freeze and the freeze response passes through the band like lightning. When the leopard is safely past, and one monkey begins to move, they all start to move again – they need to eat and can't stay in their frozen postures for too long. That capacity – to accurately, silently and quickly read messages of 'safe/unsafe' from the gestures and behaviour of another – is a huge evolutionary advantage.

We also have a remarkable capacity to read changing facial micro expressions. Paul Ekman, the world's foremost expert on the link between emotions and facial expression,[3] has shown how the basic emotions of happiness, sadness, anger, fear, disgust and surprise show up as fleeting micro expressions in the face that can be reliably detected even when people attempt to conceal their feelings. These micro expressions occur prior to the conscious control of the person having the emotion and they happen so quickly that they are frequently misidentified or not perceived by others.

Although the sample size referred to here is too small to allow for accurate generalisation, it's interesting to note that when Ekman presented two western Buddhist monks – accomplished meditators – with a video used in his research design, the monks accurately identified micro expressions of emotion at a level two standard deviations higher than the score previously rated as the most accurate.[4] They scored significantly higher than any other group taking this test – lawyers, police officers, customs agents, psychiatrists, and secret service agents (the group previously identified as the most skilled in this task).

It may be that mindfulness training is an effective means of increasing our capacity to read micro expressions and therefore our capacity to read the emotional states of others and to empathise with them.

We'll be discussing the wider subject of mindfulness and empathy in more detail in Chapter 4. For now, one of the main messages of the current section of our course is that our bodies matter. When we are on our own, our bodies are a rich source of information about our current inner climate. When we're with others, their bodies – and their inner climate – impacts on us too and our inner system is inevitably changed by that impact. We can read what is happening with others partly by sensing how we are internally impacted by them. And we get important information about the relationship between us by observing their bodies, as well as our own, when we come into contact.

Taking this wider still, the systems within which we operate impact on us and impact on others. By paying attention to what is moving in ourselves and in others, we get important information about what is moving in the wider system.

Bodily awareness is a hugely valuable resource of information in the coaching context and the good news is that mindfulness training can increase this, allowing for a deeper, subtler and more accurate reading of ourselves, others and the system within which we move.

Staying present

> The ways in which we are grounded in ourselves and open to others, and participate fully in the life of the mind are important aspects of our presence at the heart of relationships that help others to grow.
>
> Daniel Siegel, *The Mindful Therapist*[5]

There is much that can be said about this mysterious term 'presence' and we'll discuss it more fully in Chapter 8, but for now it's worth reflecting on what you found as you did 'the body scan' and the 'mindfulness of breathing' meditations as part of home practice in the past two weeks.

You set out to pay attention to parts of the body in 'the body scan' or to the breath in the 'mindfulness of breathing' practice and very soon your attention drifts away from that. You bring it back and it drifts away, bring it back and it drifts away – over and over.

Each time you bring your attention back you're coming back to presence. Each time it drifts, you're going away from presence. It may be startling – and for coaches perhaps salutary – to notice just how often you lose that sense of presence. The good news is that for most people who do these practices it's relatively easy to come back to being present. All that it takes is the act of noticing that you're *not* present. The moment you notice that, you're present again. It's like magic.

By working with and developing this latent capacity to 'come back to yourself', in Siegel's terms, quoted earlier, to become more 'grounded' in yourself, you enhance and develop your coaching presence. A key aspect of this is the ability to stay anchored in your body – in your moment to moment physical experience.

One of the things that this calls for is a greater attention to the senses. We often speak of the senses as if there were just five of these: hearing, sight, touch, taste and smell. But when you move your attention inwards and explore your immediate experience, a few more may emerge. Think about proprioception – the sense we have of how our bodies are located in space in any one moment. Or kinesthesia – the sense we have of the body's movement. There is interoception – our overall sense of the physiological condition of the body. There is chronoception – our sense of the passage of time. There may be more senses – this list isn't definitive. But however you categorise the way experience is fed by the senses, direct experience of the sensory moment is different to *thinking about* the senses.

We can come back here to the exercise we did in the previous chapter where we invited you first to *think about* your hands, then to clap them together twice and *feel* your hands. No amount of the former is ever the same as the latter.

Narrative mode – experiential mode

Distinguishing in the same way, the research neuroscientist Norman Farb, some of whose work we will discuss in much more detail in the next chapter, speaks of two different modes of mind: the narrative mode and the experiential mode. When we are involved in the narrative mode, we are thinking, planning, dreaming and so on. In the experiential mode we simply experience the world as it comes to us via the senses. Part of Farb's work has been to map the different brain regions that are involved in these two distinct processes. His studies have shown that when people have trained in mindfulness they're more readily able to notice which mode they are in and they're relatively more capable of switching between the two modes.[6]

The ability to think, to plan, to dream and to abstract is what makes us so wonderfully human. But when the narrative mode of mind predominates at the expense of the experiential mode then we become strangely misshapen. We lose that quality of here-and-now presence that is vital to the helping – and indeed every other – relationship.

We can instinctively feel somehow when another person is present with us and giving us their full attention – experientially fully present – and we can feel what it's like when they drift off into one or another inner narrative: momentarily planning a meal perhaps, or thinking about what they want to do next, or reminded by what we said about a problem they have at home or at work and thinking about that for a time.

When clients do that in the coaching context, when they lose their 'presence' and slip into an inner narrative, it's fairly easy to notice. By the same token, when coaches do that, then clients – consciously or unconsciously – are very likely to sense that too.

One of the greatest gifts that a coach can offer a client is simply their continuous, open, non-judgemental presence. The capacity to stay present in that way is hugely helped when we can anchor our attention, to some extent at least, in our own immediate embodied experience.

Mindful movement

'The body scan' and the 'mindfulness of breathing' meditation help us to develop the capacity to be mindfully present from moment to moment. In this chapter we begin to work with practices that help to develop that capacity outside of the context of static meditation. We begin to pay attention to the body as it moves.

Mindful stretching

In the first two weeks of the course you meditated lying down with 'the body scan' and you did a sitting meditation in the 'mindfulness of breathing' meditation. Now we're going to practise mindfulness in movement, bringing that same quality of present-moment attention to the sensations in your body when you stretch it.

There are audio instructions for the 'mindful movement' stretches you'll be doing for home practice this week on the download site (Track 7). You might want to have a go at doing them now, as what you've read above is still fresh in your mind. If you do that, remember that it's the mindful attitude that you bring to these stretches that is key.

If now is not a good time for you to do a full sequence of stretches, you might try just this one. Above all, do take care of yourself, only going as far as is right for you and only holding the stretch for as long as feels right for you.

- Stand up with your arms by your side. (If you'd prefer, you can also do this stretch sitting down).
- Begin by getting a sense of what it feels like to be standing or sitting here right now. Feel your feet making a strong contact with the floor; your height rising up, your weight going down.
- Feel the breath moving in the body.
- Your chest is open, your belly and shoulders softened.
- When you're ready, let both arms float up away from your sides until they come to shoulder height. There should be a straight-ish line from your left fingertips, across the shoulders, to your right fingertips.
- Stand for a moment, breathing.
- Now check in. Notice any tensing, any holding. Look for any part of the body that's tensing up and doesn't need to. Soften ... open ... keep breathing.
- Really press those finger tips away from the body. And keep breathing.
- Now, lift your fingers upwards as far as they'll go, pointing your fingers up towards the ceiling while you press outwards with the palms. Feel the stretch across the backs of your hands, across the palms, along the arms. Keep breathing ... keep softening ... keep stretching.
- See what it's like now, to just stay with that stretch for a few moments. Try letting any sensations of discomfort just *be* sensations. See what it's like to move towards them, with an attitude of kindly curiosity – allowing, letting them be just as they are. Exploring, investigating.
- And, when it's right for you, let go of the stretch and check in again.
- What's here now?

Working the edge

For many of us, stretches like these might take us to the edge of our comfort zone – and that's no bad thing. This isn't because 'if it doesn't hurt it isn't doing you good'. Quite the opposite. The intention here is to begin a mindful – gentle and kindly – exploration of the edges of your comfort zone, because it's at the edge that fruitful experiences often show up.

Much of the time, we arrange our lives – physically, mentally and emotionally – so that we stay within a familiar zone of comfort. The foods we eat, the places we go, the thoughts we allow, the people we associate with, the way we dress, the movements we make: all of these settle in time into a pattern of comfortable familiarity. The known, the familiar – even if it's often a painful place to be, at least it's ours.

With the stretches, you should begin instead to discover your edge. This is a safe opportunity to gently drop your defences and see what it's like to experience your body just as it is in each moment, noticing any tendency to compete with yourself or with imagined others. The intention here is to find a way to work that brings you to an edge but not over it.

Always treat yourself with kindness and consideration. Learning to do that can be an edge in itself for some people.

If a stretch feels too demanding, see how you can work with it in a way that is right for you, because all of our edges are different – we're all working with the very particular circumstances of our own bodies. There can be no 'one size fits all' here – make your own decision. Be challenging, but above all be kind.

The discomfort you encounter when you practise mindful stretching provides an ideal situation to learn how to approach the difficult and unwanted with curiosity, gentleness, kindness and courage. The skills of 'allowing' that you learn in a situation of physical discomfort can then be applied later to situations of mental or emotional discomfort.

For some of the coaches we've spoken to, the need to stay present with a client when he or she is experiencing acute emotional turbulence brings them to an edge. When a client is experiencing rage, for example, a coach may feel a strong impulse to back-off or to shut-down and go inward.

By learning to work with such edges differently in the context of their mindfulness training, however, many of them report a stronger capacity to simply be with whatever is emerging for them – their *own* experiences of fear, for example, might show up in that moment as a tightening in the chest and a churning in the stomach. Noticing that, 'allowing' it, bringing a kindly, curious awareness to it — they find themselves more able to stay present and resourceful for the client.

In the stretches that are part of home practice, you may be instructed to raise your hands above your head, stretching upwards with your whole body, and you might find that it begins to feel slightly uncomfortable in your shoulders and upper arms. One possible response to this – the avoidance option – is to back off as soon as you feel any discomfort. You might just lower your arms, or take your attention out of the body altogether, perhaps into a stream of thoughts or images. Another possibility – the unkind option – is to grit your teeth, tell yourself you just have to put up with the increasing pain and discomfort and not make a fuss, as if that were actually the aim of the practice. You might put even more effort into pushing yourself to stretch further. Or you might habitually numb out your awareness of the discomfort, losing awareness of the body instead of increasing it.

Mindfully working the edge involves taking a fourth option and one that may feel a bit counter-intuitive at first. Instead of avoiding or pushing harder, try seeing what it's like to adopt an 'approach' and 'allowing' attitude. Bring an attitude of gentle allowing to each moment, using these stretches to extend your ways of relating to discomfort. Try striking a balance between the tendency to withdraw at the first sign of discomfort, which would just reinforce any avoidant tendencies you may have, and forcing yourself to meet some standard of endurance that you have set for yourself in a driven mode of mind.

You begin to find that balance by a process of trial and error – moving your attention right into the area of discomfort, perhaps, using the breath to carry awareness right into the place of greatest intensity, just as you did in 'the body scan'. Then, with a gentle and kindly curiosity, explore what you find there. Notice your body sensations moving and changing. Feel them directly, maybe sensing how they change in intensity over time.

With the stretches, you can find the zone where you're 'working the edge' by varying the stretch itself. This can give you some sense of control. It can give you a way to take a gentle and kindly orientation towards yourself while still learning how to do things differently.

Mindful movement as a formal mindfulness practice

Treat these stretches differently from the way you might previously have stretched to warm up in the gym, for example. What distinguishes the stretches you're going to do for home practice is that you engage in them as a mindfulness practice.

So, as well as cultivating a kindly, curious, allowing approach to any challenging sensations that may emerge, there is also a definite intention here to keep your attention in each present moment, with what's actually showing up in the body from changing moment to changing moment. The mind will wander and, when it does, just briefly notice where it went – 'Uhuh, there I was thinking again . . .' or 'Hmm . . . planning . . .' – and then gently and kindly return the attention to the stretches and to your present-moment body sensations.

Approach and avoidance

Throughout these stretches, we're working to cultivate an 'approaching', 'allowing' attitude. That attitude is central to the whole mindfulness endeavour. To understand this from another perspective, we can make a short detour into some of the neuropsychology that underlies a part of our experience.

The prefrontal cortex is a small part of the brain just behind the forehead. It plays a significant part in your overall experience of mood and it's one of the key brain regions that seem to be impacted by mindfulness training.[7]

People who have damaged their prefrontal cortex have different experiences depending on whether that damage is to the left or the right. If the damage is to the left side, they are often unable to experience joy. Instead, they sometimes experience strong increases in sadness and even uncontrollable crying. If the damage is to the right side, however, that can leave them indifferent to injury and they might find themselves often laughing inappropriately.

The neuroscientist Richard Davidson has shown that the extent of activation on either the right or the left side of a person's prefrontal cortex can predict something significant about their inner experience. Those with generally higher activity in the left part are energised, alert, enthusiastic and joyful. Such people enjoy life and show a greater overall sense of well-being. By contrast, when there is greater activity in the right prefrontal cortex, people report experiences of worry, anxiety and sadness.[8]

Davidson came to study the brains of highly experienced meditators. One factor stood out from all the rest – while his subjects were meditating, activity in their left prefrontal cortex swamped activity in their right prefrontal to an extent never before recorded.[9]

As we've seen, left prefrontal activation is associated with happiness and right prefrontal activation is associated with unhappiness and states such as anxious vigilance. Davidson's results suggested that emotions could be transformed by mental training.

That gave rise to a question. Would similar results be obtained in an ordinary population group? Would mindfulness training change their emotional dispositions?

In collaboration with Jon Kabat-Zinn, Davidson set out to answer this question – this time studying the brains of people who had never meditated before and who were enrolled on an eight-week mindfulness course.[10]

They taught two eight-week mindfulness courses to people who worked at a high-pressure biotech company. One group undertook the eight-week course and a comparison group received the training later. The relative left–right prefrontal activation of both groups was tested before and after the training. Before the course – as so often for those who work in high-pressure environments – both groups were tipped on average somewhat towards the right and spoke of feeling highly stressed. After the training, the group who had received the mindfulness training reported that their moods had improved; they felt more engaged with their work, more energised and less anxious. Their brain scan results bore this out. Their left–right prefrontal cortex activation ratios had shifted significantly leftwards. These results persisted at the 4 month follow-up.

The subjective experience of participants accorded with that objective data. The mindfulness training, it seemed, left them feeling healthier, more positive and less stressed.

Mindfulness training also improved the robustness of the meditators' immune systems. Both groups were given flu jabs. Participants in the mindfulness group produced significantly more flu antibodies in their blood after receiving the jab. The greater the leftward shift in their prefrontal cortex activation, the larger the increase in their immune response.

Another way of understanding what happened here is that the mindfulness group became more 'approach-oriented' while the group who received the training later remained somewhat 'avoidance-oriented'.

The history of these modes of mind – approach and avoidance orientation – goes back in evolutionary terms to the emergence of two distinct neurological processes: approach systems and avoidance systems. Since the 1970s, researchers have proposed that two motivational systems play a large part in shaping our experience: a behavioural inhibition system (BIS) and a behavioural activation system (BAS).

We can call these the 'avoidance system' (BIS) and the 'approach system' (BAS).

The approach system turns us towards potential rewards. When we feel attracted to a person or to our favourite food, and we want to approach the person or that food, this system is in play. The avoidance system, on the other hand, alerts us to potential punishment or danger and motivates us to avoid things. The fear of rejection by someone we love, or the fear of snakes, along with our wanting to avoid such things, comes from the avoidance system.

Davidson and others have shown that the approach system correlates to left prefrontal-cortex activation. This system is reward-seeking and is associated with positive emotions such as joy and with the optimistic anticipation of good events. The avoidance system, on the other hand, which correlates to right prefrontal cortex activation, inhibits us in our movement towards desirable goals and is associated with feelings of fear, disgust, aversion and anxiety.

There's a significant evolutionary value to these two systems. They play a key part in the way in which we approach things we think will be good for us and avoid things that threaten us. But our genetic inheritance and our life experiences can skew them so that, at one extreme, some of us have developed a chronically overactive avoidance system – causing us to be overanxious or prone to depression.

Mindfulness training can change that. It can help you become more approach-oriented. This course offers opportunities to move towards what is difficult and to find new ways of being with it – approaching, rather than avoiding, what you have previously found to be uncomfortable. Working the edge.

Another approach to stress

Stress runs at epidemic levels through the contemporary workplace. Michael's book, *The Mindful Workplace*, published in 2011, gives the following data:

> The Labour Force Survey conducted by the UK's Office for National Statistics in 2007/08 estimated that 442,000 individuals in Britain who worked in the last year believed that they were experiencing work-related stress at a level that was making them ill.[11] Around 13.6% of all working individuals in the UK in 2007 thought their job was very or extremely stressful.[12] An estimated 237,000 people, who worked in 2007/08 became aware of work-related stress, depression or anxiety, giving an annual incidence rate of 780 cases per 100,000 workers and in the same year stress, depression and anxiety accounted for an estimated 13.5 million lost working days.[13] Commenting on the cost of stress to business, Ben

Pressure-Performance Curve

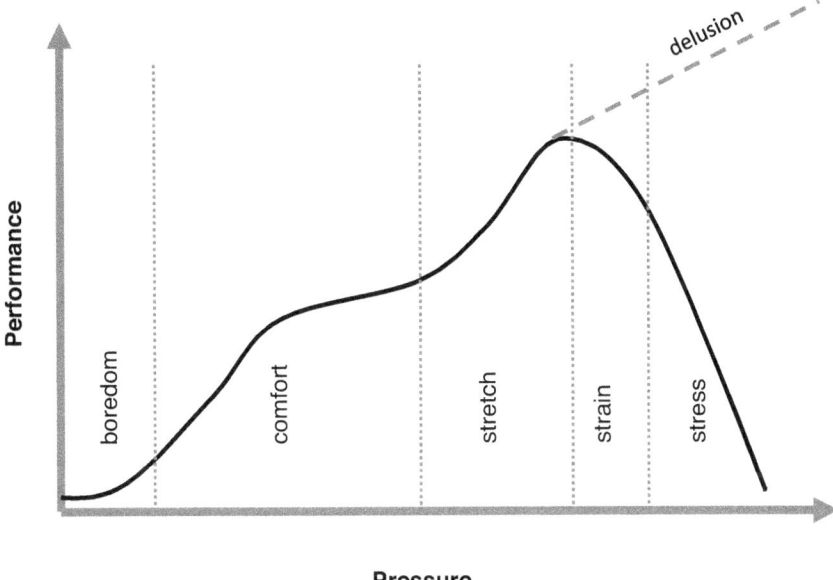

Figure 2.1 The pressure-performance curve

Wilmott, employee relations adviser at the UK's Chartered Institute of Personnel Development, estimates that the direct and indirect costs of employee absence to UK businesses is around £1,800 per employee per year.[14]

We're not able to do an exact cross-comparison with these data, but there seems to be no reason to presume that they've improved much since then. One study[15] published in 2011 suggests that 20 per cent of British adults are stressed because of their work and the coaches we work with increasingly report that one of the biggest factors affecting their clients is the unrelenting demand of the contemporary workplace.

Of course, many people find the pressure of their work is stimulating. But the tipping point between 'stretch' and 'stress' isn't always easy to spot and, as Figure 2.1 shows, that has consequences for your work. The fact that sometimes helping clients deal with the pressure of their own work is a part of any coaches' job shouldn't blind us to the fact that coaching itself – whether as a self-employed coach or as someone working in an organisation – can be stressful.

Figure 2.1, adapted from Stephen Williams' *Managing Pressure for Peak Performance*,[16] is in many respects self-evident. As the demands on us increase, so our capacity to respond to those demands also increases. But only ever up to a certain point. Beyond that point our capacity to respond falls off – sometimes quite dramatically.

The optimal point to work at is where you are managing the balance between 'stretch' and 'strain'. Work that stretches is enlivening, engaging, energising. It's likely to slip into 'strain' from time to time – that's very hard to avoid – and strain, for short periods of time, isn't really harmful. People who are generally resilient bounce back from strain when they notice and can take remedial action.

Prolonged stress, however, is dangerous. Thyroid or endocrine burnout, obesity, diabetes, the inability to experience pleasure from normally pleasurable events, immune suppression, psoriasis, lupus, fibromyalgia, chronic fatigue, chronic pain, cancer, heart disease, infertility and irritable bowel syndrome or other digestive disorders – all of these may be connected to the experience of stress.[17] Too much stress can literally kill and we ignore it at our peril.

But in these days of the corporate 'super-athlete' many of us will have come upon clients and even organisational cultures that deny the simple facts of stress. Notice the dotted line that heads upwards to the right from the peak of the curve. This is the line of delusion and it marks out a space that people can enter where they blank-out certain key and simple facts of their own experience in order to just keep going. People in such a space may believe that they're doing well, but they are not. They may tell themselves and others that they can handle things, but they can't. And whatever the inner or outer narrative that accompanies such an experience may be, it will be a simple fact that their performance will be suffering. They may think and speak as if they're doing OK and managing the demands that are being made on them, but they are not and their performance will have markedly declined.

We'll be introducing the idea that each of us has our own particular 'stress signatures' more fully towards the end of this course. Your stress signature is the collection of signals you can learn to recognise from your own thoughts, feelings, sensations and behaviour that you're moving from strain and into stress. For now we'll simply say this: when you're more mindful – and especially perhaps when you're more mindful of your body – you stand a much greater chance of accurately reading your own stress signature and of taking some remedial action when you notice it. That can help you to notice when you're moving from stretch to strain to stress and it can give you a way of moving out of stress and back to the much more creative domain of stretch.

One such remedial action is the 'three-step breathing space'.

The 'three-step breathing space'

The 'three-step breathing space' is a very handy 'pocket-sized and portable' meditation that you can do pretty much anywhere and in any posture. You can do it while standing, waiting for a bus or train. You can do it while being driven in a cab. You can do it in bed and you can do it while sitting at your desk.

It takes more or less 3 minutes to do (although it's important not to get hung up around timings but just to give it as long as is needed).

As the name suggests, the practice is divided into three parts:

1) Acknowledge
In the first stage, you simply acknowledge what's up with you – right now.

Try that. In this moment, what thoughts are here? What feelings? What sensations are you mainly aware of? And what impulses?

It's not that there is anything you *should* be thinking, feeling, sensing or whatever. It's just a case of noticing, allowing and acknowledging. So – what's up?

2) Gather
In the second stage, you bring your attention to the breath and – for just a short while, maybe a minute or so – you deliberately focus your attention on the breath and you follow each in-breath and each out-breath. Just breathing. You're not going to do this for long and, when you're doing it as part of home practice in the hurly-burly of life, it may be an opportunity to find some moments of calm in a full and busy life, it may be worthwhile being a bit more deliberate here. Really keeping your attention with each breath, just for a short while.

3) Expand
In the third and final stage, you're getting ready to re-engage with the world around you and maybe bringing some of the calm you may have found in the previous stage into that re-engagement. So begin by broadening the focus of your attention. Become aware of the body as well as the breath. Feel the whole body breathing. Breathe with any sensations you find – especially, if there are any, with any challenging sensations. Just allow them, breathe with them, and feel the whole body breathing. Do that for a little while and then gradually begin to become more aware of the space around you and, when you're ready, open your eyes and bring that short practice to a close.

We can think of these three stages as roughly following the shape of an hour-glass:

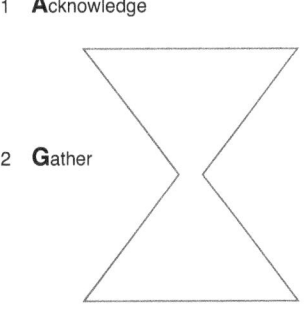

In the first stage your range of attention is quite broad – acknowledging whatever is going on for you.

In the second stage, you gather your attention together. And in the third stage you gradually expand your attention out again and then re-engage with the world around. If it helps you to remember, you could think of the acronym AGE: acknowledge, gather, expand.

This 'three-step breathing space' is so handy and portable that it's going to form part of home practice every day for the rest of the course. We suggest you do it three times a day at times you have decided in advance. You might want to make a note in your calendar of when these will be. It's a really helpful practice, but what we hear back from our course participants is that although they recognise its helpfulness, they often struggle to remember to do it. If it helps, you might set aside three short periods of time in your diary, well in advance, and set an alarm to remind yourself to do the practice. It's only 3 minutes or so long, but it can make a real difference.

Mindfulness of the breath and body

Another new practice for this week is the meditation 'mindfulness of the breath and body'. It's very like the 'mindfulness of breathing' practice we shared in the previous chapter, but this practice has a slightly broader focus.

You could think of your attention as being like a beam of light moving about a dimly lit space. Wherever the beam falls, wherever your attention moves, is more brightly lit than the surrounding area. What is more, you're able to regulate the focus of that beam. Sometimes it can be almost laser-like in its sharpness of focus. Sometimes it can be broader. Sometimes it can be almost like a floodlight, illuminating everything around it.

The spotlight of your attention was fairly tightly focused during the 'mindfulness of breathing'. For the 'mindfulness of breath and body', you begin to broaden that focus. One of the outcomes of working like this is that we can begin to become more intentional around the breadth and stability of our attentional focus in daily life – and also in the coaching context. We'll say more about that later.

Mindfulness of the breath and body meditation

1. Allow your attention to rest with the breath, as it moves in and as it moves out of the body, staying with the breath – however it shows up for you – for a few breaths.
2. When the attention is a little stable, begin to allow it to expand and start to include in its field some of the many and various sensations throughout the body. Staying with the sense of breath moving in the body, allow the primary focus now to begin to be a sense of the body as a whole – breathing.

3. You might, for example, become aware of sensations down at your feet – any sense of touch, pressure or contact. And you may become aware of sensations where your body meets the seat. As best you can, let whatever sensations you find simply be the sensations. Maybe notice sensations at the hands, at the shoulders, in the face – keeping these in awareness, feel the body breathing.
4. Stay with all these sensations, together with the sense of the breath and of the body as a whole, in a broad, spacious awareness. Just resting, with a gentle attention, to the changing field of sensations throughout the body from one moment to the next.
5. And when the mind wanders, notice where it went – you might want to lightly label that: 'Oh, there's thinking . . . ' or 'ah yes, planning . . .' and then gently and kindly return the attention to the breath and the body as a whole.
6. Let it all be simple – staying with the changing flow of sensations throughout the body – from one moment to the next.
7. You might find that you experience particularly intense sensations in some part of the body, and your attention may be repeatedly drawn to these sensations – away from the breath or the body as a whole. If that happens, you could gently shift your posture, staying aware of the intention to move and of all the sensations involved in the actual movement. Or else you might bring the focus of your attention right into the region of greatest intensity and with a gentle curiosity explore the detailed pattern of sensations there. What, precisely, are the qualities of those sensations? Where, exactly, are they located? Do they vary over time or shift around even with the region of greatest intensity? Just sensing what is there – directly experiencing it.
8. You might explore using the breath to carry your awareness right into the region of intensity, breathing into it, breathing out from it. Not tensing and bracing, instead opening and softening. As far as you can, just be with whatever's there – allowing, letting it be.
9. In the final few minutes of the meditation, bring your attention back to the breath alone. Perhaps seeing how the breath is always there – an anchor to return to in order to give yourself some calm or balance and a sense of simple self-acceptance.

Formal and informal practice

Before we describe the next meditation practice that forms part of our course, it's important to distinguish two broad types of mindfulness practice: formal practice and informal practice.

When we speak of formal mindfulness practices we're usually referring to one or another kind of meditation practice. Traditionally, it's said that there are four basic postures for meditation: sitting, lying down, standing and walking. We've already discussed sitting meditation, such as the 'mindfulness of breathing' or the 'mindfulness of breath and body' meditations. We saw that you can do 'the body scan' meditation lying down and we begin our mindful stretching with a short period of standing meditation. The next formal meditation practice we'll introduce is walking meditation, and it's important to notice the difference between the formal practice of walking meditation and simply walking mindfully, which is a great informal mindfulness practice.

Informal mindfulness practices should be popping up here and there in your daily life as the course progresses. You might find yourself stopping on your way into work in the morning and being captivated by the startling beauty of a cloud formation. Or you might notice and enjoy the feeling of warmth in your hands as you hold a warm drink. Or you might notice a repeating pattern in your own thinking and become curious about how it works and about the feelings and sensations that accompany it. All of that is wonderful, and important, informal mindfulness practice and you can't have too much of it.

Formal practices, on the other hand, are somewhat more structured. You set some time aside where you won't be disturbed, adopt a chosen posture, reduce input from the senses and you work intentionally with your chosen attentional focus, over and over.

'Walking meditation' is one such practice.

Walking meditation

1. Find a place where you won't be disturbed and where you can walk for five to ten paces in a straight line. It could be inside or outside.
2. Stand with your feet parallel and slightly apart, your knees are 'unlocked' so that they can flex slightly and let your arms hang by your sides.
3. You don't do this meditation with the eyes closed but you don't want to be looking around too much either. Just let your gaze rest on the floor 5 or 10 feet in front of you. Perhaps let your gaze be unfocused – you just want to see enough that you don't bump into anything.
4. Move your attention to the sensations where your feet meet the floor. Weight going down, height reaching up. It might be helpful to flex your knees slightly a few times to give you a clearer sense of the sensations in the feet and legs.
5. Stand and breathe – for a few breaths.
6. When you're ready, let your left heel slowly rise up from the floor. Keep your attention with sensations in your legs: sensations in the calves, the thighs and knees . . . Continuing the movement, let the whole of the left foot gently lift up as your weight shifts quite naturally to the right leg. Feel the sense of weight shifting. Staying aware of sensations in the left foot and leg, carefully swinging the leg forwards, let the left heel come into contact with the floor. Then the rest of the left foot makes contact with the floor. Feel the weight of the body shifting forwards onto the left leg and foot, as the right heel now comes off the floor.

7 When your weight is fully on the left leg, allow the rest of the right foot to lift up, swinging it slowly forwards, aware of the changing patterns of sensations in the feet and legs. Feel the right heel making contact with the floor. Sense weight shifting forwards onto the right foot as you place it gently on the floor, and feel the left heel rising up again.
8 Keep walking slowly through the space you've chosen, being particularly aware of sensations at the soles of the feet and heels as they contact the floor, as well as sensations in the legs as they swing forwards.
9 When you have gone as far as you want to in one direction, let your body turn about – it knows how to do that – and stay aware of the complex pattern of movements involved here as you continue walking in the opposite direction.
10 Walk up and down in this way, staying aware of sensations in the feet and legs. Feel the contact of the feet with the ground, keeping your gaze softly on the floor in front of you.
11 When your mind wanders, and you're no longer attending to the sensations of walking – gently bring the focus of attention back to the sensations in the feet, perhaps using the sensation of contact with the floor to anchor your experience and to reconnect with the present moment.
12 If your mind becomes agitated, it can be helpful to stop for a moment: just standing, feet together, breathing. Give the mind and body a chance to re-stabilise themselves, and then continue to walk.
13 Walk for 10 or so minutes – or longer if you wish.
14 At first, try walking at a pace that is slower than usual, giving yourself a chance to be fully aware of the sensations of walking. When you're comfortable walking slowly with awareness, you can experiment with walking faster – even quite quickly. If you feel particularly agitated, it might be helpful to begin walking quickly, with awareness, and to slow down naturally as your mind settles.

People often report that when they first start out with walking meditation the process is quite 'clunky' and feels very artificial. That's natural. When you begin to do consciously what you've always done unconsciously, it's very different and it can feel almost as if you're learning to walk again. If this happens for you, do persist. After a little while you'll likely find a greater sense of ease as you begin to become more familiar with the processes of walking meditation.

Coaching exercise for session 2

Focusing attention within

This exercise may be familiar to those who have trained in a Gestalt-based approach to coaching.

The thoughts, metaphors, images and sensations that arise within us as we are listening to our coachees may have significant bearing on what it is that they are trying to access and communicate from their side.

Or it may not.

The coach's task, while carefully attending to the client, is also to attend to what may be moving in their own field of experience – their thoughts, feelings, sensations and impulses. These may be 'private' to the coach, or they may have a relational significance in the moment – they may be pointing to something in the client's inner world.

The coach's task here would be to offer lightly to the coachee what it is they are noticing in themselves and to check whether that has any resonance for their client. The information that emerges from that kind of enquiry can lead to powerful insights in the coachee.

This exercise is designed to foster the capacity to engage in that kind of experience during a live coaching session.

Find someone with whom you can partner up for this exercise.

One of you will listen while the other talks (about any subject) for about five minutes without interrupting.

The listener's task here is to pay attention both to what the speaker is saying and also to how their own inner experience – their thoughts, feelings, sensations and impulses – are being impacted and are changing from moment to moment as the conversation unfolds.

When the conversation ends, the listener shares with the speaker both what they heard the speaker saying as well as what was coming up for them as the conversation unfolded – their own thoughts, feelings, sensations and impulses.

It is important here that the listener keeps their attention with the speaker, not getting too fixated on trying to remember every passing detail of their own changing experience. Instead, they should trust that they will remember what they were meant to when the time comes to share it. Every conversation leaves an imprint. Our task as mindful coaches is to attend to these.

Home practice for week three

- Practise the movements on the track 'Mindful Movement (Shorter Version)' (Track 7) daily for 6 days. The point of these movements is to connect directly with the body. Working with your body in this way can allow you to experience more of yourself and to connect up your experiences of body sensations, feelings, thoughts and impulses. If you have any back or other health difficulties that may cause problems, make your own decision as to which (if any) of these exercises to do, taking good care of your body.
- At a different time, practise 5 minutes of 'mindfulness of breathing' each day. Use the track 'Mindfulness of Breathing (5 Minutes)' (Track 5) for guidance here.

- Practise using the 'three-step breathing space' three times a day at times that you have decided in advance. For one of those times, use the track 'Three-Step Breathing Space' (Track 8) for guidance.
- Complete the unpleasant-events diary (*see page 50*), making one entry per day. Use this as an opportunity to become more fully aware of the thoughts, feelings, sensations and impulses that come with one unpleasant event each day. Notice these and record them as soon as you're comfortably able to. For example, you might try to record any words or images that occurred with your thoughts, or the precise nature and location of bodily sensations. But don't strain at this – it's just a guide to help you to notice.
  - What are the unpleasant events that 'pull you off centre' or 'get you down' (no matter how big or small)?
  - What do you most not want to look at?
  - Notice when you move into automatic pilot – under what circumstances does this occur?

As best you can, try to 'capture' the moments of your day.

Home practice for week four

- Practise 20 minutes of sitting meditation at least three times this week (Track 16)
- On the days when you're not doing 20 minutes of sitting meditation, practise the 'mindfulness of breathing' meditation, using the track 'Mindfulness of Breathing (10 Minutes)' (Track 4), and, either straight afterwards or at another time, do 10 minutes of 'walking meditation', using the track 'Walking Meditation' (Track 9) for guidance.
- Practise the 'three-step breathing space' at least three times a day. Either when you think of it or connecting it to three regular activities you do or places you go to every day (maybe on waking up and/or going to bed; before a television programme you usually watch; before a particular meal; on first sitting down in your car, or on the bus or at your desk.)
- In addition, practise the 'three-step breathing space' whenever you notice unpleasant feelings or come to feel unbalanced.
- Take some time to reflect on these halfway-review questions:
  - What am I learning through this process?
  - What do I need to do over the next four weeks to get the most out of the rest of the course?

Table 2.1 Unpleasant-events diary; notice one unpleasant event each day.

Day	What was the experience?	How did your body feel – in detail – during the experience?	What feelings came along with the event?	What thoughts went through your mind at the time?	What impulses came along with the event?	What are you thinking right now, as you write this?
Example	On an overcrowded train, stuck on the tracks, late for work.	Tight jaw, churning stomach, tight shoulders.	Frustration, anger, restlessness.	I'm going to have such a hassle explaining this at work – again!	Phone the CEO of the train company and scream at him!	That was quite a reaction!
Monday						
Tuesday						
Wednesday						
Thursday						
Friday						
Saturday						
Sunday						

Notes

1 www.scribd.com/document/265348695/Microsoft-Attention-Spans-Research-Report.
2 Bartley, T. (2002) *Mindfulness-Based Cognitive Therapy for Cancer*, Oxford: Wiley-Blackwell.
3 Ekman, P. (2007) *Emotions Revealed: Recognizing Faces and Feelings to Improve Communication and Emotional life*, New York: Times Books.
4 Flanagan, O. (2007) *The Bodhisattva's Brain*, Cambridge, MA: MIT Press.
5 Siegel, D. (2010) *The Mindful Therapist: A Clinicians Guide in Mindsight and Neural Integration*, New York: W.W. Norton & Co.
6 Farb, N.A. *et al.* 'Attending to the present: mindfulness meditation reveals distinct neural modes of self-reference', *SCAN*, 2(2007): 313–322.
7 Davidson, R. J. (2010) 'Empirical explorations of mindfulness: conceptual and methodological conundrums.' *Emotion*, 10(1): 8–11.
8 Davidson, R.J. (2002) 'Anxiety and Affective Style: Role of Prefrontal Cortex and Amygdala', *Biological Psychiatry*, 51: 68–80.
9 Begley, S. (2007) *Train Your Mind, Change Your Brain: How a New Science Reveals Our Extraordinary Potential to Transform Ourselves*, Ballantine Books.
10 Davidson, R.J. *et al.* (2003) 'Alterations in brain and immune function produced by mindfulness meditation', *Psychosomatic Medicine*, 65: 564–570.
11 HSE. (2008) 'Health and safety statistics 2007/08', *Labour Force Survey*, www.hse.gov.uk/statistics/overall/hssh0708.pdf.
12 Webster, S. *et al.* (2007) *Psychosocial Working Conditions in Britain in 2007*, Health at Work Group, Statistics Branch, Health and Safety Executive.
13 HSE. (2008) 'Health and safety statistics 2007/08', *Labour Force Survey*, www.hse.gov.uk/statistics/overall/hssh0708.pdf.
14 Government Business (2011) *The Fine Line Between Pressure and Stress,* as quoted in Chaskalson, M. (2011) *The Mindful Workplace: Developing Resilient Individuals and Resonant Organizations with MBSR,* Chichester, UK: Wiley-Blackwell.
15 Houdmont, J. *et al.* (2011) *Work-related stress case definitions and prevalence rates in national surveys,* Occupational Medicine, *60: 658–661.*
16 Williams, S. (1994) *Managing Pressure for Peak Performance: The Positive Approach to Stress*, London: Kogan Page.
17 Britton, W.B. (2005) 'The physiology of stress and depression and reversal by meditative techniques.' Integrating Mindfulness-Based Interventions into Medicine, Health Care, and Society. 4th Annual Conference for Clinicians, Researchers and Educators. Worcester, MA, April 1–4.

3 Session 3
Working with thoughts

Here's a brief exercise you might want to try that will help to illustrate some of the themes of this chapter.

We will outline two scenarios – scenario A and scenario B. We'll describe scenario A first and then invite you to imagine your way into it and reflect on what you might think or feel when you've imagined your way into it. Then we'll outline scenario B and invite you to do the same.

Both scenarios are designed for someone who is running their own coaching practice. If that doesn't fit your own circumstances, feel free to tweak the scenarios towards something that more closely fits your own circumstances.

> **Scenario A:** There's a really interesting piece of work going that you've been invited to pitch for. You turned up, made your pitch, which seemed to go well, and you're told that you'll hear back from them with a decision by 5pm on Friday next week.
>
> Friday comes around and it's been one of those weeks. You feel as if you've been trudging through treacle the whole time. You can't get on top of your emails; your to-do list is overflowing and none of your coaching sessions have seemed all that sparky. One of those weeks. By Friday, you're feeling pretty low and, at 5:30pm, no one's called or emailed about the pitch.

What do you think? What do you feel?

Just sit with that for 15 seconds or so, imagining your way into this scenario.

> **Scenario B:** There's a really interesting piece of work going that you've been invited to pitch for. You turned up, made your pitch, which you think went reasonably well, and you're told that you'll hear back from them with a decision by 5pm on Friday next week.
>
> Friday comes around and it's been a really great week. Everything seems to have gone really well. You feel on top of your workload and you've had some really stimulating coaching sessions. Come Friday, you're feeling pretty good and, by 5:30pm, no one's called or emailed about the pitch.

What do you think? What do you feel?

Just sit with that for 15 seconds or so, imagining your way into this scenario.

When we run this exercise on our courses we now ask just one question: 'Scenario A and scenario B – was there any difference in the way you responded to not being called or emailed?'

Although some people may say that they didn't feel different in either case, what we usually find is that people report that they have divergent sets of thoughts and feelings as a response to the two different scenarios. They feel differently about what happened and they tell themselves different stories about what the lack of response from the client means.

That tells us something important about the nature of our thoughts.

In one frame of mind we interpret events one way, in another frame of mind we interpret them another way.

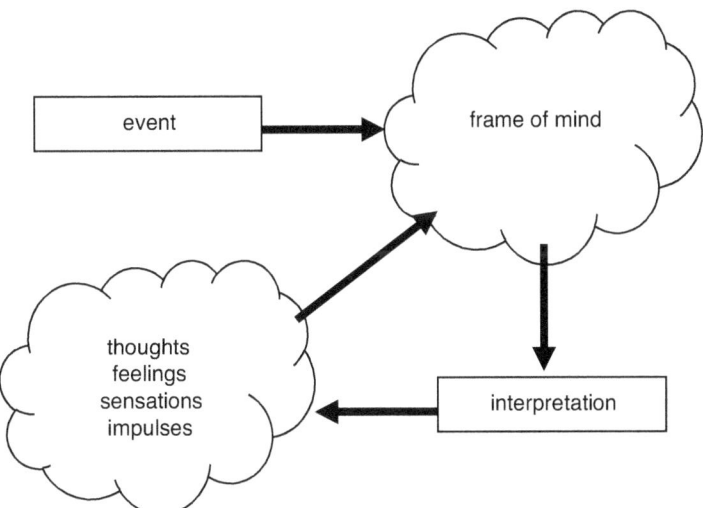

Figure 3.1

What we see above is that an event encounters a frame of mind.

That frame of mind colours how we interpret the event (when we were low after a tough week, we interpreted the fact that no one came back to us after the pitch in one way; when we were feeling more buoyant after a good week, we interpreted the same event in a different way).

That interpretation gives rise to a set of thoughts, feelings, sensations and impulses, and those thoughts, feelings, sensations and impulses, in turn colour our frame of mind.

So, we may *say* that we're feeling low, or frustrated, or angry because of an event – because, in the case of our exercise, the person never called or emailed as they said they would. But what the exercise reveals is that really it's the way we *interpret* that event that gives rise to our thoughts, feeling and so on – and that interpretation was strongly influenced by the frame of mind it came out of.

It's the interpretation – the story we tell about events – that drives much of how we respond to things.

We tell ourselves stories about the events we encounter and that's a key part of the process by which we continually shape and reshape our experience, and the interesting thing about this process is that by and large, we can't *not* do that.

Think about this:

- John was on his way to school.
- He was worried about the maths lesson.
- He didn't think he could control the class today.
- After all, it's not part of the caretaker's duties.

See how your mind worked as you read through those tiny vignettes. At each stage you'll most likely have formed some kind of mental picture, told yourself a kind of mini-story. Each time you were given new information, that story was re-written, but it's probably only at the final line – 'it's not part of the caretaker's duties' – that you get to see what you've been up to.

We're constantly involved in a process of creating inner narratives that make sense of the world we encounter and by and large we're not aware of ourselves doing that. We don't see these narratives for what they are. They're just narratives, just stories we tell about how things are.

To understand this process and its implications for mindful coaching more deeply, imagine yet another scenario:

> You're on a family holiday by the seaside, somewhere warm, and you're just beginning to unwind. You find yourself taking a solitary hour or so by yourself along the beach and you're noticing how good it feels to be there. You can feel the sand under your feet, the sea air smells just great, there's the sound of the gulls, the changing patterns of the waves and the warmth of the sun. It's all helping you to ease into just being present with it all.

Right now, it feels good.

Then, you start to wonder. What will you give the family for dinner this evening? You mentally review the food cupboard back at the cottage you're renting and you start to work out a recipe. Then you think 'hmm . . . no, they won't enjoy that . . . Last time I made it, they didn't enjoy it.'

Now the thought-pump starts going.

'You know, that happens a lot. They often don't like what I give them. In fact, lots of the things I try to do for them don't work out. . . And actually, quite a lot of what I've been trying to do lately hasn't worked out.'

And the thought-pump speeds up.

'Actually, when I think about it, a lot of what I've tried in the last while hasn't worked out.'

Now the pump is really going.

'If things keep on not working out like that, I don't know where I'm going to end up! My career – am I really cut-out for this kind of thing? Can I keep going? But if I give up now, what's going to happen to us?'

And on and on.

Now whether or not that kind of scenario feels in any way familiar, we hope you can see that what it describes are two different modes of mind. We referred briefly to these in the previous chapter. There is the experiential mode of mind and there is the narrative mode of mind – and we experience these quite differently.

When you're doing things like walking along the beach, just being present with all the various sensory inputs, you're in experiential mode. Although the scenario we outlined describes a pleasant set of experiences, experiential mode isn't confined to what is pleasant. You can be present to unpleasant or to challenging experiences too. We'll discuss that further in the section below on working with the difficult. For now though, the main thing to notice is that the experiential mode is very different to the narrative mode. It is sense-based and present-centred.

Narrative mode comes about when we start abstracting from our experience – thinking, remembering, imagining and so on. Again, it's important to realise that although the scenario we gave featured an unpleasant and unhelpful pattern of narrative, a pattern of catastrophisation, narrative mode is not always negative – far from it. When you sit down to review your to-do list, plan a presentation, write a book, these are all examples of narrative mode. The capacity to work in that mode is a vital ingredient in what makes us human and it hugely underpins our culture. But, as we saw above, there can be a downside.

Norman Farb, whose work we spoke about in the previous chapter, has looked at how these two modes show up in people who have trained in mindfulness.

Using neuroimaging, Farb and his colleagues have shown that people at large have great difficulty in disengaging from narrative, judgemental modes of experience, whereas people who are trained in mindfulness are better at noticing which mode they are in and are more easily able to switch modes at will.[1]

One of the benefits of this is that the experiential mode simply gives you a break from the incessant demands of the narrative mode. As we've seen, the narrative mode of mind can be truly wonderful – it's the place of poetry, planning and all creative thought. But it's also the space where we catastrophise, criticise ourselves and others, engage in mood lowering and self-undermining ruminations and so on. These are all variants of what one of our course participants called 'the poison-parrot' who sits on your shoulder continually whispering unhelpful sentences into your ear.

Rather than get into a fight with that parrot, the capacity at such times to deliberately move your attention just to your changing body sensations can be hugely liberating, helping you to come away from problems that are created or perpetuated through negative thinking. Turning to the present moment, using the body as an anchor to do that, can be a powerful technique for disengaging from catastrophisation and rumination and it can disrupt unhelpful cycles of self-criticism. This can be significantly more effective than the usual strategy of simply trying to suppress unhelpful thoughts and feelings.[2]

In the coaching context, when you find yourself going off down a track of excessively 'thinking about' the session rather than simply being present with the coachee, you can use the interoceptive capacity you are building through your regular mindfulness practice to come back to the body, back to presence, back to just being with the coachee – right here, right now.

Metacognition

As you've been going through this course and doing the home practice week after week, your sessions of formal mindfulness practice probably go through a cycle somewhat like this:

You sit down to practice, maybe for example with the intention of letting your awareness rest just with the breath, and then you find you start to think about things. A stream of thoughts and feelings comes up and you get carried away with the stream. Then you notice that you're doing that – that you're thinking, not simply following the breath – and so you let go of the stream of thoughts, at least to some extent, and you come back to the breath again.

You do this over and over and over. In that way, you're learning and practising four key cognitive skills:

1   The skill of seeing that your attention is not where you want it to be.
2   The skill of unhooking your attention from where you don't want it to be.
3   The skill of placing your attention where you want it to be.
4   The skill of keeping your attention where you want it to be – at least for a while.

Using the skills you develop through meditation in the context of daily life, you can begin to choose to bring your attention to your body and your senses when you notice that your mind has wandered – during a coaching session, for example. And you can do the same when you find yourself lost in unresourceful modes of thinking and feeling. When you notice the poison-parrot at work, whispering (or even shouting) unhelpfully in your ear, rather than trying to suppress that, which most often doesn't work, you can turn your attention to what you're sensing right now – in this body in this moment: a tightening in your jaw, a churning sensation in your stomach, whatever's there. That shift from narrative to experiential processing can leave you feeling very much more resourceful and better able to manage what troubles you.

The process, of *noticing* your thoughts and feelings rather than just being lost in a stream of thinking and feeling, is a state of metacognitive awareness. In that state, your mental processes become the object of your attention rather than you being lost in them as a perceiving subject. That shift, a subtle rotation of consciousness through 90 degrees so that you can *observe* the stream of thoughts and feelings rather than just being thinking and feeling is a key component in mindfulness training.

In an article published in 2015, Eric Garland and colleagues suggested that the capacity to enter into states of metacognitive awareness from time to time can powerfully facilitate the creation of a new sense of meaning and purpose in our lives.[3]

They begin their discussion by distinguishing between hedonic and eudaimonic well-being. This is a distinction which goes back in time to ancient Greek philosophy, most notably to the philosophers Aristotle and Epicurus, who took different views on the subject. Hedonic approaches to happiness – the Epicurean approach – depends on obtaining pleasure and avoiding pain. Eudaimonic well-being – the Aristotelean approach – is characterised by a sense of purpose and meaningful, positive engagement with life that arises when one's life activities accord with deeply held values, even at times of adversity.

Garland and colleagues propose a 'mindfulness-to-meaning theory', which asserts that by modifying how one attends to the thoughts, feelings and sensations that come along with moments of distress, mindfulness introduces a new flexibility into the creation of autobiographical meaning. This stimulates our natural human capacity to positively reappraise adverse events and to savour the positive aspects of experience. By fostering positive reappraisals and emotions, they suggest, mindfulness has the capacity to generate deep eudaimonic meanings that promote resilience and engagement with a more valued and purposeful life.

They illustrate this theory with a diagram.

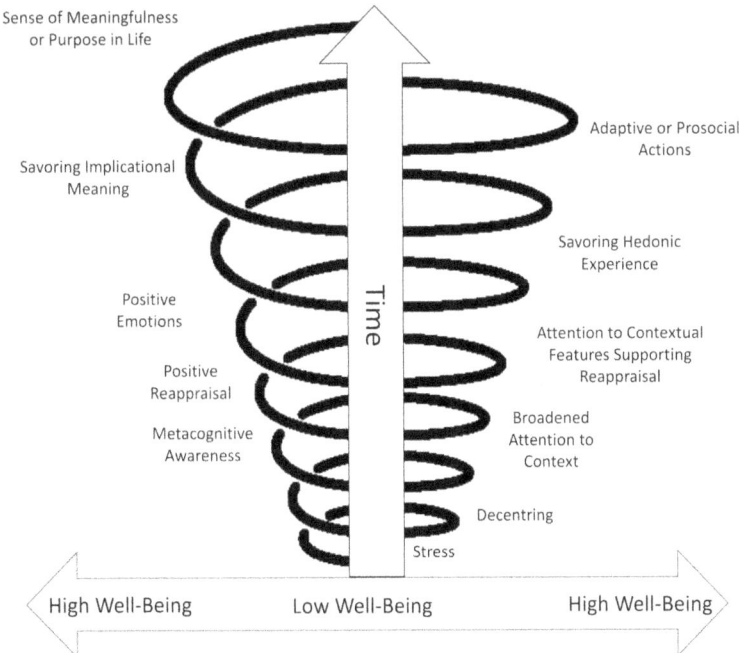

Figure 3.2 The mindfulness-to-meaning theory

The diagram illustrates a process, unfolding over time, in which an increase in the width of the spiral describes an increase in the magnitude and depth of eudaimonic well-being.

To understand this diagram, we need first to understand their term 'decentering'. As an experience, it is probably a little bit familiar at this part of the course. Decentering describes the move we described earlier, where instead of being lost in your thoughts, feelings, sensations and impulses as an experiencing *subject*, you instead see them just *as* thoughts, feelings, sensations and impulses. In other words, your thoughts and so on become *objects* of your experience that you can attend to.

Consider the difference between (1) the experience simply being irritable and (2) the experience of noticing that you're scowling and that you're having irritable thoughts and feelings. The move from state (1) to state (2) is a metacognitive shift that is accompanied by the experience of decentering.

Starting at the bottom of the spiral above, the practice of mindfulness meditation enables one to decentre from the way one appraises the experience of stress or other forms of distress.

You enter a state of metacognitive awareness which de-automatises your previously habitual cognitive sets. As a result, you feel more resourceful and the scope of your attention broadens to take in new, and previously ignored, information about yourself and your context.

That positive tuning of the attentional system allows you to take in fresh information with which to formulate a more positive reappraisal of the stressor.

As a result, more positive emotions may arise and these can then be savoured in a way that infuses eudaimonic meaning into the hedonic processing of the various contextual features that support the reappraisal. Garland and colleagues refer here to the way you now savour the 'implicational meaning' of moments of experience. Implicational meaning refers to the 'felt sense' we have of what we're experiencing – as opposed to the logical, rational meaning of it, which would be 'propositional meaning'.

Based on that new sense of meaning, the possibility of now engaging in more adaptive and/or prosocial activities emerges. You begin to feel more engaged in the stream of life around you, and this leads to an enhanced sense of meaningfulness or purpose in life.

To give this idea more concrete meaning, Garland and colleagues illustrate it with an example from some moments in the life of a cancer survivor who had been taught mindfulness as a part of his hospital treatment.

One morning, after completing a gruelling series of surgeries followed by several chemotherapy and radiation treatments, this patient found himself overwhelmed by thoughts of his impending doom.

As he had been trained to do, he started a session of mindfulness of breathing practice and was able to acknowledge and accept the presence of those thoughts without suppressing them. He mindfully decentred from the stress appraisal 'My life is over – I'm doomed,' and began to metacognitively

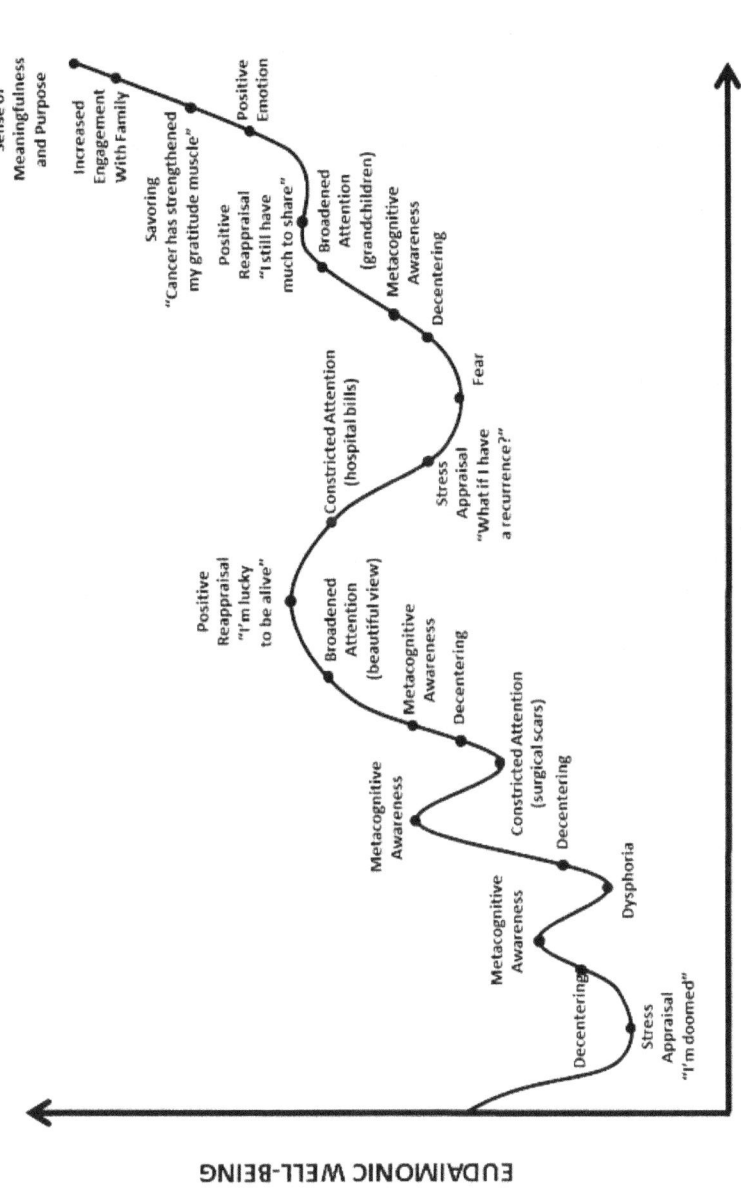

Figure 3.3 The mindfulness-to-meaning theory in action, as exemplified by a case example from a cancer survivor

observe a feeling of great despair, along with intense sensations of heaviness in his chest and a gnawing emptiness in his gut.

He returned the focus of his attention to his breath in order to decentre from that negative emotional state and this enabled him to adopt a fresh meta-cognitive perspective of his own experience. After sustaining that for several moments, he found his attention captured by the fresh scars on his belly where the cancer had been surgically removed.

Becoming aware of how the focus on his scars constricted his attention, he was then able to re-engage in the meditation and again he decentred into a mode of metacognitive awareness. As a result, his attention broadened and he found he was able to encompass, in a broad focus of present-centred awareness, both the sensations of his breath and the beautiful view out his window to the snowcapped mountains beyond.

Attending to these, a positive reappraisal arose: 'I'm lucky to be alive,' he thought, and he felt a sense of relief and contentment.

A little while later though, as he was filing his bills from the hospital, he was distressed by the thought 'What if I have a recurrence?' Again, he turned to his practice of mindfulness, becoming aware, in his body, of feelings of fear.

Acknowledging these emotions, allowing the 'felt sense' of it, he returned his attention to the breath and once more decentred from the thoughts of cancer recurrence into a state of metacognitive awareness. From that space of broader awareness, he watched the fearful thoughts and feelings dissipate 'like clouds dissolving into mist'.

His difficult feelings were gradually replaced by a sense of equanimity, out of which arose a positive, buoyant state as his attention broadened to take in the photograph of his grandchildren on a shelf. Enjoying the image of their smiling faces, he made another positive reappraisal: 'Cancer or no cancer, I still have so much I want to share with them.'

His attention broadened still further, encompassing other positive aspects of his past and present; his long marriage to a loving partner, his significant professional accomplishments, the activities that he loved. As he began to savour the positive emotions that arose during these moments of contemplation, he came to see that 'cancer has strengthened my gratitude muscle'.

From a coaching perspective, one of the interesting things about the various arcs of this journey is that it echoes some of the ways in which a productive series of coaching sessions might play out. Coaching, at its best, can facilitate positive reappraisal. But what's perhaps most interesting here is the way the patient described led himself through the journey. In a certain sense, by being able to stand back and observe his own unfolding thoughts, feelings, sensations and so on, metacognitively – he coached himself.

Working with the difficult

The humanistic psychologist Carl Rogers spoke of three core conditions for therapeutic change in helping contexts – congruence, unconditional positive regard and empathy.[4] We will discuss unconditional positive regard and empathy in the next chapter. Here, we want to focus on congruence.

Incongruence is a discrepancy between your actual experience and the way you represent that experience to yourself and others.

Rogers suggested that the more the therapist or coach is simply themselves in the relationship, the more congruent they are, with no front or facade, the greater the likelihood that the relational process that unfolds between them will enable the client to change in a constructive manner.

As a coach, that requires you to be aware of – and to adopt an allowing and accepting attitude to – the thoughts, feelings, sensations and impulses that are flowing within you from moment to moment. Mindfulness training significantly enhances your ability to do that.

One of the things this calls for is a greater capacity to stay with, and to allow, whatever difficult or challenging thoughts, feelings, sensations or impulses arise – without reacting to them. Instead of denying them, suppressing them, immediately acting on them or in any other way reacting to them, we learn to mindfully allow what emerges simply to emerge and then we can choose how best to respond to what has emerged.

This capacity to respond, rather than just react, to what is difficult is a key outcome of the Mindfulness for Coaches programme.

This isn't just a matter of opinion – although it's borne out time and again by our own observations. Research from a variety of studies, as cited by the researchers Davis and Hayes[5] has demonstrated that mindfulness meditation enables people to become less reactive and have greater cognitive flexibility. Mindfulness practitioners develop skills of self-observation that disengage the automatic neurological pathways that were created by prior learning, and this enables what emerges in their present moment experience to be integrated in new ways. Meditation appears to activate regions of the brain associated with more adaptive responses to stressful or negative situations, and the activation of these brain regions corresponds with faster recovery from negative provocations.

'Sitting with the difficult' meditation

With the 'mindfulness of breathing' we established some calm and focus. With 'mindfulness of the breath and body' we broadened the field of attention to become more aware of what was going on in the body from moment to moment. Now, we add another dimension to this. In the 'sitting with the difficult' meditation we begin consciously to explore what it's like to allow whatever difficult or unwanted experiences showed up in meditation simply to be as they are. As much as possible, we bring an attitude of gentle, kindly curiosity to those experiences: allowing them, letting them be.

– Begin by practising a session of 'mindfulness of breathing' followed by 'mindfulness of the breath and body'.

- Scan through the different elements of your experience right now. What thoughts are here? What feelings, sensations and impulses – if any? Just acknowledging these, noticing them with no attempt to change them. You're not trying to move your attention away from these right now, or to make them any other way than they are.
- If any of these thoughts, feelings, sensations or impulses feel in any way challenging or unwanted, try seeing what it's like to be with them differently – allowing, letting them be.
- If you notice challenging thoughts or feelings, see what body sensations or impulses come along with these. If you encounter unwanted sensations in the body, see what thoughts, feelings and impulses come along.
- You may find connections here or you may not. It's not important to *think* about what you're noticing, simply to notice. See what's here and allow it to be so.
- If you sense unwanted body sensations, you might see what it's like to move your attention right into the heart of the sensation – approaching, rather than avoiding, what is difficult.
- Experiment with 'breathing into' unwanted sensations, 'breathing out' from them, approaching this imaginatively – just as in 'the body scan'.
- Keep your attention with the physical aspect of what is unwanted, staying with that part of the body where the sensations are strongest, holding what you find there with an attitude that is welcoming, curious, kind, allowing. This isn't a cold and clinical investigation, it's gentle and warm.
- Whatever feelings, sensations, thoughts or impulses show up – they're all allowed. See what it's like to treat them honourably, with warmth and kindness.
- Keep noticing, watching sensations shifting, noticing their changing intensity.
- When your attention settles for a time and you're able to stay with the changing flow of sensations for a while, try deepening the allowing attitude. You could, for example, inwardly say 'it's OK – I can be with this. Here it is. It's allowed. Let me be open to it.' Or any other set of phrases that work for you. Not tensing or bracing against unwanted sensations, instead opening and softening. If it helps, on the out-breath you might say to yourself 'opening', 'softening' over and over.
- By saying 'it's OK – I can be with this' or 'it's allowed' you're not pretending or saying that everything's fine. You're just staying open to what's here, letting what *is* the case *be* the case. You might even inwardly say to yourself 'it's OK not to want these feelings and sensations, but here they are. Let me be open to them.'
- You don't have to *like* what you're experiencing right now. Just see what it's like to stay with it – allowing, letting it be.
- Not all unwanted physical sensations come with a strong emotional charge. If you don't find any strong emotions as you're sitting through

this practice that's fine – just stay with whatever body sensations turn up – especially those that aren't pleasant.

As well as experimenting with this meditation as part of home practice in the next week, you could try doing a version of it in your daily life.

As you're going about things, see what it's like to bring an attitude of gentle and kindly curiosity to whatever thoughts, feelings, sensations or impulses your mind is repeatedly drawn towards. Notice how you relate to what arises there.

If you do that, you might notice that sometimes you experience your thoughts, feelings, sensations and so on in a non-accepting, reactive, way. It's part of the human condition to try to hold on to those experiences you like, becoming attached. Or to push away experiences you don't like – out of fear, irritation or annoyance, tightening and contracting in the face of these.

Allowing and letting your experience be – making space for whatever is going on, rather than trying to create some other state – lets you settle for a while into a simple awareness of what is present.

The allowing approach we're discussing here isn't a clever way of 'fixing' your experience or getting rid of the unwanted. Nor is this about trying deliberately to change your feelings. Instead, the intention here is to soften the way you hold unwanted experiences in awareness. The intention is to ease and to open out of the aversion that underlies much of our distress. Sometimes the feelings or sensations may change, sometimes they may not. The main thing you're trying to do here is to change how you *relate* to them – and that changes everything.

Mindfulness of sounds and thoughts meditation

You begin this meditation by letting your attention rest with the breath and the body as a whole and then, letting go of the particular attention to the breath and the body, instead open your attention wide to take in sounds from all directions. Just let sounds come and go as they do. You're not *thinking about* sounds here – you're simply *experiencing* them. Not thinking about the meanings or implications of sounds, just allowing them to be patterns of sense experience. Each has their own rhythm, pitch, timbre and duration. Let them come, go and change as they do, letting them be.

After a while, drop that attention to sounds and move on to the second part of the practice – turning your attention to what's moving in your mind.

This can be a little trickier. You will most likely have noticed in all the meditation practices that the mind is rarely still. Thoughts, images, memories, emotions, come and go all the time. Up till now, whenever you've noticed that mental activity has pulled your attention away from your intended focus, the instruction has been simply to notice that this has happened, see where the attention went and then gently bring it back to the breath and so on.

Now we're going to do something different. Instead of noticing a thought or other kind of mental activity and shifting the focus away from it, the intention here is instead to observe it – to 'let it be' as it changes and flows. The intention here is simply to notice, paying attention from moment to moment, to whatever is moving in the space of the mind.

This is a subtle practice and here it's even more important than usual to let go of any attempt to 'get it right'.

There are a few tricky points to deal with.

When you turn your attention to thoughts or images or other mental activity, it's very easy to get swept up into them. One moment you may be observing a thought, then very quickly you find yourself *thinking* that thought. That's just how it sometimes goes. It's not a mistake, but see what it's like to come back to that 'observer' perspective, over and over.

There can be an interesting mechanism at work here. When you become mindful of a thought or other mental activity, that process of mindful attention can shift your brain away from the default mode network of activation that was driving your thoughts, and so your mind may calm. Previously when you meditated there might have been lots of thoughts, now you may find that when you consciously seek to attend to thoughts they are not there to be attended to.

This is quite common and it's not a problem. If it happens to you, just enjoy the process and wait. Something will turn up.

You may also find that without a definite focus such as the breath, the mind can become quite agitated in meditation. If that happens for you, just notice it and gently and kindly bring your attention to the breath for a few moments to get some steadiness before broadening the focus once more.

- Let your attention rest with the breath, as it moves in and out of the body.
- Aware of the body as a whole, breathing, begin gently to attend to the field of sensations throughout the body, from one moment to the next.
- Begin to focus on the sense of sound. Move your attention to what you're hearing right now and let that awareness open and expand, becoming receptive to whatever sounds arise.
- Not searching for sounds or listening out for particular sounds. Instead, simply becoming receptive to sounds from all directions – obvious sounds and subtler sounds; be aware of the spaces between sounds; aware of silence.
- Staying aware of sounds *as* sounds. Noticing any tendency to interpret sounds, to attach stories and meanings to them. Instead, see what it's like to just sit with an awareness of their sensory qualities: their changing pitch, loudness, rhythm and duration.
- After a short while, let go of your awareness of sounds and, instead, open your attention to whatever's moving in your mind – thoughts, images, dreams, emotions . . .
- Just as sounds are experienced in the mind, so too your thoughts and other mental activities are simply experiences in the mind. Just as sounds arise, linger and pass, so too thoughts arise, linger and pass.

- There is no need to try to make thoughts come or go – just let them arise and pass naturally, as they will.
- Like clouds in the sky, thoughts arise, they drift through the mind and they pass away again. Whether these clouds are dark and stormy or white and feathery, just notice them and let them be.
- You may find other analogies helpful here: you might see your thoughts like the carriages of a railway train, passing through a station. But it's not your train. You don't have to get onto it. You can just be content to watch it go by.
- Or maybe your thoughts are like leaves on a stream, just floating downstream while you're sitting on the bank watching.
- If any thoughts come to you with intense feelings or emotions, pleasant or unpleasant, as much as you can just note their 'emotional charge' and intensity and simply let them be.
- If your mind becomes unfocused and scattered, if it gets repeatedly drawn into the drama of your thinking and imagining, perhaps come back to the breath for a few moments, using the breath as an anchor to gently steady your focus.
- Before bringing the practice to a close, spend a few moments coming back to the breath again and following each in-breath and each out-breath.

Coaching exercise for session 3

Noticing judgements

Get into a pair. The idea in this exercise is that one person listens, the other talks (about any subject) for about 5 minutes without interrupting.

The task of the listener here is to notice any tendency on their own part to begin to judge what the client is saying. Inner statements like 'You're wrong', or 'You're missing the point', or 'You just don't get it' or even more extreme – 'You're coarse', or 'You're greedy', or 'You're an idiot'.

What we find on our courses is that when we raise issues like this in the group, we're often told things like 'Oh, I never think like that about my clients'. But we also often notice on the same courses that coaches will sometimes talk amongst each other about some clients – obviously anonymised, in ways that can be quite disparaging.

So, it's important to notice that the mind judges. It's not wrong, it's not right – it's just what the mind does. The question is can we notice that, and when we have done so are we able to suspend that tendency – at least for a time.

Home practice for week five

1 Practise the 'sitting with the difficult' meditation once this week – using the tracks 'Mindfulness of the Breath and Body' and 'Sitting With The Difficult' (Tracks 10, 13) in sequence.

2 For your regular practice, do a 20-minute meditation – 'Mindfulness of the Breath and Body' and 'Mindfulness of Sounds and Thoughts' (Tracks 10, 11). If you'd like to, you might try a few sessions of sitting without audio guidance. If you want to keep to time and have a smartphone, there are several apps available to help with this. I use Insight Timer myself – but do look around and choose your own.
3 Practise the 'three-step breathing space' three times each day. You could either do this when you think of it or you could connect it to three regular activities you do or places you go to, such as on first waking up or before going to bed, before a television programme you regularly watch, before a meal, on first sitting down in your car or on the bus or train, or when you get to your desk or workstation.
4 Whenever you notice yourself starting to feel stressed, practise the 'three-step breathing space' to cope, exploring ways of responding with greater mindfulness and more friendliness to yourself and the situation.
5 Bring awareness to moments of reaction and explore options for responding with greater mindfulness and creativity. Practise opening up space for responding in the present moment. Explore how using the breath can bring you into the present moment.
6 When you find yourself willing to 'embrace the unwanted', what does that feel like?

Home practice for week six

1 Do 20 minutes of meditation each day, using 'Mindfulness of the Breath and Body' and 'Mindfulness of Sounds and Thoughts' (Tracks 10, 11). If you'd like to, you might try a few sessions of sitting without audio guidance.
2 Practise the 'three-step breathing space' three times each day. You could either do this when you think of it or you could connect it to three regular activities you do or places you go to, such as on first waking up or before going to bed, before a television programme you regularly watch, before a meal, on first sitting down in your car or on the bus or train, or when you get to your desk or workstation.
3 Notice how you are relating to your thoughts day to day, as well as in the meditation practice.

Notes

1 Farb, N.A. *et al*. 'Attending to the present: mindfulness meditation reveals distinct neural modes of self-reference', *SCAN*, 2(2007): 313–322.
2 Garland, E.L., Farb, N.A., Goldin, P.R. and Fredrickson, B.L. (2015) 'Mindfulness broadens awareness and builds eudaimonic meaning: a process model of mindful positive emotion regulation', *Psychological Inquiry*, 26(4): 293–314.
3 Garland, E.L., Farb, N.A., Goldin, P.R. and Fredrickson, B.L. (2015) 'Mindfulness broadens awareness and builds eudaimonic meaning: a process model of mindful positive emotion regulation', *Psychological Inquiry*, 26(4): 293–314.

Garland, E.L., Farb, N.A., Goldin, P.R. and Fredrickson, B.L. (2015) 'The mindfulness-to-meaning theory: extensions, applications, and challenges at the attention-appraisal-emotion interface, *Psychological Inquiry*, 26(4): 377–387.
4 Rogers, C.R. (1980) *Way of Being*, New York: Houghton Mifflin.
5 Davis, D.M. and Hayes, J.A. (2010) 'What are the benefits of mindfulness? A practice review of psychotherapy-related research', *Psychotherapy*, 48(2): 198–208.

4 Session 4
Empathy

Even if we have never been coached in a formal sense, many of us have an important figure in our lives who has acted as an informal coach to us. We have warm feelings when we recall people like that: perhaps our parents, or grandparents, other relatives or school teachers. They leave a deep impression.

One of the great values of having a coach, formal or informal, is the experience of someone really being there for you – encouraging you to believe in yourself and achieve your goals. According to Peter Bluckert[1], Chairman of the Standards and Ethics Committee of the European Mentoring and Coaching Council, 'When clients look back, years later, on their earlier experience of being coached, more often than not, they bring the coach as a person to mind, not the tools or psychological frameworks they used.'

The quality of the coaching relationship, he says, is not just *a* critical success factor, it is *the* critical factor in successful coaching outcomes. Good coaches create a safe enough space for the individual to take the risks necessary to learn, develop and change.

Bluckert isn't alone in drawing attention to the centrality of the coaching relationship. Erik de Haan and other theorists make similar claims[2] and Bluckert calls on coach training programmes that are model- and technique-based, to adapt to include a greater emphasis on the coaching relationship and on equipping coaches with a higher level of relationship-building skills.

At the heart of this, we suggest, will be the three core conditions laid out by Carl Rogers over half a century ago[3]: *unconditional positive regard; empathy*; and *congruence*. The presence or absence of these, Rogers asserted, will determine the quality of the therapeutic relationship and it's our contention that effective mindfulness training is a highly effective means of developing all three.

Coaches who show unconditional positive regard communicate a deep, genuine, non-judgemental attitude of care for their client. Those who show congruence act in accordance with their own values and belief system: they come across as genuine in their interactions with their client. While those who are empathic understand the client's world from the perspective of their subjective reality – they are able to 'walk in their shoes'.

There is extensive literature that supports the contention that these conditions are central in determining the quality of the therapeutic relationship[4] and, although there may be much more to say about this – and one can point to factors outside of these conditions that are also important – we suggest that coaches who embody the three core conditions will establish more effective coaching relationships than those who don't. What is more, however good a coach you are, however well you have already developed your capacities around these core conditions, none of us are perfect. Each of these skills can be further developed.

In training programmes for coaches, Bluckert,[1] for example, recounts that he often hears delegates honestly admit their difficulties in taking a non-judgemental stance, speaking instead of holding strong opinions about the behaviours and values of their coachees. Many also have problems expressing empathy, thinking that if they *understand* the clients' thoughts and feelings then that should be enough. But, empathy is about more than thinking that we understand the other person's world, although such understanding is important.

This chapter and this part of the course focus on the issue of empathy. This isn't because we don't regard the other two core conditions as important. We do. But to some extent we've already covered the issue of unconditional positive regard as we've explored the non-judgemental dimension of mindfulness training. That, along with the themes of kindness and openness, flavours the whole approach. Congruence too is threaded through the whole mindfulness approach. As you begin to deepen your experience of mindfulness, self-awareness naturally increases and – as our experience of working with coaches and others tells us – there will often follow a natural impulse to bring one's coaching, indeed all of one's behaviour, into line with that increased self-awareness.

Empathy, though, is sufficiently complex a subject to merit a chapter and a section of the course all of its own.

Does mindfulness training increase a coach's levels of empathy? That is the question that a large-scale global corporation brought to Michael several years ago. They were in the process of training up a large cohort of internal coaches. Drawn from amongst their senior executives around the world, few of the potential internal coaches had any specific previous training in empathic relating, nor had their career paths to date made any explicit requirement on them to develop that. Those leading the training for the would-be internal coaches wondered whether mindfulness training, along with its many other benefits, might enhance the novice coaches' capacity for empathy.

They put together a pilot trial group of sixteen internal coaches and Michael led them in an eight-week mindfulness programme, similar to the one outlined in this book. The coaches' levels of mindfulness and empathy were measured before and after the course.

To measure mindfulness, we used the self-report Five Factor Mindfulness Questionnaire (FFMQ).[5] To measure empathy, we used the self-report Inter-personal Reactivity Index (IRI).[6] According to these measures, participants' levels of both mindfulness and empathy increased after doing the course. This small pilot study was never formally published, but its findings accord to varying degrees with those we have seen in other parts of the overall literature.[7]

To understand these outcomes more fully, we'll need to investigate Davis's Interpersonal Reactivity Index a little more deeply. The IRI is a self-report measure that uses four primary sub-scales to measure empathy. These four are:

Fantasy: the tendency to get caught up in fictional stories and imagine oneself in the same situations as fictional characters. You could think of this as measuring 'imaginative empathy' ('I really get involved with the feelings of the characters in a novel.')
Perspective Taking: the tendency to take the psychological point of view of others. You might think of this as 'cognitive empathy'. It addresses one's tendency to take another's point of view. ('When I am upset at someone, I usually try to "put myself in his shoes" for a while.')
Empathic Concern: this is a measure of one's concern for others in distress. You could think of this as 'emotional empathy'. ('When I see someone being taken advantage of, I feel kind of protective towards them.')
Personal Distress: this is a measure of the anxiety or other distress one personally experiences when confronted with the pain or distress of others. ('In emergency situations, I feel apprehensive and ill-at-ease.')

It is important to realise when using the IRI that it is not a method proposed for calculating a total empathy score which could be obtained by summing the individual subscale scores. This is because the four subscales are not all positively correlated[8] so increases in every subscale are not indicative of greater levels of empathy. Instead, the findings that turn up when one uses the instrument will always have to be interpreted – what does it mean when one or another of the sub-scales shifts?

In the case of our own small pilot trial, we found that scores for Fantasy, Perspective Taking and Empathic Concern all increased while the score for Personal Distress decreased.

So, it could be said that the training increased our coaches' capacity to imagine the lives of their clients (Fantasy scale). They were better able to understand their client's perspectives, to think what it was like to have their lives and their situations (Perspective Taking scale). They were more likely to be concerned for their coachees and to want to help them (Empathic Concern scale). And yet, for all that, the training *decreased* the likelihood of their being thrown off their own centres in the presence of their client's distress (Personal Distress scale – which went down).

That, we think, is a wonderful outcome from the Mindfulness for Coaches training. It describes an enhanced capacity to be there for the client, to step into their shoes and understand what their situation is like for them – and to be able to hold all of that while staying present, centred and open.

Given the small sample size we are talking about here, and given the lack of a control group and several other experimental factors, one needs to be wary of reading too much into this outcome. It needs to be replicated under more rigorous conditions and with a larger sample and it's important to discover how long such effects last. But, as mentioned earlier, several other studies, such as those cited in Dekeyser *et al.*,[9] have found a similar shift when measuring the impact of mindfulness and empathy using the IRI. The reduction of Personal Distress alone is certainly something one would expect from a mindfulness course that aimed, amongst other things, to enhance participants' capacity to be with what is difficult without reacting or being thrown.

But it is not only from studies such as these that we have come to believe that mindfulness training can significantly enhance a coach's capacity for empathy.

The psychiatrist and neurobiologist Daniel Siegel[10] uses the term 'attunement' to describe how one person focuses their attention on the internal world of another person. As that happens, he observes, a range of neural circuits are harnessed and activated in a way that allows both persons to 'feel felt' by one another. This state is crucial, he says, if people in relationships are to feel vibrant, alive, understood and at peace. Research, Siegel adds, has shown that attuned relationships promote resilience and longevity.

For Siegel, mindfulness training can lead to enhanced interpersonal and intrapersonal attunement. When we are mindful we can more readily attune to others and, importantly, also become better attuned to ourselves. By training in mindfulness, we engage in processes of attunement that lead the brain to grow in ways that promote balanced self-regulation via processes of neural integration, that enable flexibility, self-understanding and understanding of others.

The way we experience the satisfaction of feeling felt by others and so feeling connected to the world, can help us to understand how becoming attuned to ourselves through mindful awareness can promote the same physical and psychological dimensions of well-being that arise when we're attuned to others.

We will return to the theme of self-care later in this chapter. For now, let's consider the evolutionary basis of our capacity for empathy and very briefly explore some of the mechanisms that enable it.

It was only around 10,000 years ago, that human beings began to live in large-scale settled societies. Before then, we lived in small tribal bands – typically no larger than 150 members.[11] There we had to compete with others for scarce resources. Once we left the family campfire and ventured out into the wild to search for food we were constantly at risk – from predators and other humans. In that harsh environment, those who were better able to co-operate generally lived longer and left more offspring.[12] Those whose teamwork was better usually beat those whose teamwork was weak, they were more likely to survive and it is their genes we mainly inherit.[13]

The evolutionary processes that have shaped humans for more than 2.6 million years have endowed us with neurobiological mechanisms that enable us to empathise with others. We have the capacity to read the inner states of others to an extraordinary extent. These capabilities are driven by three distinct neural systems. We have the capacity to sense, and to simulate within our own experience, other people's *actions, emotions* and *thoughts*.[14]

The networks in your brain that become active when you perform an action, also become active when you see someone else perform it. That gives you, in your own body, a felt sense of what others experience in their bodies.[15] The way these networks 'mirror' the behaviour of others gives them their name: mirror neurons. When we see people grimacing in distress, for example, or beaming with elation, we feel what they are feeling – although usually to a lesser extent – in our own bodies.

There are also affective, emotion-related circuits that play a part in forming our experience. The same neural circuits that are activated when you are experiencing strong emotions are sympathetically activated in you when you see others having the same feelings. The networks that produce your own feelings allow you to make sense of the feelings of others,[16] and so the more aware you are of your own feelings and body sensations, the better you will be at reading these in others.

A different set of circuits come into play when you come to 'read' the thoughts and beliefs of other people. The prefrontal circuits involved in helping us to guess the thoughts of others (a form of 'cognitive empathy'), work alongside the circuits involved in sensing the feelings and actions of others to produce our overall perception of their inner experience.[17]

The more mindful you are – the more you are attuned to your own thoughts, feelings, sensations and impulses – the better you will be able to attune to the thoughts, feelings, sensations and impulses of others. When you're more mindful you are better able to notice – from a variety of sources and with non-judgemental care – what is moving in the inner life of your coachee.

Just like me practice

This practice is designed to help you to see the essential humanity we share with everyone else on the planet. We first heard of it when it was taught at a meeting we attended by Chade Meng-Tang, the founder of Google's Search Inside Yourself Programme.

You can do it face-to-face with another person, or you can do it alone, simply calling another person to mind. Here's how it goes:

Become aware that there is a person in front of you, or that you have called one to mind – in either case, they're a fellow human being, just like you.

Now, turn the following thoughts, or ones very like them, over in your mind. Spend a few moments with each of them – don't rush:

> *This person has a body and a mind, just like me.*
> *This person has feelings, emotions and thoughts, just like me.*

This person has at some point been sad, disappointed, angry, hurt or confused, just like me.
This person has in his or her life, experienced physical and emotional pain and suffering, just like me.
This person wishes to be free from pain and suffering, just like me.
This person wishes to be safe, healthy and loved, just like me.
This person wishes to be happy, just like me.

Now, allow some wishes to arise:

I wish for this person to have the strength, resources, and social support to navigate the difficulties in life.
I wish for this person to be free from pain and suffering
I wish for this person to be happy.
Because this person is a fellow human being, just like me.

Coaching exercise for session 4

Attending empathically to the felt sense of a conversation

Get into pairs. The idea in this exercise is that one person listens, without interrupting, as the other person talks about a subject that deeply concerns them for about 5 minutes.

The task of the listener here is to notice in particular what feelings may be moving in the client and what feelings are moving in themselves as the conversation unfolds.

When the conversation has naturally concluded, after a mindful pause, the listener relates to the speaker what they sensed to be particularly charged in the speaker's flow of feeling. Then, they tell the speaker how their own flow of feeling was changed and impacted by what they heard.

Then swap around.

Taking care of yourself and others

For coaches, as for all those engaged in helping professions, taking care of oneself is a crucial part of taking care of others. The stale adage that this is like the instructions you hear on take-off in aircraft about the need to fit your own oxygen mask first if they deploy before helping others, is only stale because it's recounted so often – and that's because it's so pertinent. If we don't take care of ourselves, we'll not be in a position to help others – and that is profoundly self-defeating.

This section of our course often raises complex issues for some of the coaches who take part. The idea that you might choose to take better conscious care of yourself, that you might, from time to time, prioritise your own needs over the needs of your coachees, family, friends or organisation seems simply wrong to some people. To some, it feels somehow selfish.

74 *The eight-week programme*

Figure 4.1 The exhaustion funnel

But it's worth taking the time to reflect on that. Is it really selfish? After all, if you don't take care of yourself, who will? And if you don't take care of yourself, how will you be able to be there effectively for others?

Given the frenetic pace of working life today, the 'exhaustion funnel', which we describe below, is becoming all too familiar to many of the people we meet on our courses.

It's a variant on the 'exhaustion funnel' that was first described by Professor Marie Åsberg at the Karolinska Institute in Stockholm. She is an expert on burnout and the image of the funnel graphically conveys how this can happen to anyone.

We tend to think that the activities described on the left side of the funnel – choir singing, time with friends, going to the movies, taking walks in the country, doing yoga, gardening and so on – are optional. While those described on the right are non-optional – work, childcare, housework, yet more work, emails, yet more emails etc.

When you're at the top of the funnel, things are more or less in balance. There's the world of work and there are all the things that support the world of work, that make life even more enjoyable and worthwhile and which sustain a good level of well-being.

But when life gets busy, as it unavoidably seems to, what can happen is the apparently optional activities on the left are progressively dropped in favour of those that are presented as non-optional. As a result, one begins to slip lower and lower into the funnel. As you do that, the scope of your life narrows and the levels of tiredness, stress, worry and so on simply seem to increase. They're not being offset anymore. Near the bottom of the funnel lies exhaustion and, at the very bottom, burnout.

It turns out that the activities on the left aren't really optional. They're actually essential – they keep the possibility of a functional, balanced work-life alive.

Nourishing and depleting activities exercise

Most people's days include a wide range of activities. Some of these we enjoy, they nourish and uplift us and give us a sense of well-being, of being more fully alive. Some of them deplete our energies – we just do them because we must, although often we might wish we didn't have to. And some activities are more or less neutral. They're a necessary part of our lives, but they neither lift us up or bring us down.

At some point this week, take a sheet of paper, and write down everything you do in a typical day. Don't get into too minute a detail here, and don't skip over too much. Here, for example, is what the first few hours of one of Michael's typical days looks like when he's not travelling for work:

Wake up
Reflect on the day ahead
Get out of bed
Cup of tea
Feed the cat
Chat with Annette
Walk to garden studio
Meditate
Walk back to kitchen
Breakfast
Say good-bye to Annette as she heads for work
Walk back to garden studio
Boot computer
Emails
Write books, articles, blogs
Make calls
And so on . . .

Then, when you've listed a typical day, go through the list and mark each activity. If it nourishes you and gives you a sense of enhanced well-being, mark it (+). If it depletes you and lowers your feeling of well-being, mark it (–). If it's neutral, neither lifting you up or bringing you down, mark it (/).

Now take a look at the list again. Start with the neutrals. Is there anything you could do with any of these to turn them into plusses? Then go on to the minuses. Is there any way you could change any of these? Spend less time on them, for example, or maybe adjust something so that they become a little more neutral or even a bit plus? Finally, consider the plusses. Is there any way you could spend more time with any of these? Or do more of them?

We're not looking for a radical life-change here (although that's never ruled out), but even a very few percentage points of improvement in your overall level of well-being can make a huge difference to your experience of life – to say nothing of your overall physical and mental health. Even small changes and tweaks can make a real difference.

One participant on one of our Mindfulness for Coaches courses, for example, reported how life-changing she found it to stop watching the late news before going to bed. All of that bad news had previously just brought her down and left her heading up to bed anxious and low-spirited. That affected her sleep and that in turn affected her overall sense of well-being all the next day. To drop that habit was only a tiny tweak in the overall shape of her life, but its impact was enormous.

An empathic coach can spend a lot of their working time being with other people's trouble and distress. To be able to really be there for them, fully, authentically present and open, you need to be in good shape yourself. It's therefore of crucial importance, and vital for your effective functioning as a coach, that you take an active responsibility for looking after yourself.

Keeping your mindfulness alive

We hope that by now you'll have been engaging in some degree of formal mindfulness practice for at least six weeks. And we hope you'll have experienced the benefits of doing that.

When we deliver this course face-to-face with groups of coaches, it's a real joy at this stage in the course to look around the room and to see how much some people appear to have changed at this point in the journey. Shoulders that we saw were up have lowered, faces that were marked by stress and worry seem somehow softer. The tone of the overall conversation in the room is more open, more 'allowing', more receptive (but not uncritical).

Some of that is no doubt due to the fact that we've had four meetings of 4 hours together and we know one another better, we may even have made some friends and we're all less on-guard with one another.

But we're certain that some of those changes are also the results of people having been practising mindfulness meditation, with varying degrees of regularity, over a period of weeks. The task now is to somehow keep it all going once the defined structures of a course are no longer there.

Here are a few tips for that and one word of caution:

1) Informal practice is great, but formal practice is the bedrock.

Research conducted by Michael and his colleague Megan Reitz with a group of senior leaders at Ashridge Business School[18] showed that simply attending a mindfulness course, similar to the one described here yielded certain benefits. It increased attendee's resilience, for example. But the real benefits showed up when people formally practiced for more than 10 minutes a day.

We're not aware of any research that describes what happens when people who have practiced regularly stop practising, but our personal experience of teaching in other contexts suggests that, over time, the benefits that were previously experienced decline and ultimately fade away.

What a waste that would be.

It's like getting fit. You don't do it once – you need to keep it up.

2) Keep a routine going.
By now you will have figured out which time of day best suits your own practice. Keep it going. Michael and Megan's Ashridge attendees often cited the value of routine in maintaining their practice. Like anything, once it becomes a habit it's much easier to sustain.

3) Regularity may be more important than duration.
Again, we know of no studies that would back up this assertion, but our own experience and the anecdotal evidence we have gathered from years of teaching suggests that doing some practice every day yields more benefit than doing a bit more but at weekends only, for example. But experiment – see what works for you.

4) Begin to come away from the audio guidance – if you haven't already.
People tell us that the audio is really helpful to them. But meditating is not about listening to instructions: it's partly about learning to work your 'attention muscles' for yourself. When you can do it without guidance you're better equipped to work those muscles outside of meditation, when you need to focus on a client, for example.

5) And the word of caution: don't be in any rush to teach others.
You may be really impressed by what you've gained from the course yourself, and you may really want to share it with others. What is more, clients might begin to ask if you can help them in this area. Proceed with great caution. Mindfulness teaching is a real skill. It's one that can be trained, and if you're interested in that we'd recommend that you look out for some suitable training.

The field of mindfulness teaching and teacher training lags some decades behind the world of coaching in terms of in-depth training and teacher accreditation, but bodies such as the UK Network for Mindfulness Teacher Trainers[19] have made a start and their Good Practice Guidelines give a sound indication of how we think you should approach the question of teaching.

Home practice for week seven

1. Let's presume that you're going to keep up your formal mindfulness practice for at least 1 month after the course finishes. Then you can assess what you want to go forward with. So, from all the different forms of formal mindfulness practice that you have experienced so far in the course, use this week to settle on a form of practice that you intend to use on a regular, daily basis for the next five weeks. You might try using the audio guidance only on alternate weeks – or even less. But make your own choice about what is most helpful.
2. Practise the 'three-step breathing space' whenever you need it.

Home practice for week eight

1 Continue the practice from the previous week, following this format:
   a Sit somewhere quiet and choose how you are going to practice.
   b Do that practice.
   c When your mind wanders, see where it went and gently and kindly bring it back.
   d Repeat – several billion times.

Notes

1 Bluckert, P. (2005) 'Critical factors in executive coaching – the coaching relationship', *Industrial and Commercial Training*, 37(7): 336–340.
2 de Haan, E. *et al.* (2011) 'Executive coaching in practice: what determines helpfulness for clients of coaching?', *Personnel Review*, 40(1): 24–44.
   Boyce, L.A., *et al.* (2010) 'Building successful leadership coaching relationships: examining impact of matching criteria in a leadership coaching program', *Journal of Management Development*, 29(10): 914–931.
3 Rogers, C. (1961) *On Becoming a Person*, New York: Houghton Mifflin.
4 For example, Kirschenbaum, H. and Jourdan, A. (2005) 'The current status of Carl Rogers and the person-centered approach', *Psychotherapy: Theory, Research, Practice, Training*, 42(1): 37–51.
5 Baer, R. A. *et al.* (2006) 'Using self-report assessment methods to explore facets of mindfulness'. *Assessment*, 13(1): 27–45.
6 Davis, M.H. (1980) 'A multidimensional approach to individual differences in empathy'. *JSAS Catalog of Selected Documents in Psychology,* 10: 85.
7 Beitel, M. *et al.* (2005) 'Psychological mindedness and awareness of self and others'. *Journal of Clinical Psychology*, 61: 739–750.
   Thomas, J.T. (2012) 'Does personal distress mediate the effect of mindfulness on professional quality of life?' *Advances in Social Work*, 13(3): 561–585.
   Beddoe, A.E. and Murphy, S.O. (2004) 'Does mindfulness decrease stress and foster empathy among nursing students?' *Journal of Nursing Education*, 43(7): 305–312.
8 Davis, M.H. (1980) 'A multidimensional approach to individual differences in empathy', *JSAS Catalog of Selected Documents in Psychology*, 10: 85.
9 Dekeyser, M., Raes, F., Leijssen, M., Leysen, S., & Dewulf, D. (2008) 'Mindfulness skills and interpersonal behaviour', *Personality and Individual Differences*, 44(5), 1235–1245.
10 Siegel, D.J. (2007) *The Mindful Brain: Reflection and Attunement in the Cultivation of Well-Being*, New York: W.W. Norton & Co.
11 Norenzayan, A. and Shariff, A.F. (2008) 'The origin and evolution of religious prosociality', *Science*, 332: 58–62.
12 Wilson, E.O. (1999) *Consilience: The Unity of Knowledge*. New York: Vintage Books.
13 Nowak, M. (2006) 'Five rules for the evolution of cooperation,' *Science*, 314: 1560–1563.
14 Hanson, R. and Mendius, R. (2009) *Buddha's Brain: The Practical Neuroscience of Happiness, Love and Wisdom*. Oakland, CA: New Harbinger Publications.
15 Preston, S.D. and de Waal, F.B.M. (2002) 'Empathy: its ultimate and proximate bases', *Behavioral and Brain Sciences*, 25: 1–72.
16 Singer, T. *et al.* (2004) 'Empathy for pain involves the affective but not sensory components of pain', *Science*, 303: 1157–1162.

17 Singer, T. (2006) 'The neuronal basis and ontogeny of empathy and mind reading: review of literature and implications for future research,' *Neuroscience and Biobehavioral Reviews*, 30(2006): 855–863.
18 Reitz, M. *et al.* (2016) 'The mindful leader: developing the capacity for resilience and collaboration in complex times through mindfulness practice' http://ashridge.org.uk/Media-Library/Ashridge/PDFs/Publications/Ashridge-Mindful-Leader-for-web-low-res.pdf.
19 www.mindfulnessteachersuk.org.uk.

Part two
Joining the dots

5 Further development

It's common for coaches completing the eight-week programme to ask 'where do I go next?', and if you already have an established personal practice you may be asking the same question.

The field of mindfulness is vast and when it comes to deepening your practice, one way to do that is to find a regular group to sit with. No matter how diligent you are in your own practice, questions and obstacles often arise. Having experienced teachers and a group to draw on can be hugely supportive: not least because every time you come to sit together, you do so with a shared intention. That shared intention can be nourishing and sustaining, particularly if other aspects of your life seem to pull you away from living and working mindfully. Finding a regular group to sit with provides a supportive environment for your personal practice to develop in its own time. Bear in mind, though, that – at the time of writing – most sitting groups have a Buddhist background to them and some groups are more open-minded than others.

Beyond this, there may be further development of specific interest and relevance to you as a coach. In this chapter we point to mindfulness and positive emotions as a means to cultivate unconditional positive regard, interpersonal mindfulness as a means to bring mindfulness into relationship, and we also discuss teaching mindfulness to others. Finally, we explore self-compassion practices as a means to deepen self-acceptance and self-care.

Mindfulness and positive emotions

Barbara Fredrickson is one of the world's leading experts in the study of positive emotion. Martin Seligman, the founding father of positive psychology, describes her as 'the genius of the positive psychology movement.'[1]

The Broaden and Build theory

Fredrickson's Broaden and Build theory of positive emotions[2] is summarised in Figure 5.1.

Prior to Fredrickson's work, positive emotions were generally regarded by psychological theorists – at best – as markers of optimal well-being. However,

84 *Joining the dots*

the Broaden and Build theory created a paradigm shift, suggesting that positive emotions actually *produce* optimal functioning and fuel human growth and flourishing.

While negative emotions have played their part in our survival as a species, positive emotions have played an equally important role in our evolution. By broadening our 'thought-action repertoire' and building enduring resources, positive emotions have enabled us to adapt.

Two decades of experiments by Isen and colleagues[3] have shown that people experiencing positive emotion demonstrate patterns of thought that are notably creative, flexible, integrative and open to information. People experiencing positive emotions also show an increased preference for variety and accept a broader array of behavioural options.

By broadening an individual's momentary thought-action repertoire, Fredrickson suggests that positive emotions promote the discovery of novel and creative actions, ideas and social bonds which in turn build that individual's personal resources. These range from physical and intellectual resources to social and psychological resources. Those of our ancestors who succumbed to the urges to play and explore – sparked by positive emotions – would have accrued more personal resources. When these same ancestors later faced inevitable threats, their greater personal resources would have translated into greater survival odds.

Thus, according to Fredrickson, our capacity to experience positive emotions has been genetically encoded and this supports our capacity to adapt to changing environments.

This has important implications for both individual and organisational development.

The Broaden and Build theory specifically explores the form and function of a subset of positive emotions including joy, interest, contentment and love.[2]

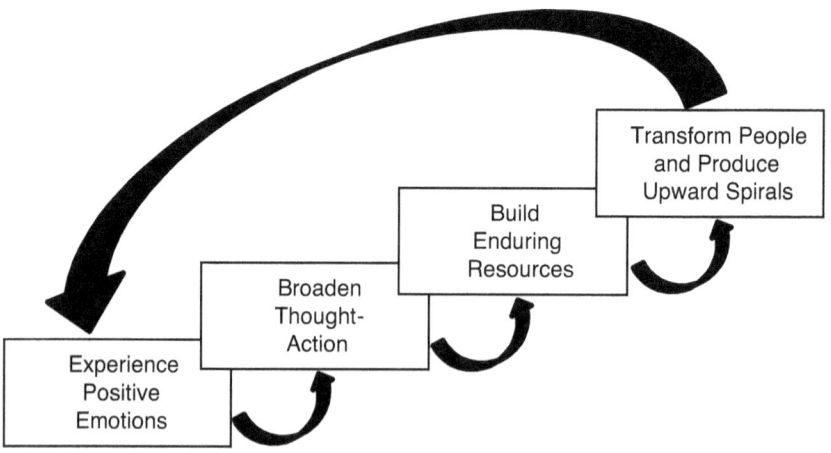

Figure 5.1 The Broaden and Build theory

Joy sparks the urge to play, push the limits and be creative. Interest sparks the urge to explore, take in new information and experiences and expand the self in the process. Contentment sparks the urge to sit back and savour current life circumstances and integrate these into new views of self and the world. And love creates recurring cycles of urges to play, explore, savour and integrate, thereby broadening habitual modes of thinking or acting.

The Broaden and Build theory suggests that positive emotions broaden people's attention and thinking, undo lingering negative emotional arousal, fuel psychological resilience, build personal resources, trigger upward spirals towards greater well-being and prompt human flourishing. It also implies that people should actively cultivate positive emotions not just because it makes them feel good in the moment, but because it also sets them on paths towards flourishing. When positive emotions are in short supply people get stuck and become predictable but when they are in ample supply people become generative, creative, resilient and ripe with possibility – they take off.

Love 2.0 *and positivity resonance*

Fredrickson's 2013 book, *Love 2.0*,[4] fundamentally reframes our understanding of love – our supreme emotion. It suggests that it's not just that unique feeling you reserve for your spouse or romantic partner, or even the feelings you have for your children, parents or close friends. Fredrickson suggests that love is that micro-moment of warmth and connection that arises anytime two or more people, even strangers, connect over a shared positive emotion – something she refers to as 'positivity resonance'.

Like other positive emotions, beyond simply feeling good, love literally changes your mind. It expands your awareness of your surroundings, even your sense of self. The boundaries between you and not-you become more permeable and your ability to really see, hear and feel others increases.

Unlike other positive emotions, positivity resonance creates deep interpersonal resonance. In micro-moments of love, your own warmth and openness evokes and is simultaneously evoked by, the warmth and openness arising in the other person. This is amplified further by synchronised changes in biochemistry and behaviour. Love reverberates between people and alters activity in your body and brain in ways that trigger parallel changes in another person's body and brain.

Positivity resonance doesn't just spring up at random – it emerges under certain conditions. The first condition is a perception of safety – if you assess your current circumstances as threatening, then love is not a possibility in that moment. The second condition is connection – feelings of oneness surface when two or more people 'sync up' and come to act as one. When positivity resonance arises between you and another person you begin to mirror each other's postures and gestures and a synchrony also unfolds internally, as the physiological responses in your bodies and brains come to mirror each other as well. Fredrickson suggests that true connection requires sensory and temporal co-presence of bodies – and particularly eye contact. One reason why eye contact seems to be the most potent trigger for connection is that smiles and other micro expressions require eye contact for accurate interpretation.

Paul Ekman, the world's leading expert on human facial expressions, estimates that humans regularly use some fifty different types of smiles.[5] Eye contact is the key that unlocks your intuition – when you meet another person's smiling gaze their smile triggers activity in your own brain circuitry that allows you to simulate the emotions you see emanating from theirs. As Fredrickson suggests,

> your smiles, nods, and other gestures of your own positivity and attunement don't just exist 'out there' in you. When we meet each other's gaze, they also come to exist, in a very real way, inside me. Within milliseconds my brain and body begin to buzz with your enthusiasm and appreciation, and your attunement to me . . . Increasingly, with each passing micro-moment you and I come to feel the same way. We're in sync, attuned . . . your and my brain activity and biochemistry increasingly become one and the same. A positivity infused interweaving of our hearts and minds emerges, a momentary state scientists have called *intersubjectivity*.[4]
>
> p. 23

For Fredrickson, there are three key players in the biology of positivity resonance – the brain, oxytocin and the vagus nerve.

In terms of the brain, Uri Hasson at Princetown University has found ways to measure multiple brains connecting while in conversation and what he calls 'neural coupling'.[6] Prior to this, the discovery of mirror neurons was a significant breakthrough, but it now seems that the concept of isolated mirror neurons was just the tip of a larger iceberg. Hasson uncovered far more extensive neural coupling than previously imagined and he argues that communication is a single act performed by two brains.

According to Hasson, one of the key brain areas where coupling is evident is the insula. This is an area associated with conscious feeling states in the body. Evidence suggests that in good communication, two individuals come to feel a single, shared emotion – there's synchrony in their insulae. In other studies Hasson has also shown that people's brains come particularly into sync during emotional moments,[7] so neural coupling becomes all the more likely when you share the same emotion. Shared emotions, brain synchrony and mutual understanding emerge together.

The second key player is oxytocin. Often nicknamed the 'love hormone', oxytocin plays a key role in social bonding and attachment. It surges during sex, childbirth and lactation. Recent research reveals the effect of oxytocin on levels of trust, suggesting that through synchronous oxytocin surges, trust and cooperation can quickly become mutual.[8]

Oxytocin doesn't induce trust indiscriminately – the effects are sensitive to interpersonal cues.[9] Under the influence of oxytocin, you attend more to people's eyes and become more attuned to their smiles – and so become a better judge of their feelings.[10]

Oxytocin also modulates the activity of your amygdala – it mutes the aspect of amygdala activity that tunes into threats and it amplifies the aspects that tune into positive social opportunities.

Oxytocin also appears to play a key role in the 'calm and connect' response – it calms fears that might steer you away from interacting with strangers and sharpens your skills for connection.[11] Your own oxytocin flow can also trigger someone else's. In studies of infants and parents, positive behavioural synchrony (the degree to which an infant and parent laugh, smile and coo together) goes hand in hand with oxytocin synchrony.[12]

The final key player in the positive emotion system is the vagus nerve, which connects your brain and your heart. It's your vagus nerve that soothes your racing heart after a fight or flight response by orchestrating, along with oxytocin, your calm and connect response. It also supports connection by stimulating tiny facial muscles that better enable you to make eye contact and synchronise your facial muscles with another person.

The strength of your vagus nerve is referred to as your 'vagal tone'. This can be measured by tracking your heart rate in conjunction with your breathing rate. Like muscle tone, the higher your vagal tone is, the better. According to Fredrickson (p. 55)[4] science has shown that people with higher vagal tone are more flexible across a range of physical, mental and social domains – they simply adapt better to changing circumstances. High vagal tone allows people to be more agile, attuned and flexible as they navigate social exchanges and the ups and downs of life. It's a key indicator of the health of your parasympathetic nervous system; it reflects the strength of your immune system[13]; and it can predict your likelihood of heart failure.[14]

Even if you're not advantaged with high vagal tone today, research suggests that just as you can build muscle tone through regular physical exercise, you can build vagal tone through regular mental exercise.

As we will see in the next section, by learning how to generate positivity resonance from your own side, you can raise your vagal tone. And with higher vagal tone your attention and actions become more agile and more attuned to others.

Similarly, evidence suggests that positivity resonance raises your oxytocin levels. And under the influence of oxytocin, you grow calmer, more attuned to others, friendlier and more open. Positive connections with others also create neural coupling and synchronise brain activity between people. With repetition, positivity resonance produces structural changes in the brain; you become healthier, happier, more socially integrated and your wisdom and resilience grow.

But of course, as a coach, it's not all about you. Positivity resonance can synchronise your brain and oxytocin waves with others. As one of our mindful coaches observed:

> The quality of thinking is impacted by something else that has no language – it's the person's energy, quality of connection, being in the present moment. And that's the bit that connects with mindfulness. There's something about the quality of contact and energy that the coach brings in that creates a possibility for something quite amazing to happen. So there's something else for which we have very little language that goes on which makes a difference. It's hard to put language to. The only words that come to mind are 'heart' – there's a quality of human contact that is felt and is not spoken – and the other, in coaching terms, would be called unconditional positive regard. But the language that came to my mind was love. Fundamentally, it's that which creates the connection.
>
> Alyse Ashton

Loving-kindness meditation

In researching positive emotions, Fredrickson wanted to compare one group of people who increased their daily diets of positive emotions to another group who didn't. To do this she introduced the ancient Buddhist mind-training practice of *metta-bhavana* – which translates as 'the cultivation of loving-kindness'.

Fredrickson found that when people learned to quiet their minds and expand their capacity for love and kindness, they transformed themselves from the inside out. They experienced more of every positive emotion they measured. Although they typically meditated alone, their biggest boosts in positive emotions came when interacting with others. The kind-heartedness they learned to cultivate during meditation practice warmed their connections with others. In studies at Fredrickson's Positive Emotions and Psychophysiology (PEP) Lab they found that vagal tone also significantly increased. Participants in the study devoted a little more than an hour each week to loving-kindness meditation yet within a matter of months their vagal tone had increased.[15]

Loving-kindness meditation (LKM) conditions your heart and mind to be more open and loving and it helps create the safety and connection required for positivity resonance. It's a bit like guided imagery, but it encourages warm feelings to arise by repeating phrases silently to yourself.

It might seem a little contrived, but it isn't possible to fabricate authentic positivity. You can, however, create the conditions for positivity by contemplating certain thoughts and wishes and being open to positive emotions that may arise.

With loving-kindness meditation, you set an intention and then see what follows – the key is to stay open to and accept whatever arises.

While LKM is not a silver bullet for all our troubles, whatever positive feelings you generate are likely to imbue the rest of your day. This can show up as more openness in your posture, face and breathing – openness that can be readily spotted by others.[16] Since non-verbal gestures are contagious, your openness also allows others to become more open and relaxed.[17] It also informs the way you make sense of things – you'll be more likely to see things in a good light and be optimistic about the future and others' potential.[18] Your intonation also becomes more upbeat and inviting.[19] Well after you practice, your verbal and non-verbal behaviour may remain changed, such that others feel a greater sense of safety in your presence – more likely to open up and connect.

With regular practice you can systematically cultivate the conditions for positivity resonance by slowing down and preparing your heart and mind to be truly open to others. You might wish to try 20 minutes of daily practice but keep in mind that research from Fredrickson's PEP lab reveals a wide range of benefits after just a few months of practicing LKM for an average of 60 minutes a week.

Try Barbara Fredrickson's *Loving-Kindness Meditation* and other practices from her website, available at www.positivityresonance.com.

Insight Dialogue and interpersonal mindfulness

Insight Dialogue (ID) is a formal practice of interpersonal meditation developed by Gregory Kramer.[20] It breaks the paradigm of individual, intrapersonal mindfulness practice by explicitly cultivating mindfulness while in relationship. Kramer highlights that in the field of psychotherapy, outcomes have been shown to depend mostly on the character and quality of the therapist-client relationship and that 'meditative practices . . . are able to address this training gap in important ways' (p. 196).[21]

While he acknowledges that traditional intrapersonal mindfulness practice can help, Kramer suggests that ID can foster changes in the quality of relationships 'much more directly than solitary approaches to the cultivation of mindfulness' (p. 197).[21] In particular, he suggests that ID supports greater therapist self-awareness and acceptance of dysphoric experience, greater presence to and acceptance of the client and provides concrete practice in exploring the present moment with another person with respect and curiosity. Modelled loosely on MBSR, the Interpersonal Mindfulness Program (IMP) is an important offshoot of ID and presents the basics in a secular format. Both formats are rooted in and shaped by the use of guidelines (meditation instructions) and contemplations.

Guidelines

The guidelines are: *Pause, Relax, Open, Trust Emergence, Listen Deeply* and *Speak the Truth*.

Pause refers to a temporal pause from habitual thoughts and reactions. By pausing you become better able to step out of conditioned reactions and learn to create space between what is heard, seen or thought and your responses.

Relax invites the practitioner to calm the body and mind, and to accept whatever thoughts and feelings are present in the moment. *Relax* points to an attitude of acceptance of difficult thoughts and emotions.

Open invites the practitioner to extend mindful awareness to another person and is the extension of meditation into the relational moment as you become aware of others with simple acceptance.

Trust Emergence means entering practice without an agenda. It involves mental flexibility, an appreciation of the impermanence of moment to moment experience and cultivates 'don't know' mind.

Listen Deeply begins with mindful and attuned listening and then develops into full energetic presence and an open receptivity to words, meaning, emotions and other elements of the interaction.

Speak the Truth begins with the articulation of the simple truth of your subjective experience and an authenticity of emotion. Discernment of what to speak, and mindfulness while speaking, are also elements of this guideline.

At a basic level, if we see the 'three-step breathing space' as a systematic way to shift state and break out of patterns of personal reactivity, we can begin to experience *Pause, Relax, Open, Trust Emergence, Listen Deeply and Speak the Truth* as a systematic way of breaking out of patterns of interpersonal reactivity and of shifting to another state in relationship with another.

Contemplations

Contemplations are the second central element of ID/IMP practice. These are topics of conversation drawn from wisdom traditions and more modern framings of human experience. They facilitate deeper insight into the shared human experience and encourage a re-evaluation of assumptions and behaviour patterns at a personal level. Traditional topics such as aging, compassion and the desire for pleasure and recognition are used alongside topics like the roles assumed at work, at home and in one's intimate relationships. The guidelines and contemplations work together synergistically. Self-knowledge deepens in relation to the contemplation themes and trust builds as participants realise that individual responses reflect shared experience. Mindfulness, energetic presence and exploration are balanced by kindness, joy and equanimity, and through practice participants learn to choose ease and compassion over stress and self-identification.

Relational skills cultivated through ID/IMP

For Kramer, ID and IMP support the client relationship in a number of ways. One important group of factors can be described as coach self-awareness and acceptance. This includes acceptance of dysphoric experiences during a coaching session, such as not knowing what is going on and not knowing what to do, as well as countertransference. *Pause* provides an interruption to responding automatically, particularly in moments of not knowing. The pause enables the coach to notice any self-identification with being the knowing one who should provide answers and to step back from identification with negative feelings, allowing a meeting of the client with 'beginner's mind'. In this way the coach is better able to put aside their own knowledge, beliefs and opinions, minimising any preconceptions and meeting the client with an open mind.

Trust Emergence extends this further by freeing the coach from having an agenda or having to accomplish a particular goal.

Speak the Truth fosters patience and discernment, creating ease in accepting silences and waiting for what is relevant to emerge in the moment.

Countertransference may be seen by some coaches as embarrassing, confusing or even inadmissible, but through the guidelines of *Pause* and *Relax* a coach is better able to recognise, accept and respond effectively to his or her own reactivity and/or countertransference. *Pause* introduces a buffer in the moment between reaction and action or expression and when it reveals difficult matters, *Relax* provides the support of acceptance and compassion towards whatever is arising. Over time, meeting difficult inner experiences in this way means they are not fed and their energy begins to drain away.

Another group of relational factors cultivated by ID and IMP are coach presence and empathy. The stance of unconditional presence is known to assist the change process[22] and is represented through the presence of the whole person, present moment empathy and the coach's genuine interest and close attention.

The guideline *Open* is the main reminder to the practitioner to extend meditative awareness from the personal to the interpersonal. When applied to the coaching relationship, *Open* invites the coach to notice the 'between' of the relationship, and the sense of an isolated self and separate other gives way to an I–Thou relationship. The mindfulness and calm concentration of meditation are then repurposed for the relationship and open the way for the emergence of present moment empathy.

Empathy with the client in the present moment is particularly supported by the guidelines of *Relax* and *Open*. Some commentators on Buddhist psychology speak of aversion as a kind of tension or stress. Through the guideline of *Relax* – the letting go of tension – a state of non-aversion and open receptivity arises. Equanimity is also strongly evoked by *Trust Emergence* and develops the balance needed to remain available and responsive in emotionally challenging situations.

Finally Kramer refers to other 'fruits of practice' from Interpersonal Meditation. Deep listening takes on an entirely new dimension and speaking the truth is understood as arising from a more embodied place in the felt sense of the moment. Through ID and IMP these qualities are developed and explored while in relationship with others. Coaches can benefit from ID practice through a variety of different routes – IMP, weekly ID practice groups, on-line dialogue, and retreats.

In the UK, Jane Brendgen, an associate of Michael's Mindfulness Works, has trained to teach the IM programme and has also developed a programme that brings Positivity Training into the IM meditative format. Other international Insight Dialogue (ID) offerings, both in person and on-line, can be accessed through www.metta.org.

Teaching mindfulness

After an eight-week programme it's not uncommon to feel a greater sense of personal well-being and it's understandable when coaches wish to share these insights and benefits with clients. If it's appropriate for the client we would certainly encourage coaches to refer to reliable books, materials and sources for mindfulness training.

However, we wouldn't encourage explicitly teaching mindfulness without appropriate training. In the same way that the coaching profession has developed standards and ethics of practice, so too has the mindfulness community. We trust that ethical professional coaches will work on the basis of referring when outside areas of their own expertise. People respond to guided practices in all kinds of ways and in some cases, with particular personal history, those reactions can be adverse. It's as important for mindfulness teachers to know how to work with reactions to practice as it is to guide the practices themselves.

Ultimately this is about teaching based on extensive personal experience of practice. When people start navigating the inner world of their minds it's helpful for them to have a guide who is familiar with the terrain. To use a metaphor – if you want to climb a mountain it's better to travel with an experienced guide who has climbed the mountain thousands of times than someone who has heard about a map of the mountain, who has read a map of the mountain or who has climbed it once or twice. But this isn't as simple as sharing experience in a traditional sense – that might be more like mentoring. There is an expression that mindfulness is 'caught not taught' through the embodied presence of the teacher. In part, this is about guiding mindfulness practice from an embodied place. As McCown *et al.* note:

> This is the most critical dimension of guidance: the connection of the teacher to her own practice while speaking. Guiding a meditation is not an empty performance; the teacher herself is engaged in the practice from moment to moment as she speaks . . . In training and development of new teachers, it is quite easy to perceive whether a teacher is 'dropped in' to the practice she is guiding; the listener will have a felt sense of authenticity when the connection is there.[23]

In addition, perhaps the true act of teaching mindfulness has more to do with facilitating a process of inquiry that brings an individual closer to their own direct personal experience of practice. Meeting all experience, even the difficult or unwanted, with a warm, kindly curiosity. This is more about an embodied way of being that emerges through regular personal practice. Certainly this is something Segal *et al.* discovered in the early days of teaching Mindfulness Based Cognitive Therapy (MBCT):

> ... it is important that instructors have first-hand, ongoing experience of mindfulness practice ... First, it is inevitable that some patients will experience difficulties with the practice that the instructor will not be able to answer with 'intellectual' knowledge alone ... It is not just an issue of credibility or competence, but of a teachers' ability to embody 'from the inside' the attitudes they invite participants to adopt ... Our own conclusions, after seeing for ourselves the difference between using MBCT with and without personal experience of using mindfulness practice, is that it is unwise for instructors to embark on teaching this material before they have extensive personal experience with its use.[24]

However, if you've established a solid personal mindfulness practice for more than a year and you're committed to teaching mindfulness to others, we'd like to point you towards the *Good Practice Guidelines for Teaching Mindfulness-Based Courses* in Appendix C. Published by the UK Network of Mindfulness Teacher Training Organisations in 2015, it highlights a number of important facets to good practice. If you would like to pursue teacher training in the UK, a list of current providers can be found at www.mindfulness teachersuk.org.uk. At the time of writing, there is a masterclass series at the Oxford Mindfulness Centre that offers workplace-specific sessions. This is being carried out in conjunction with the Centre for Mindfulness Research and Practice at Bangor University and is intended to be a precursor to a training pathway for those interested in teaching in workplace settings. For more information, visit http://oxfordmindfulness.org/about-us/courses/omc-master classes/.

We're not suggesting here that mindfulness cannot and should not be brought explicitly into coaching. Just as Germer *et al.*[25] identify Mindfulness-Based Psychotherapy, we're aware that Mindfulness-Based Coaching is already being offered by professional coaches who are also trained mindfulness teachers. We look forward to hearing more about this and about the outcomes from this approach as it evolves.

What we are recommending here however is that professional coaches do not teach mindfulness to clients without appropriate training. More than that, we are suggesting that, just as Germer *et al.* identify 'mindfulness-informed psychotherapy' and 'the practicing therapist' as a significant part of mindfulness-orientated psychotherapy, 'mindfulness-informed coaching' and being a practicing coach can have profound effects on the way you show up as a professional coach and on the outcomes you co-create with your clients. All without ever discussing mindfulness with clients or guiding practices.

Given the current growth and interest in mindfulness amongst professional coaches we fully expect to see more including mindfulness in their coaching frameworks and models when asked to do so as part of the professional coach training. In such cases their coaching will include a relational/psychodynamic understanding that values the coaching relationship as a central vehicle of transformation and sees the part that mindfulness has to play in this.

Mindfulness, self-compassion and self-care

When we ask participants why they signed up for the Mindfulness for Coaches programme many simply state 'I'm here for me.'

When we spend so much of our time extending ourselves to others it's important that we have reliable ways to nourish and renew ourselves. While coach well-being might be a good outcome in itself, research in the field of psychotherapy confirms that a therapist's own mental health has a significant bearing on outcomes.[26] Mental health and well-being is thus likely to be important for coaching work as well as for coaches themselves.

In this respect, we trust that the coaching professional bodies will share an interest in how mindfulness might support its members to do their very best work.

In this section, we will hear mindful coaches talking about the personal benefits of regular mindfulness practice. We will then explore the role self-compassion practices might play in supporting well-being and the outcomes we co-create with clients.

Mindfulness and personal well-being

Here's what some of our mindful coaches said in response to the question 'What beneficial effects has your mindfulness practice had on you personally, if any?'

> I am more grounded and present in day to day life. I'm happier and enjoy life more. I'm calmer and better able to deal with stressful situations; less reactive in relationships and better able to make good decisions.
>
> Emma Donaldson-Feilder

> I have a more anchored sense of self, which in turn builds my confidence. I feel calmer. I'm able to rationalise with wider choice when things go wrong unexpectedly. I ruminate less. My practice helps me know how I am and what's going on. I'm able to identify areas of my body where I'm holding tension – which gives me choice about what I do with those areas. I'm more compassionate. I'm more accepting of myself and others.
>
> Lindsay Wittenberg

> Significantly improved sleep patterns. Zero incidents of my previous sinus and ocular migraine problems. Lower blood pressure.
>
> Angus Fisher

I have become significantly less self-judgemental and judgemental of others. My capacity to feel compassion has deepened. I'm more able to be vulnerable and own my shadow stuff without experiencing shame. I feel my life has simplified a lot. My relationships with others are so much deeper, richer and more heartfelt. I appreciate the simple things more and my capacity to take care of myself has improved a lot.

Jane Brendgen

For many years I used it privately for two main purposes – helping me to be more present in my clinical work and also helping to offset some of the stress and fatigue of doing clinical work.

Arnie Kozak

It's made me more compassionate to myself and others. Calmed me down, helped me focus, and reduced anxiety. It helped me to cope with my daughter's (major) illness and I do believe – made me a better coach.

Sally Woodward

It enabled me to cope with my husband's two year illness and death. The mindful self-compassion especially has helped me to focus on what is here on a daily basis, to keep focused with compassion for others and me, and to manage anxiety and rumination.

Wendy Briner

Sometimes when we're so focused on supporting other people we might forget, or put to one side, the fact that we have our own stresses and emotional challenges. In some cases this may simply be the stress of daily life or emotionally demanding work and on other occasions, more seismic events that present us with our biggest life challenges. Whatever the circumstances, mindfulness practice allows us to meet all of our experiences with greater awareness and compassion.

Compassion fatigue

Typically, coaches support leaders to successfully navigate the demands placed upon them in highly complex and stressful environments. Focusing a lot of energy on helping others in this way can lead to 'compassion fatigue'. In clinical settings compassion fatigue is a type of exhaustion experienced as a result of continually dealing with traumatised clients. Sometimes it's known as 'secondary traumatic stress', as therapists often relive their client's trauma. Symptoms can include nightmares, emotional numbing, an exaggerated startle response, decreased feelings of safety, increased cynicism and disconnection from loved ones. Therapists who are the most empathic tend to be most at risk. Other negative consequences of stress on helping professionals include increased depression, emotional exhaustion, anxiety, psychological isolation, reduced self-esteem, disrupted personal relationships, and loneliness. Further stress can increase burnout, involving depersonalisation, emotional exhaustion and a sense of low personal accomplishment.

Of course coaches are *not* therapists. We're not working in clinical contexts with clients who have experienced abuse, trauma or who have personality disorders. However, research suggests that secondary stress is just as real for coaches. In Negative effects of coaching for coaches, Carston Schermuly[27] found that 94 per cent of coaches had experienced at least one negative effect in recent coaching and 99 per cent over their career. The following were the highest negative effects:

1. I felt insecure (over coaching career, 80 per cent; last coaching assignment, 38 per cent).
2. Personally affected by topics discussed – direct relation to own life and problematic areas (78 per cent; 44 per cent).
3. Disappointed I couldn't observe the long-term influences of the coaching (77 per cent; 45 per cent).
4. I felt emotionally exhausted (74 per cent; 26 per cent).
5. I experienced anger towards the coachee (73 per cent; 20 per cent).
6. Scared that I would not fulfil my role as coach (71 per cent; 40 per cent).
7. I was scared to do something wrong (71 per cent; 28 per cent).
8. Frustrated that the problems the coachee was facing could not be resolved (70 per cent; 36 per cent).
9. I felt underpaid (69 per cent; 36 per cent).
10. Felt under pressure as a result of high expectations (68 per cent; 29 per cent).

We cannot say for sure how much of this is transference, but one cannot hope to come into a relationship and not be affected in some way.

So, if we choose to undertake relational work of this kind, how do we best take care of ourselves?

In *The Art and Science of Mindfulness*,[28] Shauna Shapiro and Linda Carlson dedicate an entire chapter to 'Mindfulness and self-care for clinicians'. Shapiro shares from personal experience,

> As . . . professionals, we often forget to 'care' for ourselves. I learned this during my first clinical position . . . I believed I was responsible for 'saving' all of the people I encountered . . . I scheduled patients after hours and at lunch breaks, taking home notes to review and thinking about 'my' patients all the time . . . after about 2 months my supervisor called me into his office and said . . . 'I've noticed you are taking on extra patients, staying late, have no social life, always seem to be rushing and seem chronically exhausted' . . . At this point my supervisor offered me a metaphor that I have carried with me. He said, 'the heart pumps blood first to itself, before pumping blood to the rest of the body. If it didn't, it would die and then

the rest of the body would die. The art of caring for others is learning how to first care for yourself. Remember this.'[28]

p. 108

Self-compassion

Christopher Germer, a clinical psychologist affiliated with Harvard, suggests that the antidote to compassion fatigue is *self-compassion*. Ironically, he also highlights that the term 'compassion fatigue' is a misnomer because compassion itself isn't fatiguing. It's actually 'attachment fatigue' – we wear ourselves out when we're attached to outcomes. Research suggests that self-compassion is an emergent quality that arises from mindfulness training. In research studies of therapists who participated in MBSR programmes, significant increases in self-compassion were found after training (in addition to decreases in stress and burnout).[29] This shouldn't be surprising since the attitudinal qualities cultivated through mindfulness practice are warmth, kindness, non-judgement and acceptance towards whatever is arising in our field of experience. However, as Germer suggests

> we don't need to wait for self-compassion to dawn on its own in mindfulness practice. When we're in intense emotional pain and need a helping hand, we can make the implicit quality of compassion explicit – we can directly deliver kindness and compassion to ourselves.[30]
>
> p. 90

This is where self-compassion practices come in, designed specifically to deepen the cultivation of this attitudinal quality.

What do we mean by self-compassion? Compassion comes from the Latin roots *com* (with) and *pati* (suffer) or to 'suffer with'. Being compassionate means that we recognise when someone is in pain, we abandon our fear or resistance to it and a natural feeling of love and kindness flows toward the suffering individual. It's full acceptance: of the person, of the pain and of our own reactions to the pain. Self-compassion is simply extending that same kindness to ourselves. But it does require that we stop to recognise our own suffering first. In our Western culture of having a 'stiff upper lip' that isn't so usual.

Self-compassion is also the foundation of compassion for others. According to the Dalai Lama, '[Compassion] is the state of wishing that the object of our compassion be free of suffering ... Yourself first, and then in a more advanced way the aspiration will embrace others.'[31]

As its title implies, in *The Mindful Path to Self-Compassion*,[30] Christopher Germer suggests two core components of practice – mindfulness and self-compassion. Mindfulness helps us see what's going on in our lives and ourselves more clearly and self-compassion helps us embrace our experience in a kind and warm-hearted way.

Kristin Neff,[32] another pioneer in the research of self-compassion, suggests three main components to self-compassion:

1. *Mindfulness* – observing our negative thoughts and emotions with openness and clarity through non-judgemental awareness.
2. *Self-kindness* – being warm and non-self-condemning towards ourselves and our suffering.
3. *Common humanity* – recognising suffering as part of the shared human experience rather than feeling ashamed or alone.

Mindfulness is non-attached awareness – it gives us the ability to *be with* painful thoughts and feelings in an even and balanced way. The opposite of mindfulness – over-identification – happens when we lose ourselves in emotional reactivity. Mindful awareness helps us recognise when we're in pain, when we're criticising or isolating ourselves and it points the way out. As Neff notes,

> If we can be mindful of the pain associated with failure or the stress and hardship entailed by difficult circumstances we can take a step back and respond to our pain with kindness. Not only am I suffering, *I am aware that I'm suffering*, and therefore I can try to do something about it.[32]
>
> p. 93

Self-kindness is the opposite of self-judgement. When things don't go our way many of us tend to judge ourselves harshly for that, which only adds insult to injury. *Self-kindness* involves stopping the constant disparaging internal commentary and actively comforting ourselves, just as we would with a dear friend.

Sadly, many people believe that they shouldn't be kind to themselves, especially if they received that message during childhood. John Bowlby, perhaps the best known researcher of attachment, proposed that children develop a secure attachment bond if they are supported by caregivers when they are upset or frightened.[33] This allows them to use their parents as a 'secure base' to safely explore the world around them. However, if parents provide inconsistent support, or are cold and rejecting, children develop an insecure attachment bond which impairs their confidence in exploring the world and this often extends into adulthood.

The good news is that our attachment system can be reset. Sometimes this happens through a loving partner or through a therapist providing unconditional positive regard. But with self-compassion practice we offer this to ourselves. When we soothe our own pain we tap into our caregiving system and release oxytocin. When we cultivate warm and tender feelings toward ourselves we alter our bodies and minds.

Rather than feeling worried and anxious we feel calm, content and secure. Self-kindness allows us to feel safe as we respond to painful experiences, so we no longer operate from a place of fear.

As Neff notes,

> When we treat ourselves as a kind friend would we are no longer totally absorbed by playing the role of the one who is suffering. *Yes, I hurt. But I also feel care and concern. I am both the comforter and the one in need of comfort. There is more to me than the pain I am feeling right now. I am also the heartfelt response to that pain.*[32]
>
> p. 50

Common humanity brings relief from feeling alone and isolated. When we experience misfortune we can feel we're the only person in the world who is suffering. And when we fail, we sometimes feel isolated, becoming absorbed in feelings of insufficiency and insecurity rather than framing our imperfection in the light of our shared human experience.

Even when we're having a painful experience that is not our fault, it can feel isolating. For example, consider a dying 90-year-old man whose final words are 'why me?'.

In contrast, feelings of connectedness, like feelings of kindness, activate the brain's attachment system. As Neff suggests,

> The 'befriend' part of the 'tend and befriend' instinct has to do with the human tendency to ... come together in groups in order to feel secure. For this reason, people who feel connected to others are not as frightened by difficult life circumstances ... If we can compassionately remind ourselves in moments of falling down that failure is part of the shared human experience, then that moment becomes one of togetherness rather than isolation.[32]
>
> pp. 64–65

Self-compassion and loving-kindness

Germer and Neff both draw on loving-kindness practice as a core part of their approach to self-compassion. What distinguishes compassion from loving-kindness is the presence of pain.

Loving-kindness is wishing happiness for another person while compassion is wishing for that person to be free from suffering. It's a kindly response to pain, whether physical or emotional.

Traditional loving-kindness phrases are designed to cultivate feelings of goodwill, but not necessarily compassion. So, in order to target the feeling of compassion more directly, Germer and Neff offer a variant of traditional loving-kindness practice *with compassion phrases* in their Mindful Self Compassion (MSC) programme.

Try Christopher Germer's *Compassion for Self and Others Meditation* www.chrisgermer.com/wp-content/uploads/2017/02/Compassion-for-Self-and-Others-16-min.mp3.

Suffering and acceptance

In the Buddhist context, out of which the mindfulness approaches arose, human life is seen as being marked by 'dukkha'. Often, perhaps inadequately, translated as 'suffering', the term is etymologically related to the idea of an ill-fitting cart-wheel. When you've got one of those on your cart, things are pretty bumpy. So, it's not so much that human life is a state of continuous suffering. Often it's wonderful. But however wonderful life can be, that never lasts. Things go well for a time, then they go badly for a time. It's how life goes and there's no escaping that in its own terms. You can try to craft the perfect life for yourself, completely free from suffering, but good luck with that – illness, separation from loved ones, loss – in all sorts of unforeseeable ways, these will turn up. The wheel of human fortune keeps on turning. There is comfort, joy and happiness, and there is discomfort, pain, loss and distress.

From this perspective, pain and loss are inevitable. They're a part of being human. But suffering – that's optional. This is because the suffering we're speaking of here comes from a single source. We experience it when reality doesn't match our wants and desires.

From this perspective, the key to happiness is understanding that suffering is caused by our tendency to try to resist unavoidable pain.

$$\text{Suffering} = \text{Pain} \times \text{Resistance}$$

There is the unavoidable pain of life – accidents, illnesses, the death or loss of those we love – and there is suffering – the mental anguish caused by fighting and resisting pain and loss.

'Resistance' here, refers to any effort to ward off pain, such as tensing the body or ruminating about how to make the pain go away.

The good news is that since most of the pain in our lives is really 'suffering' – in the terms we've outlined above, we can do something about it.

Self-compassion is a form of acceptance and while resistance creates suffering, acceptance alleviates it. Whereas acceptance usually refers to what's happening to us, as in accepting a feeling or a thought, self-compassion is acceptance of the person to whom it's happening. It's a full acceptance of ourselves while we are in pain.

As Tara Brach puts it in *Radical Acceptance*,

> The way out of our cage begins with *accepting absolutely everything* about ourselves and our lives . . . By accepting absolutely everything . . . we are aware of what is happening within our body and mind in any given moment, without trying to control or judge or pull away. I do not mean that we are putting up with harmful behaviour – our own or another's. *This is an inner process of accepting our actual, present moment experience* . . . Clearly recognizing what is happening inside us, and regarding what we see with an open, kind and loving heart.[34]
>
> pp. 25–26

Acceptance doesn't mean tolerating bad behaviour. Nor is it about resignation or stagnation – quite the opposite. Instead, acceptance is the deep recognition that this moment of experience couldn't be anything other than it is. It is the result of what happened before and we can't go back in time to change that. It is what it is. This experience is this experience, right now.

We have two fairly simple choices: we can be stuck in various forms of denial – trying in various ways, unrealistically, to avoid what's here. Or we can accept it, ground ourselves in the reality of what's here, then other possibilities can follow from that. Change naturally follows acceptance.

If you care to, you could try exploring this experientially through a guided practice from Kristin Neff. In the following practice she guides you in ways of coming more deeply into contact with two sources of suffering we all experience – from ourselves not being as we want and from our lives not being as we want.

Self-Compassion/Loving-Kindness Meditation www.self-compassion.org/wp-content/uploads/meditations/LKM.self-compassion.MP3.

Dealing with difficult sensations in the body

As we saw earlier, it's not uncommon for coaches to pick up secondary stress from clients. At some point most coaches will have had an experience of walking out of a coaching session with uncomfortable thoughts, feelings or sensations – we pick things up. How best can coaches work with this in order to support their own well-being and the quality of their work?

Typically, experiences like this are brought to, and processed in, supervision. In *Supervision In The Helping Professions*[35] Peter Hawkins and Robin Shohet refer to 'pit-head time' – the right of miners to wash off the grime of work in the boss's time rather than taking it home. Hawkins and Shohet view supervision as pit-head time for those working at the coalface of personal distress, disease and fragmentation. At some level, all the coaching professional bodies concur, as evidenced by their consistent reference to its importance.

But this approach creates a dependency on supervisors to help coaches raise awareness of and process psychodynamic influences. We suggest that coaches can be more empowered, as demonstrated by one of our mindful coaches:

> After a coaching session, I always run through a body scan as soon as possible. I find that I often pick up emotions and physical sensations from my client that I need to let go of before I can objectively review my coaching performance and reflect on my client's needs. Sometimes the body scan may be all of 30 seconds, sometimes I may take 10 minutes.
>
> Farah Govani

'The body scan' is one way of working with emotions and sensations after a coaching session. Another alternative is the following practice from Neff for working with uncomfortable emotions in the body.

Soften, Soothe and Allow www.self-compassion.org/wp-content/uploads/meditations/soften,soothe,allow.MP3.

This practice can be used any time you experience emotional or physical discomfort in your life, including as a result of secondary stress. However, it shouldn't be approached as a clever way of getting rid of unwanted emotions and sensations. The common element in both mindfulness and self-compassion practice is a shift toward befriending emotional pain.

Instead of fighting hard against difficult emotions, we bear witness to them and respond with kindness. Difficult emotions, like all emotions, usually express themselves in the body – anger, for example, is sometimes felt as tension in the neck, sadness as tightness in the chest and fear in the abdomen.

Such experiences aren't inherently 'destructive' – they only become so when we cling on to them or push them away. By working at the level of physical sensation, self-compassion can act as a powerful tool. It can help lessen the hold of negative emotions. But it doesn't do so by pushing them away. Rather than trying to replace negative feelings with positive ones, new positive emotions are generated by allowing and embracing negative ones.

When an emotion is released in the body, the mind lets go as well. The phrase 'soften, soothe and allow' can help the body to release what it's holding onto. We abandon the instinctive tendency of the body to tense up and reject discomfort. Given that we accumulate stress in the body all day long, *Soften, Soothe and Allow* can be a very helpful practice.

Giving and receiving compassion

Another practice that may be helpful for coaches working with secondary stress is Germer's *Giving and Receiving Compassion*, particularly if we are encountering difficulty with a specific client.

This meditation is derived, with modifications, from the Tibetan Buddhist practice of *Tonglen*. By inhaling compassion we soothe our own bodies and minds, and by exhaling compassion we send goodwill, care and comfort to others. Changing our relationship to the people in our heads is often the first step towards transforming our relationships with them in real time. When things change on the inside, they usually start to shift on the outside.

Giving and Receiving Compassion www.chrisgermer.com/wp-content/uploads/2017/01/GivingandReceivingCompassion21.21ckgamplified12-14-14.mp3.

Stages of self-compassion

Germer suggests that practitioners go through several distinct stages as they engage with self-compassion practice. A common experience at the beginning is 'backdraft'. When a fire is deprived of oxygen and fresh air is suddenly let in an explosion can occur. Similarly, people who are used to constant self-criticism can erupt with anger and intense negativity when they first try to take a kinder approach with themselves.

Such feelings are not *created* by compassion practice, and Germer's advice to practitioners is simply to recognise and feel them as they go out the door.

Once their initial resistance softens, Germer tells us, practitioners often feel great enthusiasm for self-compassion practice. During this 'infatuation' stage some people get attached to the good feelings produced by practice, but this phase eventually has to end because it's based on a narrow wish to feel good. Often, that infatuation gives way to a phase of 'disillusionment' as people realise that self-compassion doesn't magically make all their negative thoughts and feelings go away.

When people practice self-compassion as a subtle way of resisting negative emotions, such emotions will remain and may even get worse. But when people stick with the practice, Germer says, they may eventually discover the wisdom of 'true acceptance'. During this phase the motivation for practice shifts from 'cure' to 'care'. The fact that life is painful, and that we are all imperfect, is fully accepted as an integral part of being alive. It becomes understood that happiness is not dependent on circumstances being exactly as we want them to be, or on ourselves being exactly as we'd like to be. Rather, happiness stems from loving ourselves and our lives exactly as they are. When we're able to do that, growth and development more readily follow.

Mindfulness, self-care and radical acceptance

Since *Mindfulness for Coaches* draws on core aspects of MBSR we shouldn't be surprised that coaches come away with practical tools to manage their own stress levels and much more besides. Research suggests that there's a clear inverse relationship between stress and compassion[36] – when we're stressed we become less emotionally available to others. Research also suggests that MBSR training has significant effects on levels of compassion towards others.[37] Since compassion is based on a foundation of self-compassion, it's not surprising that self-compassion also significantly increases with MBSR training. Through mindfulness practice we learn to cultivate warmth, kindness, non-judgement and acceptance towards whatever is arising in our field of experience.

As we've seen, research suggests that secondary stress and compassion fatigue are as real for coaches as they are for therapists. Commentators like Germer highlight self-compassion as an antidote to compassion fatigue, so in this respect MBSR and *Mindfulness for Coaches* offer an antidote to coaches working with secondary stress. Germer also suggests that specific self-compassion practices provide a way of working with compassion fatigue and in this chapter we have explored some of these. By offering these practices we are not suggesting that they should *replace* supervision as 'pit head time' but, used together, they can significantly amplify levels of awareness and processing of psychodynamic effects.

Since transference is created in relationship, it seems natural that the best way for it to dissolve is also in relationship. For most coaches, the relationship where this is resolved is mainly that between coach and supervisor, but this need not be the only way.

Regular mindfulness practice develops one's 'witness consciousness', a growing capacity to become the objective observer of one's own experience. Combined with this clear seeing, the attitudinal qualities of mindfulness and self-compassion may help coaches to embrace and release the difficult emotions generated in relationships.

We see mindfulness training and its various transformations as complementing supervision in supporting the well-being and effectiveness of coaches. Whether this becomes reflected in coach ethics and standards we will see, but already we notice a number of coach supervisors combining mindfulness and supervision with good effect.[38]

Research suggests that people who have been trained in self-compassion are less likely to experience compassion fatigue because they have learned the skills to avoid getting overly stressed or burned out. They are more likely to engage in acts of self-care such as taking time off, sleeping more, and eating well – they stop to care for their own emotional needs. Self-compassion is a way of emotionally recharging our batteries. Rather than becoming drained by helping others, self-compassion allows us to fill up our internal reserves. In this respect, it is an altruistic act – it puts us in an optimal mental and emotional state to help others in a *sustainable* way.

By becoming more understanding and accepting towards ourselves, we also become more understanding and accepting towards others. And that matters in terms of outcomes. Research in the field of psychotherapy[39] demonstrates that therapists who lack self-compassion and are critical and controlling toward themselves are also more critical and controlling toward their clients, and have poorer outcomes. In coaching, unconditional positive regard is also central to our clients opening to their experience – it's key to transformational change.

As Tara Brach notes, practicing *radical acceptance in relationship* is a powerful source of change,

> Witnessing the power of Radical Acceptance always amazes me . . . I've watched people shift careers and pursue work that truly inspires them just because they experienced acceptance . . . When Radical Acceptance blossoms in our relationships, it becomes a kind of spiritual re-parenting that enables us to trust the goodness and beauty of who we really are. Just as good parenting mirrors back to the child that they are loveable, when we understand and accept others, we affirm their intrinsic worth and belonging. To receive this kind of Radical Acceptance can transform our lives.[34]
>
> pp. 297–300

It's important to say that we've only provided a brief introduction to self-compassion here. If you wish to practice longer than 20 minutes a day it's important you find a qualified teacher. Pioneers like Paul Gilbert caution that people with a history of parental abuse should proceed slowly down the path of self-compassion. When we start working with our early attachment patterns in this way it's important to work with someone who has gone down the road before you, knows the obstacles and can guide you through them. Germer and Neff's Mindful Self Compassion (MSC) programme and other related resources can be found at www.centerformsc.org.

Notes

1 Fredrickson, B. (2009) *Positivity*, New York: Crown Publishers.
2 Fredrickson, B. (2004) 'The broaden-and-build theory of positive emotions', www.ncbi.nlm.nih.gov/pmc/articles/PMC1693418/pdf/15347528.pdf.
3 Reviewed in Isen, A. (2000) 'Positive affect and decision making', In M. Lewis and J. Haviland-Jones (eds) *Handbook of Emotions*, New York: Guilford Press, pp. 417–435.
4 Fredrickson, B. (2013) *Love 2.0*, New York: Hudson Street Press.
5 Ekman, P. (2001) *Telling Lies*, New York: W.W. Norton & Co.
6 Hasson, U. (2010) 'I can make your brain look like mine', *Harvard Business Review*, (December).
7 Hasson, U. et al. (2004) 'Intersubject synchronization of cortical activity during natural vision', *Science*, 303: 1634–1640.
8 Mikolajczak, M. et al. (2010) 'Oxytocin not only increases trust when money is at stake, but also when confidential information is in the balance', *Biological Psychology*, 85: 182–184.
9 Mikolajczak, M. et al. (2010) 'Oxytocin makes people trusting, not gullible', *Psychological Science*, 21(8): 1072–1074.
10 Domes, G. et al. (2007) 'Oxytocin improves "mind reading" in humans', *Biological Psychiatry*, 61: 731–733.
11 Campbell, A. (2009) 'Oxytocin and human social behaviour', *Personality and Social Psychological Review*, 14(3): 281–295.
12 Feldman, R. et al. (2010) 'The cross-generation transmission of oxytocin in humans', *Hormones and Behaviour*, 58: 669–676.
13 Sloan, R. et al. (2007) 'RR interval is inversely related to inflammatory markers', *Molecular Medicine* 13(3/4): 178–184.
14 Bibevski, S. and Dunlap, M. (2011) 'Evidence for impaired vagus nerve activity in heart failure', *Heart Failure Reviews*, 16(2): 129–135.
15 Fredrickson, B. et al. (2008) 'Open hearts build lives', *Journal of Personality and Social Psychology*, 95(5): 1045–1062.
16 Kemper, K. and Shaltout, H. (2011) 'Non-verbal communication of compassion', *BMC Complementary and Alternative Medicine*, 11: 132.
17 Chartrand, T. and van Baaran, R. (2009) 'Human mimicry', *Advances in Experimental Social Psychology*, 41: 219–274.
18 Han, S-H et al. (2007) 'Feelings and consumer decision making', *Journal of Consumer Psychology*, 17(3): 158–168.
19 Singh, L. et al. (2002) 'Infants listening preferences', *Infancy*, 3(3): 365–394.
20 Kramer, G. (2007) *Insight Dialogue*, Boston, MA: Shambhala.
21 Kramer, G. et al. (2008) 'Cultivating mindfulness in relationship', In S. Hick and T. Bien (eds) *Mindfulness and the Therapeutic Relationship*, New York: Guilford Press, pp. 195–214.
22 Wellwood, J. (1992) 'The healing power of unconditional presence', In J. Wellwood (ed.) *Ordinary Magic*, Boston, MA: Shambhala, pp. 155–158.

23 McCown, D. *et al.* (2011) *Teaching Mindfulness*, New York: Springer.
24 Segal, Z.V. *et al.* (2002) *Mindfulness Based Cognitive Therapy for Depression*, New York: Guildford Press.
25 Germer, C.K. *et al.* (2013) *Mindfulness and Psychotherapy* (2nd edn), New York: Guildford Press.
26 Beutler, L. *et al.* (1986) 'Therapist variables in psychotherapy process and outcome', In S. Garfield and A. Bergin (eds) *Handbook of Psychotherapy and Behaviour Change* (3rd edn), Hoboken, NJ: John Wiley & Sons.
27 Schermuly, C.C. (2014) 'Negative effects of coaching for coaches', *International Coaching Psychology Review*, 9(2): 165–180.
28 Shapiro, S.L. and Carlson, L.E. (2009) *The Art and Science of Mindfulness*, Washington DC: American Psychological Association.
29 Shapiro, S. *et al.* (2007) 'Teaching self-care to caregivers', *Professional Psychology*, 1(2):105–115.
30 Germer, C.K. (2009) *The Mindful Path to Self-Compassion*, New York: Guildford Press.
31 Davidson, R. and Harrington, A. (2001) *Visions of Compassion*, New York: Oxford University Press.
32 Neff, K. (2011) *Self-Compassion*, London: Hodder & Stoughton.
33 Bowlby, J. (1969) *Attachment and Loss. Vol. 1: Attachment*, Basic Books.
34 Brach, T. (2003) *Radical Acceptance*, London: Rider.
35 Hawkins, P. and Shohet, R. (1989) *Supervision in The Helping Professions*, Maidenhead, UK: Open University Press.
36 Darley, J. and Batson, C. (1973) 'From Jerusalem to Jericho', *Journal of Personality and Social Psychology*, 27: 100–108.
37 Condon, P. *et al.* (2013) 'Meditation increases compassionate responses to suffering', *Psychological Science*, 24: 2125–2127.
38 See Graham Lee at www.graham-lee.co.uk
39 Henry, W. *et al.* (1990) 'Patient and therapist introject, interpersonal process, and differential psychotherapy outcome', *Journal of Consulting and Clinical Psychology*, 58: 768–774.

6 Mindfulness and coaching approaches

In this chapter we will investigate the overlaps between mindfulness and various coaching approaches. We will also explore how mindfulness practice might support, enrich and deepen the application of these approaches. What is presented here is simply an outline – a sketch of a much richer tapestry. There is so much here that this chapter could become a book in its own right, with mindful coaches contributing from their particular psychological specialisms – combined with their personal experience of mindfulness practice.

A person-centred approach

> One of the most . . . growth-promoting experiences for the other person . . . comes from my appreciating this individual in the same way that I appreciate a sunset . . . I don't find myself saying, 'Soften the orange a little on the right hand corner, and put a bit more purple along the base . . .' I don't try to control a sunset. I watch with awe as it unfolds . . . this is a somewhat Oriental attitude.
>
> Carl Rogers,[1] p. 22

When we asked our mindful coaches which models informed their coaching approach and how their mindfulness practice deepened or supported these, many referred to Roger's person-centred approach.

Jane Brendgen, for example, told us that her own mindfulness training had helped her to cultivate the core therapeutic conditions of unconditional positive regard, authenticity and empathy. Liz Gooster echoed that, saying:

> Mindfulness supports the unconditional positive regard I want to hold for my clients . . . the impact it has on my general way of being facilitates this and if I'm feeling stressed or finding a client challenging, I will deliberately use a loving kindness meditation to help me bring a more open attitude.

The humanistic vision underlying Rogers' person-centred approach is often described in terms of the acorn analogy. When provided with the appropriate nurturing conditions, acorns grow into oak trees. However clichéd the analogy, it describes an essential truth of life as Rogers saw it. Given the right conditions, living things grow as potential pushes towards actualisation.

Rogers identified three 'core conditions' necessary and sufficient for a growth promoting climate in which people can realise their inherent potential:

1. Congruence or genuineness
2. Unconditional positive regard and acceptance
3. Accurate empathic understanding.

Rogers believed that through authenticity, the therapist serves as a model of a human being struggling towards greater 'realness'.

> The more the therapist is himself or herself in the relationship ... the greater is the likelihood that the client will change and grow ... This means that the therapist is openly being the feelings and attitudes that are flowing within at the moment ... there is a ... congruence, between what is being experienced at the gut level, what is present in awareness, and what is expressed to the client.[1]
>
> pp. 115–116

Rogers' second core condition is a deep and genuine caring toward clients that is unconditional.

> When the therapist is experiencing a positive, acceptant attitude toward whatever the client is at that moment ... change is more likely to occur. The therapist is willing for the client to be whatever immediate feeling is going on [and] prizes the client in a total rather than a conditional way.[1]
>
> p. 116

Finally, the therapist strives to walk in the client's shoes, understanding their subjective experience by reflecting back understanding of what was said, as well as the meaning and feelings underlying the words.

> When functioning best, the therapist is so much inside the private world of the other that he or she can clarify not only the meaning of which the client is aware but even those just below the level of awareness.[1]
>
> p. 116

Rogers maintained that these attitudes bring about change as the client comes to listen to and trust their own inner experience. As a person is accepted they develop a more caring attitude toward themselves. As a person is empathically heard, they are able to listen more accurately to the flow of their inner experience. And as a person understands and accepts their self, they become more congruent with their inner experience. While Rogers identified these core conditions as necessary and sufficient for change, he didn't provide a concrete means to develop them.

We suggest that mindfulness offers that systematic method.

Congruence involves being fully focused on the present moment and able to flow with the client's, and one's own, moment-to-moment experience. Mindfulness allows one to become more present to whatever is arising in the field of experience. Not only do we become more aware of thoughts in the moment but, by quietening the mind, we also become more aware of feelings and sensations. We develop a more refined intuition and a felt-sense experienced at 'the gut level'.

Mindful awareness helps us get in touch with our inner experience and, by having the courage to disclose this in relationship, we resonate more deeply with clients.

As we've seen, theorists such as Gregory Kramer[2] suggest that mindfulness has an interpersonal dimension. His 'Interpersonal Mindfulness' programme is designed to enable participants to access their own embodied wisdom more readily and to develop their capacity to speak from that.

As the person-centred approach developed, Rogers placed an increasing emphasis on congruence as the foremost attitudinal condition. For him, the integration and wholeness of the therapist was a key predictor of client outcomes. In his later years, Rogers commented that, when he was at his best, 'then, simply my *presence* is releasing and helpful' (p. 129).[1]

As Jane Brendgen notes, this is one of the features of Rogers' concept of a psychologically mature person, where the authentic self is facilitated through self-transparency and self-awareness, the readiness to experience 'what is' without defending against it, and the willingness to be an embodiment of all that one truly is. Since mindfulness practice is essentially a process by which we become more aware of and accept and integrate more and more aspects of ourselves and our experience, we suggest that it has a key role to play in developing more integrated coaches, thereby supporting the outcomes co-created with clients.

When we practice mindfulness we also cultivate acceptance – we learn to greet whatever feelings come up, even the uncomfortable or unwanted, with an attitude of warmth, kindness and non-judgement. This repetitive practice also helps us welcome our client's feelings more easily – it helps us develop unconditional positive regard. This non-evaluative, non-judgemental attitude contributes to the 'holding environment' of any coaching. Our receptivity, containment and tolerance to receive whatever emotions are present help to bring forward our client's seemingly 'unacceptable parts'. And as we saw in the last chapter, these attitudinal qualities are further deepened through self-compassion practices.

Finally, research also suggests that regular mindfulness practice increases empathy. Rather than teaching techniques for empathic listening, mindfulness offers the opportunity to develop empathy from 'the inside out'. Through regular practice, mindfulness develops the insula, a part of the brain associated with self-awareness and empathy. As we will see in the next chapter, Dan Siegel suggests our ability to deeply attune to ourselves at a felt sense level is inextricably linked to our capacity to deeply attune to and resonate with others.

Clearly there are a number of similarities in the philosophy and attitudinal foundations of mindfulness and a person-centred approach. In his later years, Rogers entitled his book *A Way of Being* to convey that it is a way of being to adopt a person-centred approach. Similarly, mindfulness is also a way of being – a way of opening to ourselves, others and life exactly as it is moment by moment.

Time to think

Many of our mindful coaches found a strong resonance between their experience of mindfulness and Nancy Kline's 'Time to Think' approach.

For Alyse Ashton, Time to Think 'feels like mindfulness in practice' – there's a certain quality of attention that goes beyond listening, she says. Liz Gooster says that in the Time to Think sense, mindfulness gives her a greater sense of ease in silence, allowing her to give clients a higher quality of attention.

Lindsay Wittenberg builds on that. For her, Kline's concept of 'generative attention' is all about mindfulness, as are the encouragement of ease and her recognition of the importance of feelings.

People who meet Nancy often speak of her palpable presence. She fully embodies what she teaches and we would suggest that it is this that is transformative. Ironically, when *Time to Think*[3] was first published, there may have been some questions within the coaching profession as to whether it was actually coaching. Since a significant part of the approach has to do with non-doing, it doesn't readily lend itself to the assessment of more verbal coaching competencies. However, its influence seems to be firmly recognised today as reflected by her invitation to provide the keynote address at the inaugural BACP Coaching Conference. Speaking to the title *What Happens in the Silence? The Real Art of Coaching*, she began by drawing on the inspiration of W.B. Yeats:

> We can make our minds so like still water
> That beings gather around us,
> That they might see, it may be,
> Their own images,
> And so live for a moment,
> With a clearer, perhaps even with a fiercer life,
> Because of our quiet[4]
>
> Yeats, 1998

She then went on to suggest that clients first, and possibly only, need from their coaches the most powerful coaching expertise of all: generative attention and its uncorrupted silence. All other tools, she suggested, can wait.

I wonder what new levels of superb we might reach if we could become expert at generating this kind of attention, this silence. Could we begin by seeing that attention ... creates thinking in our clients? That in the presence of our silent, profound attention, clients can generate all of the connections, insights, challenges, feelings, plans and actions they want from the session ... Could we notice that all of this can happen even if we say nothing, other than to ask, 'What do you want to think about?' And then, only if needed, 'What more do you think, or feel, or want to say?'[5]

This captures the essence of Kline's approach in its purest and simplest form. More fully, her *Thinking environment* consists of ten components and her *Thinking partnership* consists of a six stage format. We do not propose here, to go into detail regarding all of these but simply to examine Part 1 (*Free exploration*) and those components most obviously relating to mindfulness.

In our own experience, when the thinker and thinking partner are in a state of mutual mental absorption and flow, '*Free exploration*' is the only stage required. At its simplest, this consists of the coach asking, at most, the two well framed questions highlighted in the previous extract and then not interrupting.

While doing that, the mindful coach or thinking partner brings an attitude of *ease* to the dialogue – silently offering their own freedom from tension or internal rush, allowing the thinker's mind to broaden, open and expand. For Kline, people who are at ease while someone is trying to think in their presence can 'work near-miracles ... to pay attention with a heart and mind at ease is what produces results' (pp. 69–70).[3]

The mindful coach or thinking partner also brings an inner attitude of *encouragement* to the dialogue. Even if you don't verbally interrupt, any sign of an internal narrative on the part of the listener that says 'you're wrong', 'you're missing the point' or 'I've got a better idea' can discourage the thinker from opening up or thinking innovatively and can subtly close them down. This can leak out through a frown, a subtle shake of the head, or a change in the eyes. An encouraging attitude lets the thinker know that you believe they have great thinking of their own. It communicates 'say more' and 'keep going with your thinking', but without words. 'A Thinking Environment' says Kline, 'sets up a wholehearted, *unthreatened* search for good ideas' (p. 72; our emphasis added).[3] As we saw in the last chapter, Barbara Fredrickson's research on positivity resonance points to the role that positive emotion can play in broadening our 'thought-action repertoire'.

The mindful coach or thinking partner's attitude of *allowing* when it comes to their own and others' *feelings* is vital to the thinking partnership. Thinking is often inhibited when emotional pain is repressed and the question 'What more do you think, or feel, or want to say?' is an invitation to enter the affective, as well as the thinking realm. However, the willingness of another person to accept that invitation will depend on their intuitive, felt sense of the listener's capacity to safely hold emotion. When training coaches, Kline advises that when people are trying to think for themselves they, just occasionally, might cry, get angry or say they are frightened. 'Don't stop them' she says 'be with them. Pay respectful attention to them . . . They will stop sooner rather than later. And then they will think more clearly' (p. 78).[3]

The most potent component of a *Thinking environment* is *Generative attention*. 'Attention', says Kline, 'the act of listening with palatable respect and fascination, is the key to a *Thinking environment*' (p. 37).[3]

The key here is Kline's revolutionary recognition that attention from one person generates thinking in another. High calibre listening ignites the mind of the person being listened to.

You signal attention of this kind in three ways: your face, your eyes – and by not interrupting.

'To be interrupted is not good. To get lucky and not be interrupted is better. But to *know* you are not going to be interrupted allows your mind to dive, to skate to the edge and leap' (p. 43).[3] Kline suggests that the fact that the person can relax, knowing that you are not going to take over, talk, interrupt, manoeuvre or manipulate, contributes to the quality of their thinking.

As we've already noted, your facial expression can encourage or discourage the thinker.

> If you look bored, the Thinker will be boring. If you look scared, they will censor. If you seem angry, they will tiptoe. If you worry between your eyes, they will stop and begin to take care of you . . . The point is to be interested and to show it.[3]
>
> p. 44

Finally, Kline instructs coaches to keep their eyes on the person thinking, no matter what. 'Don't look away even for a second . . . It is a basic indicator of attention' (pp. 44–45).[3]

So: attention, ease, encouragement and a capacity to be with strong emotion. Much like Rogers before her, Kline highlights key components for transformative change to occur. But how do you systematically train attention of this kind and these inner attitudes?

With Kline, much of this comes down to her own modelling of the approach – she embodies what she teaches.

If you're able to watch her sit in stillness, completely at ease with the thinker's free exploration, you get a sense of what is possible. You might then begin to mimic and practice that for yourself, learning to sit in silence, at ease with yourself and with the thinker. This can be challenging at first. You might find yourself metaphorically sitting on your hands and biting your lip – itching to ask a well-intended question.

But mindfulness training helps. With its emphasis on present-moment attention, self-regulation, perspective taking and allowing; we believe that regular mindfulness practice can produce the capacities of ease, encouragement and generative attention that 'Time to Think' calls for.

That leads us to wonder whether mindful attention and generative attention might be similar or the same thing. Attention and presence are interconnected – when we train our attention to reside in the present moment rather than the future, the past or abstraction, we become more present in each moment. In his later years, Rogers' writings suggest that the relational conditions that are central to his approach emerge from the ground of presence and that presence itself is an embodiment of the therapeutic conditions.

We suggest that generative attention is a form of coaching presence, and in this we share Kline's curiosity – 'I wonder what new levels of superb we might reach if we could become expert at generating this kind of attention, this silence.'

As more and more coaches are drawn to regular mindfulness practice we may be about to find out.

Relational coaching

For Erik de Haan, the quality of the coaching relationship and the personal qualities of the coach are centrally important to coaching outcomes. We'll be looking at this in more depth in a later chapter, but for now it's worth noting that de Haan himself draws links between his own approach and mindfulness.

In *Relational Coaching*,[6] he suggests that 'insight meditation' – practices that are similar to those taught in the first chapters of this book – can be an important means of cultivating the capacities called for in his approach. Meditation practice, he suggests, enables the coach to focus more effectively on the present moment as it comes. This leads to a higher level of present moment awareness and enables the coach to engage in a more careful examination of the here and now. The practices also address one of the key obstacles to success in the Relational Coaching context – the coach's own anxiety about the unknown.

This is borne out by what our mindful coaches have told us about their experience of how mindfulness impacts the coaching relationship.

> I know that my mindfulness practice has an impact, even if the client isn't necessarily aware. Several say that I have a calming presence – that as soon as they see me, they feel calmer. Mindfulness gives me the courage to be open and vulnerable. If I am willing to show my true self this encourages the client to do the same and hold nothing back. Even something as simple as saying 'I don't know where to take this' shows the client that it's ok to not know, that one doesn't need to have all the answers.
>
> Farah Govani

Through greater self-awareness and somatic sensitivity, developed via mindfulness practice, I am better able to track the subtle dynamics of the coaching relationship and their relevance for the work. I find greater internal spaciousness and a reduction in automatic responses. Dis-identification from dominant coaching narratives supports greater flexibility, creativity and collaborative meaning making. There's also a greater capacity to sit in the void of not knowing – allowing new possibilities to emerge.

Simon Cavicchia

Lindsay Wittenberg said mindfulness practice enabled her to bring a more mindful approach to building what she called 'connected separateness' with her clients. She spoke of this as a way of being present to the client without judgement; allowing her to build an awareness of herself and her thinking, in the relationship and in the moment, while also being authentic and able to make choices around the interventions she used.

'Clients often mention my calmness,' she said, 'my lack of judgement and the ease they have in trusting me. Is this, at least partly, about mindfulness at work? Perhaps. My mindfulness practice can't *not* impact on coaching outcomes.'

She went on to say that she imagines that the combination of her presence, any insights that presence might bring or facilitate trust and a sense of being accepted without an agenda create a space in which the client feels safe enough to take risks. It creates an environment in which they are able, sometimes courageously, to achieve insights that lead to sustainable change which may be converted into development and sometimes even transformation.

'When I'm able to be in the moment and mindful,' said Alyse Ashton, 'surprising things sometimes happen.' She told us about a client she once worked with. 'As I sat with her and observed "that sounds emotional", she suddenly burst into tears. She followed that by saying "I don't do this, I don't cry!"'

Alyse thinks that mindful attention enables a quality of contact with herself that allows her coachees to discover an ability to connect with different ways of thinking and being which might be shocking and surprising.

She thinks that the client she was telling us about discovered for herself what had been going on beneath the surface that she hadn't been aware of. That enabled her to make new sense of things and to look at them differently.

'So I think that sense of fully being aware of what's going on physically and noticing feelings, and not just thinking about it shifts things,' she said.

> And, in that moment, for her I made a difference. I'd bet money on it. And how does mindfulness impact on the quality of the relationship? Very often it impacts not only the results we get together but how the whole process feels – it's far more rich . . . it feels like fertile ground . . . so you are in flow more of the time.

Gestalt

The fundamental intent of Gestalt approaches is to work with present-moment attention. Among other things, this might involve providing here-and-now feedback 'from the inside': sharing with the coachee some of the content of what was evoked in the coach by what they brought to the session. Or it might involve 'noticing' changes in facial expression, body language or tone of voice and bringing this into conscious awareness.

As we've mentioned, regular mindfulness practice develops parts of the brain associated with greater levels of self-awareness and empathy. Research also suggests that it enhances our ability to notice what Paul Ekman[7] refers to as micro expressions – those micro moments of unconscious communication. Regular mindfulness practice also actively cultivates the present-moment attention on which Gestalt practice is built. But there is more to it than that.

One aspect of present-moment awareness, that is common both to mindfulness-based approaches and Gestalt, is their emphasis on the need sometimes to 'stay with' the experience of resistance.

As we saw in Chapter 1, 'the body scan' is a key practice within mindfulness-based approaches. By scanning through the body we may become aware of areas where there is a sense of ease and flow, and other areas where there is tension, resistance or even discomfort and pain. As we've seen, it's a natural human reaction to wish to move away from physical or mental pain and discomfort. However, through the repetitive practice of 'the body scan' we may gradually develop a capacity to *turn towards* resistance and discomfort with an attitude of curiosity and kindness. In doing so, we might find that we are able to *soften and open* into it and that the resistance is not as permanent or as fixed as first thought. But ironically, this awareness only develops by 'staying with' it. Stay with the resistance long enough without wishing to fix or change it in any way and, paradoxically, one might find that it changes, transforms or even dissolves of its own accord. Having learnt to approach our own experience in this way, it is only a short step to extend this relationally into the coaching encounter.

As Gestalt supervisor and coach Marion Gillie notes about Gestalt coaching,

> if you are working well as a Gestalt coaching practitioner your orientation will be . . . looking to see where the energy is and where it is blocked . . . When the client is stuck somewhere in the cycle of experience your task is to help the client explore how they are creating this blockage. This involves surfacing, listening to and experiencing being stuck. Paradoxically, if you and the client can stay with the block/stuckness/ resistance, fully experience it (often by exaggerating it) we generally find that it will either dissolve or transform, thus freeing the client up to move forward.[8]
>
> pp. 36–37

As Fritz Perls and the other founders of Gestalt studied Eastern philosophy, including Zen Buddhism, we shouldn't be surprised by the parallels with mindfulness. In *The Paradoxical Theory of Change*,[9] Arnold Beisser, an early and influential Gestalt theorist, suggests that change occurs when one fully becomes what one is, rather than trying to be what one is not, and that lasting change cannot take place through coercion. The Gestalt approach rejects the role of the change agent and simply works with 'what is' rather than 'why it is' or 'what it should be'.

As Marion Gillie notes,

> The process of healthy self-regulation is the ability to be fully what *one is* and to meet one's genuine needs, as distinguished from external regulation (trying to be what I think I *should* be to meet some external demand, real or imagined).[8]
>
> p. 35

The crucible for working with 'what is' is present moment awareness and one of the key means for generating awareness of this kind arises from a coach's own presence. When a coach is aware of what is going on within him or herself and between him/herself and the client in the present moment, and is prepared to share some of this with the client this can assist greatly with the Gestalt notion of 'contact'.

Mindfulness practice can support, enhance and deepen the Gestalt approach through systematically cultivating present moment attention and coach presence. However, since mindful awareness is both an outcome as well as a process, we can also say that the act of bringing mindful attention into the coaching encounter is a way of raising awareness in and of itself.

As Simon Cavicchia, one of our mindful coaches, noted:

> Mindfulness is a very natural ally of Gestalt because of the emphasis on awareness. From a purist perspective, awareness is the only thing that is needed. Once you become aware you have choice ... I talk about mindfulness as 'the new awareness'. It's a very specific orientation to noticing, observing and being with. As a Gestalt practitioner, my own mindfulness practice is key to supporting my increased awareness and that of my clients and it has significantly sensitised me to somatic information.

Speaking of the relationship between mindfulness practice and Gestalt, Lindsay Wittenberg talked about how it sharpens her awareness of the client's 'figure' – and of her own, and of how their relationship is playing out.

> It also allows me to be more confidently creative in the design and suggestion of experiments, and builds my multi-faceted awareness of what is going on in the field. I am better able to reflect in the session on what is drawing the client's attention in comparison with what is drawing my attention.

Alyse Ashton spoke in similar terms.

> The first thing is noticing what's in the field, the figure in the ground. To do that you have to pay attention. It's harder to do that if you're not present – which is harder to do if you're not mindful.
>
> The second thing is when a figure starts to emerge, you have choice points: when to offer an experiment and how to offer it. And in that moment I need to notice what is going on for me and what I see physiologically in the client. It's the same thing – presence and awareness. What matters is the quality of attention.
>
> And then as you go through it, there's the tracking – noticing what's happening for you and the other person. This quality of being an observer and at the same time in the process. There's a lot going on.
>
> At the best of times that's hard and if you're not really there, in the moment, it's impossible.
>
> Then there's the ending of a Gestalt experiment – noticing the moment when it feels done, testing that with the client and inviting them to come out and start the sense-making process. The pacing of that matters. Mindfulness of that is what feels right energetically as you withdraw.

Cognitive behavioural approach

Some theorists say with Mindfulness-Based Cognitive Therapy and similar approaches we're currently experiencing the 'third wave' of CBT.[10] Certainly, since Segal, Williams and Teasdale developed MBCT, mindfulness and the cognitive behavioural approach have been inextricably linked. MBCT explicitly brings mindfulness into the therapeutic relationship. It has a very specific protocol as outlined in Segal *et al.'s Mindfulness-Based Cognitive Therapy for Depression*[11] as well as specific means for training MBCT teachers and therapists. For this reason, we recommend that coaches wishing to explicitly integrate MBCT into their coaching should first undertake the relevant training.

But for those coaches who already operate as cognitive behavioural coaches, what is important to share about the similarities and differences to MBCT? One answer to this is revealed in the following quote from Jon Kabat-Zinn,

> To come to our senses, both literally and metaphorically, on the big scale as a species and on the smaller scale as a single human being, we first need to return to the body, the locus within which the biological senses and what we call the mind arise.[12]

For many coaches cognitive behavioural coaching appeals not only to themselves but also to their clients because it explicitly works with cognitions. When working with highly cerebral executives, this can often serve as a natural entry point into the coaching. A simplified way of thinking about CBC is that it is about 'changing the tape', particularly where the presenting issue is one of confidence. CBC can offer a well-trodden path of helping clients become more aware of negative self-talk and offers a means to find positive reframes to this and other limiting assumptions.

While MBCT shares the focus of becoming more aware of thoughts, it differs in a subtle but significant respect. Rather than focusing simply on 'changing the tape', the MBCT emphasis is more on 'turning the volume down'. To borrow Norman Farb's[13] terminology, by equipping individuals with the means to systematically move between 'narrative' and 'experiential' mode, mindfulness equips people with the capacity to turn the volume down on unhelpful inner narrative. This in itself shifts things as it loosens the grip of unhelpful self-talk. Participants on MBCT programmes are helped to see that their disturbing thoughts are 'just thoughts' and to change their relationship to these.

The primary means of moving from narrative mode into experiential mode involves coming home to the body through practices like 'the body scan' and coming to see thoughts not as facts, through practices like 'mindfulness of thoughts'. In this respect anyone wishing to *explicitly* integrate MBCT into their coaching approach will require quite a different skill set: one based on significant personal experience of relevant guided meditation and other practices.

Arnie Kozak, one of our mindful coaches, thinks of mindfulness training as a form of CBT, where mindfulness provides the powerful option of stepping out of the cognitive, narrative stream. Similarly, Heather Rachel Johnston, another of our mindful coaches, finds that mindfulness approaches helped her to focus less on changing thoughts, which people struggled with anyway, and to emphasise more an attitude of simply noticing and being aware of thoughts.

The Inner Game

> The greatest efforts in sports . . . come when the mind is as still as a glass lake.[14]
>
> p. 23

> If there is one thing that excellence in sports and excellence in work have in common, it can be summed up in a single phrase: focus of attention.[15]
>
> Tim Gallwey, p. 43

Tim Gallwey was influential in the early development of the coaching profession. His book, *The Inner Game of Tennis*[14] evolved into the *The Inner Game of Work*[15] and, through the advocacy of coaches like Myles Downey[16] it influenced early thinking and practice. For Downey, '*The Inner Game of Tennis* is perhaps one of the most influential books on performance and learning of the last 30 years' (p. 10).[16]

We reference it here, immediately after cognitive behavioural approaches, because of its emphasis on the way unhelpful inner dialogues impede performance:

Performance = Potential – Interference

Interference can show up in many forms: fear, doubt, lack of confidence, trying too hard, trying for perfection, anger, frustration, boredom or a busy mind.

According to Gallwey, one of the ways to reduce interference is to focus attention. When attention is focused, individuals enter a mental state where they can learn and perform at their best. Gallwey called that mental state 'relaxed concentration'. Others refer to it as 'flow'.[17]

The Inner Game also speaks of Self One and Self Two. Self One is the internalised voice of our parents, teachers and those in authority – it seeks to control Self Two and does not trust it. Self One is characterised by tension, fear, doubt and trying too hard. Self Two is the whole human being with all its potential and capacities including the hard-wired capacity to learn. It is characterised by relaxed concentration, enjoyment and trust.

In *Effective Coaching*[16] Downey suggests that coaches should aim to operate from Self Two. This, he says, is where we do our best work and when we coach others the aim should be to help them get into Self Two, as this is where they will be most insightful and creative. He goes on to suggest 'there is no guaranteed method of getting into Self Two that I know of' (p. 45).[16]

We suggest that there *is* a way of regularly getting into Self Two in coaching work. While nothing is guaranteed, people who are more skilled at focusing their attention, such as meditators and high-level sports-people, are more likely to find themselves in flow.

Downey suggests that there are two major 'interferences' that get in the way of flow for coaches: trying to get it right and the coach's opinions and judgements of the coachee.

If 'the greatest efforts . . . come when the mind is as still as a glass lake', then how might a coach best attain this state of relaxed concentration where interference and unhelpful inner narrative is minimised? Regular mindfulness practice can help.

This still leaves the question of how best to help the coachee get into Self Two. If we subscribe to the assertion that attention, of a particular kind, actually generates thinking in another; and if we see the importance of therapeutic presence as an enabler of change; then we can see that by bringing mindful attention and therapeutic presence to clients we offer them the opportunity to enter states of flow alongside us.

Simply by bringing mindful attention to clients, we might enable them to access new levels of awareness. Just as emotions are contagious, so too may be mental states.

To clarify the kind of attention or 'relaxed concentration' involved in the 'Inner Game', Gallwey quotes D.T. Suzuki, the renowned Zen thinker, describing the effects of the ego-mind on archery:

> As soon as we reflect, deliberate, and conceptualize, the original unconsciousness is lost and a thought interferes . . . The arrow is off the string but does not fly straight to the target, nor does the target stand where

it is. Calculation, which is miscalculation, sets in . . . Man is a thinking reed but his great works are done when he is not calculating and thinking. 'Child-likeness' has to be restored with long years of training in self-forgetfulness.[14]

p. 22

Transactional Analysis

Even where Transactional Analysis (TA) is not central to a coach's approach, many may have used it with clients because of its accessibility. Developed by Eric Berne,[18] TA can be a helpful way of developing greater self-awareness and broadening awareness about key relationships through the use of concepts such as 'drivers', 'ego states' (PAC) and 'life scripts'.

When people begin to practice mindfulness on a regular basis, they often become more aware of their reoccurring patterns of thought, feelings and behaviour. Having labels for some of those clusters, in the form of the 'drivers' that TA speaks of, can be helpful: 'be good', 'hurry up', 'please others', 'be strong' or 'try hard'. One may even discover a heightened awareness of where these come from in the meditator's own biography. By bringing mindfulness to the coaching encounter, one increases the likelihood of spotting such patterns as they arise: either as the client describes key relationships, or as they are experienced in the coaching encounter itself.

The same may be true of 'ego states'. In broad terms, TA sees ego states as distinctive sets of thoughts, feelings and behaviours. The 'parent' ego state is the part of us which takes care of others and decides what is right and wrong in life. Responses from this ego state are copied from our actual parents or parent-like figures from our past. Similarly, the 'child' ego state is the part of us which conforms, rebels and behaves in uncensored ways. Responses from this ego state are replayed from experiences in our childhood. The 'adult' ego state is the part of us which weighs up our past experiences in the light of current circumstances. Responses from the adult ego state are directly related to 'here and now' situations.

In TA terms, conscious responses from the adult ego state are quite different to unconscious, automatic reactions from our 'life script' – the unconscious narrative we adopted as a child about who we are and our place in the world. Once formed, these scripts continue to have a deep and unconscious effect on how we live our lives. They shape our self-image and affect the decisions we make.

Related to this is the notion of 'autonomy', the ultimate goal of TA. Berne implied that autonomy was the same thing as freedom from the script. It implies becoming self-governing, determining one's own destiny, taking responsibility for one's own feelings and actions and throwing off archaic and restrictive patterns.

For Berne, autonomy developed through the release or recovery of three capacities – *awareness*, *spontaneity* and *intimacy*.[19]

Awareness refers to being fully aware in the moment of how we are thinking, feeling and behaving and whether this is being triggered by old patterns learned in childhood. Berne saw *awareness* as the first step towards integration with the 'adult' ego state as executive. For example, a person who becomes aware of acting from 'critical parent' or 'adapted child' can decide what to do about that behaviour – to knowingly keep it, own it and be it, or to choose an alternative.

In this respect, *spontaneity* points to the fact that we always have a choice in how we behave in the present moment. An autonomous person is spontaneous and flexible, having the freedom to choose the most appropriate response for the situation rather than impulsively reacting. With awareness and spontaneity we don't have to act out of old patterns. It's in this sense that awareness supports the unlearning and undoing of old 'scripts'. For Berne, moving toward autonomy was a process of developing an integrated adult ego state, filtering more and more 'parent' and 'child' material through the 'adult' and learning new behaviour patterns as part of the integration process.

In the same way, the present moment awareness and self-regulation that come from mindfulness training can offer freedom from old scripts and conditioning by enabling creative and adaptive responses to challenges and opportunities in the present moment. In doing so, we also suggest that it offers a path towards integration.

Psychodynamic

Mindfulness practice and the psychodynamic approach share several common features. Both are introspective; both assume that awareness precedes change; and both recognise the importance of unconscious processes. A central goal of the psychodynamic approach is to make the unconscious conscious. By becoming more self-aware, by understanding more about how we think, feel and act, we can exercise more conscious choices. There is a clear overlap here with the outcomes of mindfulness practice.

Another area the two approaches hold in common is their shared emphasis on 'exposure'. Both approaches identify our habitual tendency to avoid what is unpleasant and work to counteract it. Through regular mindfulness practice we notice our tendency to try to control experience, to hold on to pleasant events and reject unpleasant ones, and we learn to tolerate, and even befriend, 'unpleasant' experience. In the same way, a psychodynamic coach may pay particular attention to ways in which the client resists mental or emotional experience.

The psychodynamic approach sees the coaching relationship as a central vehicle for change. As the connection between coach and client deepens the conversation becomes more spontaneous and authentic, and the client develops the freedom to explore what is really troubling them. With the support of the relationship, the client is gently exposed to what is going on inside and discovers that he or she need not avoid difficult experience.

The coach's capacity to hold difficult experience is a primary enabler of the client opening to their experience and mindfulness practice can actively support this process by helping the coach to cultivate their capacity to be with what is difficult.

No discussion of the psychodynamic approach would be complete without mention of transference, countertransference and parallel process. As we saw in the section on Gestalt, coaching clients behave toward us in the same ways they behave toward others. By noticing parallel process and transference, we become better able to see how what is emerging in relationship in the 'here and now' relates to the 'there and then' of other key relationships.

Through regular mindfulness practice, coaches can develop a heightened awareness of what is being evoked in them by clients. By giving voice to this in an unattached way, they are then able to bring this into the client's awareness.

Mindfulness practice also heightens awareness of countertransference arising in the relationship. As well as helping us to become more aware of how we are being triggered by the client, mindfulness practice also enables us to develop greater self-regulation. It enables us to better see intrapersonal and interpersonal reactivity, and allows us to make more conscious decisions in the moment about how best to respond to the client. As we saw in the last chapter, even if we aren't able to see and respond to transference in the moment, certain mindfulness practices may help us work with it after the event.

Jane Brendgen, one of our mindful coaches, told us that her mindfulness practice allows her to be 'much more aware of those times when transference or counter-transference might be playing out in the relationship. I am therefore less likely to be unconsciously caught although of course this still happens!'

Somatic

The term *somatics* comes from the Greek word *somatikos*, which means the living, aware, bodily person. As we saw in Chapter 2, like Mr. Duffy, many of us seem to live a good distance from our bodies and the wisdom they hold. Somatic coaching seeks to address this by directly working with the body. It is based on an understanding that over 3 billion years of embodied knowledge lays largely dormant within us. It teaches individuals how to access this and develops the self through the body. Given that mindfulness practice brings us home to the body we shouldn't be surprised that meditation plays an important part in the somatic approach.

'Somatic awareness' is the process of turning our attention to the body and seeing what is there, then making choices and taking actions to shift or transform our self. The first step in this is becoming aware of sensations in the body as sources of information and a direct way of connecting with the self.

The first principle in somatic coaching is to move from the thinking self to the feeling self and to deepen that into a 'felt sense of life'. By bringing attention into the body we become more aware of gut feelings about what matters most to us. Mindfulness can play a key role in this by developing our awareness of bodily sensations.

This being the case, it's no surprise to find that meditation practices form a key part of the Somatic practices used to deepen 'Somatic awareness' and enable 'Somatic transformation'.

The somatic approaches focus on the idea of transformation through practice: we are what we practice and our bodies come to reflect this. Within the field of Somatic practices, 'generative' practices are seen as those that increase awareness and expand consciousness, and Richard Strozzi-Heckler, a key figure in the approach, suggests that 'one of the most direct and powerful generative practices is meditation. The fundamental principle . . . is to cultivate and train the attention to increase awareness . . . The more aware we are the more choice we have.'[20]

Focusing

Elizabeth English, one of our mindful coaches, told us that the combination of mindfulness practice and the practice of 'Focusing' affords her a unique pathway into the nature of human experience. 'It's an added level of emotional intelligence and sensitivity that I could not manage without when coaching,' she said.

It seems natural to follow discussion of somatic coaching with Eugene Gendlin's 'Focusing'. Both place an emphasis on working at the level of 'felt sense' and so both have a natural affinity with mindfulness.

'Focusing' is a subtle but powerful method to help find and change where life seems stuck. It opens the ability to experience from a deeper place than just thoughts and feelings. In the focusing process, one is enabled to contact with a particular kind of internal bodily awareness: 'A felt sense is not a mental experience but is a *physical* one . . . A bodily awareness of a situation or person or event. [It] encompasses everything you feel and know about the given subject.'[21]

Gendlin breaks down the inner act of focusing into six movements:

1. Clearing a space – paying attention inwardly in your body to an initial prompt such as 'How is my life going right now?'
2. Felt sense – from among the things that come, selecting one thing to focus on. Paying attention in the body and getting a sense of what *all of the problem feels like.*
3. Handle – letting a word, phrase or image come up that best describes the quality of the unclear felt sense.
4. Resonating – going back and forth between the felt sense and the word (phrase or image) and checking how they resonate.
5. Asking – enquiring inside: 'What makes the whole problem so . . .? (the quality you just named or pictured).
6. Receiving – staying with whatever comes with a shift in a friendly way.

Obviously to work in such a subtle way requires a capacity to deeply attune to the body at the level of felt sense. As we have seen, regular mindfulness practice heightens our awareness of feelings and bodily sensations. It seems natural then, that the mindfulness and focusing approaches should support one another.

Psychosynthesis

Susan Cruse, one of our mindful coaches, takes an approach informed by Psychosynthesis. Her mindfulness practice, she told us, supports the 'subpersonalities work' from Psychosynthesis. It also supplements 'dis-identification practice'.

What does this mean?

The Psychosynthesis approach to the development of human potential can broadly be split into two parts – 'personal' and 'transpersonal'. Personal Psychosynthesis focuses on ways to integrate the various parts of the personality and is based on the idea that we are dominated by everything with which we become identified or attached. But we can reverse that. Instead, we can dominate and control everything from which we dis-identify or detach ourselves.[22]

This dis-identification is achieved through contacting our 'unattached centre'. If we feel a wave of overwhelming anger, for example, we neither need to suppress it nor let it explode out. Both are ways in which it has us, rather than us having it. As we saw in Chapter 3, through regular mindfulness practice we develop a kind of 'witness consciousness': a way of seeing and being that arises from our capacity for metacognition. Rather than being immersed in the drama of our experience, we become able to stand back and simply witness it. From this place we might find ways to express anger appropriately or discharge the energy in other ways. In Psychosynthesis terms, this witness is your unattached centre or self – the you that is pure self-awareness, unattached to anything but willing to identify with the content of your consciousness as appropriate. Once you have made strong connections with this 'I', the next step of Psychosynthesis is the reconstruction of your personality around this centre.

Roberto Assagioli, the founder of Psychosynthesis, suggested that our personality is like an orchestra, made up of multiple subpersonalities. What we experience as our 'core personality' is made up out of the roles we take on in our lives, or aspects of ourselves that we readily identify with. But this ignores the more suppressed aspects of ourselves that we may be aware of but don't happily accept.

What is more, the Psychosynthesis approach suggests that hidden deeper in the 'lower unconscious' are repressed parts of us that are trapped and totally not accepted – these make up our 'shadow'.

Psychosynthesis aims to expand our awareness to integrate all three: the core, the subpersonalities and the shadow, because only by connecting with our subpersonalities can we transform them. Until then we remain fragmented. Through building a solid connection with the 'I', we enable it to act as the conductor: orchestrating a harmonious whole.

As we saw in the last chapter, as well as developing something akin to 'witness consciousness', certain mindfulness practices also help us to accept different aspects of ourselves that we discover, even those we find hard to accept. In this sense, mindfulness practice supports the processes of integration described by Assagioli, Rogers and Berne.

Psychosynthesis highlights the problems that arise when we become too identified or attached to any of our subpersonalities, so a key practice in Psychosynthesis is dis-identification. Writing about this process, Parfitt – a prolific theorist of Psychosynthesis – suggests that we need to find ways to dis-identify from our bodies, from our feelings and thoughts, from all our subpersonalities, and from everything that fills us up and creates the contents of our consciousness. Instead, he suggests, we have to become truly empty. When we have done that we may find there is something left. A sense of 'I'-ness, of being a self, or just being.[23]

Through deliberate dis-identification, Psychosynthesis suggests, we gain the freedom to choose either identification with, or dis-identification from, any aspects of our personality according to what is most appropriate for the situation. That enables the conductor to better orchestrate harmony and integration.

The next stage of development, Psychosynthesis suggests, is transpersonal. This is where, as the conductor, we also contact the composer – the 'transpersonal Self' – who supplies us with information about how to play the musical composition of life. Making contact with the transpersonal, Psychosynthesis suggests, we connect with a deep intuition, with our sense of value and meaning in life, and so are better able to make our lives more purposeful. Our 'higher' Self comes to the fore and we become more aligned with, rather than fighting against, the natural current of life.

Unsurprisingly, meditation plays a significant part in Psychosynthesis. While the approach it takes to meditation is different to mindfulness meditation, a capacity to still and focus the mind would support the Psychosynthesis approach to meditation practice.

An emerging Gestalt

What's presented here is simply an outline – a sketch of a much richer tapestry. There are many coaching approaches we've not had the opportunity to discuss. We also feel sure that those with a regular mindfulness practice and deep expertise in any of the approaches we've mentioned will have more to say on the matter. We look forward to that particular Gestalt emerging further in due course. For now, what we have sought to highlight here are not just overlaps between mindfulness and various coaching approaches, but we have tried to show how mindfulness practice can actively support, enrich and deepen their application.

As we've seen, regular mindfulness practice actively develops:

- congruence in the coaching encounter, increasing attunement to what is arising moment by moment and a willingness to bring this into awareness;
- an attitudinal quality of unconditional positive regard;
- deeper levels of empathy;
- interpersonal ease, along with a reduction of intrapersonal and interpersonal reactivity;
- a capacity to stay open to and hold strong emotions;
- present moment attention and generative attention;
- the capacity to stay with resistance or what is uncomfortable or unwanted
- the capacity to be at ease with not knowing;
- a quietening of the mind, reducing interference and unhelpful inner narrative;
- sensitivity to somatic felt sense;
- greater awareness of transference and countertransference and a means to better self-regulate in the moment; and
- a systematic process to work with psychodynamic effects as a complement to supervision.

These all support a deepening of the coaching relationship and this in turn supports and deepens the outcomes co-created from that relationship.

Regular mindfulness practice confers the possibility of enhanced presence, awareness and integration. It offers the coach a systematic path of integration and the possibility of developing a 'witness consciousness' that enables us to see our own experience more clearly.

When we cultivate a capacity to witness our thoughts, feelings, sensations and behaviour with non-attached awareness we are better able to bear witness to all the various aspects of ourselves, some of which may have been suppressed or repressed. To see the working out of our subpersonalities more clearly, moment by moment, day by day is an important first step towards integration.

When we develop a capacity to meet all experience with acceptance and non-judgement we also develop a capacity to befriend all aspects of ourselves. Based on his personal experience, Rogers suggested that all of this matters when it comes to helping relationships. He suggested that therapists who are more integrated will establish deeper levels of relationship and therefore co-create better outcomes with clients. We suggest that it is no different for the mindful coach. When we are better able to see, accept and integrate the different aspects of ourselves, we are better placed to bring that same unconditional presence to another.

Notes

1 Rogers, C.R. (1980) *Way of Being*, New York: Houghton Mifflin.
2 Kramer, G. (2007) *Insight Dialogue*, Shambhala.
3 Kline, N. (1999) *Time to Think: Listening to Ignite the Human Mind*, London: Cassell Illustrated.
4 Yeats, W.B. (2004) *The Celtic Twilight: Faerie and Folklore*, Mineola, NY: Dover Publications.
5 Kline, N. (2010) *What Happens in the Silence? The Real Art of Coaching*, www.timetothink.com/uploaded/BACP%20Speech%2017%20June%202011%20Article%20Version.pdf
6 de Haan, E. (2008) *Relational Coaching: Journeys Towards Mastering One-To-One Learning*, John Wiley & Sons.
7 Ekman, P. (2001) *Telling Lies*, W.W. Norton & Co.
8 Gillie, M. (2009) 'Coaching approaches derived from Gestalt', In D. Megginson and D Clutterbuck (eds) *Further Techniques for Coaching and Mentoring*, Oxford: Butterworth-Heinemann.
9 Beisser, A.R. (1970) 'The paradoxical theory of change', In J. Fagan and I.L. Shepherd (eds) *Gestalt Therapy Now: Theory, techniques, Applications*, Palo Alto, CA: Science and Behaviour Books.
10 Hayes, S. (2011) 'Open, aware, and active: contextual approaches as an emerging trend in the behavioural and cognitive therapies', *Annual Review of Clinical Psychology*, 7(1): 141–168.
11 Segal, Z.V. et al. (2012) *Mindfulness-Based Cognitive Therapy for Depression: A New Approach to Preventing Relapse* (2nd edn), New York: Guildford Press.
12 Kabat-Zinn, J. (2005) *Coming to Our Senses: Healing Ourselves and the World through Mindfulness*, Windmill: Piatkus.
13 Farb, N.A. et al. (2007) 'Attending to the present: mindfulness meditation reveals distinct neural modes of self-reference', *SCAN*, 2(2007): 313–322.
14 Gallwey, W.T. (1975) *The Inner Game of Tennis*, London: Pan Books.
15 Gallwey, W.T. (2000) *The Inner Game of Work: Overcoming Mental Obstacles for Maximum Performance,* London: Orion Business Books.
16 Downey, M. (2003) *Effective Coaching: Lessons from the Coaches' Coach*, New York: Texere Thomson.
17 Csikszentmihalyi, M. (2002) *Flow: The Psychology of Happiness*, London: Rider.
18 Berne, E. (1964) *Games People Play: The Psychology of Human Relationships*, New York: Grove Press.
19 Berne, E. (1972) *What Do You Say After You Say Hello?*, New York: Grove Press.
20 Strozzi-Heckler, R. (2014) *The Art of Somatic Coaching*, Berkeley, CA: North Atlantic Books.
21 Gendlin, E.T. (2003) *Focusing* (25th Anniversary edn), London: Rider.
22 Assagioli, R. (1976) *Psychosynthesis: A Collection of Basic Writings*, London: Penguin.
23 Parfitt, W. (2003) *Psychosynthesis: The Elements and Beyond*, Glastonbury, UK: PS Avalon.

7 Mindfulness and psychotherapy

Coaching and psychotherapy aren't the same. They have different purposes and different outcomes. But in its evolution, the coaching profession has drawn heavily on psychotherapeutic traditions. Most professional coach training requires some understanding of different psychological models and many publications on coaching mastery emphasise the use of therapeutic models to work at a deeper level.[1] It seems that the two professions have always been inextricably linked and always will be. In pointing to the future of coaching we think it's important to direct attention to emerging thinking and practice from the fields of psychotherapy, mindfulness and neuroscience. Here we will outline what seems most relevant so that you can decide for yourself what can be translated between the two professions. After all, both involve relational work where change of some kind is on the agenda. Against this backdrop, we believe that mindfulness has something hugely significant to contribute to both professions.

The practising therapist

One of the most comprehensive publications to shape thinking and practice has been *Mindfulness and Psychotherapy*.[2] It was the first to differentiate the *practicing therapist* from mindfulness *informed* therapy and mindfulness *based* therapy. In this book we consider these distinctions from a coaching perspective. Chapter 5 explores mindfulness based coaching (teaching mindfulness to clients) and Chapters 6 and 8 explore how mindfulness might inform coaching process. But the larger part of this book is focused on the *practicing coach* and implications for the coaching profession. For Germer and his colleagues, a *practicing therapist* is simply a therapist with a regular mindfulness practice. While this much is obvious, what was less obvious at the time of publication, was the suggestion that a regular *intra*personal practice could have a positive impact not only on the therapist, but also *inter*personally on the therapeutic relationship and *outcomes*.

Mindfulness training and therapeutic outcomes

To date, the most compelling study of mindfulness and clinical outcomes was conducted by Grepmair et al.[3] The study randomly assigned therapists to practice Zen meditation for nine weeks and 124 inpatients were then divided between the meditating and non-meditating therapists. The group treated by the meditating therapists reported subjectively better outcomes, and on ten of the eleven outcome measures the patients treated by meditating therapists excelled.

While research in this area is still in the early stages, there is evidence that mindfulness training has beneficial effects on the therapeutic relationship, so we might also take a considered view as to the likely impact on outcomes. For example, if empathy is associated with an effective treatment relationship and mindfulness training can be shown to cultivate empathy, it seems plausible that mindfulness would positively influence therapeutic outcomes.

Benefits of mindfulness training for the therapist

In *Mindfulness for Therapists*,[4] Eric McCollum highlights the benefits of mindfulness most relevant to therapists. Among non-clinical groups, he notes,

> we see that mindfulness is associated with better attentional control, more cognitive flexibility, better working memory, less emotional reactivity and better relational functioning. While there are other ways in which mindfulness appears to help therapists, these fundamental skills would seem to serve therapists well.[4]
>
> p. 24

There is also growing evidence about the impact of mindfulness practice on healthcare workers in general. Research suggests clinicians can reap the same beneficial effects as non-clinicians, including reduced anxiety and depression,[5] decreases in mood disturbance[6] and increased empathy.[7] Shapiro et al.[8] found that MBSR reduced stress and increased self-compassion for health care professionals and Cohen-Katz et al.[9] found that MBSR can combat the deeper stresses of compassion fatigue and burnout. So we see clinicians exploring mindfulness to increase resilience and well-being, but also to cultivate factors beneficial to the therapeutic relationship. These include the cultivation of attention,[10] therapeutic presence,[11] openness and acceptance,[12] self-attunement,[13] and compassion and empathy.[14] Before looking at these, let's examine the link between the quality of the therapeutic relationship and outcomes.

The therapeutic relationship and common factors

While therapeutic approaches differ, research suggests that effective treatment owes more to factors they have in common, such as the personal qualities of the therapist and the quality of therapeutic relationship, rather than the particular approaches employed.[15] In conclusion to a large-scale review Norcross and Lambert suggest that

> many factors account for success and failure: the patient, the treatment method, the psychotherapist, the context, and the relationship between therapist and the patient... the therapy relationship accounts for why clients improve (or fail to improve) *as much as* the particular treatment method.[16]

A number of meta-analyses have established a positive relationship between the therapeutic relationship and outcomes[17] and qualities clients attribute to therapists in positive treatment relationships include empathy, warmth, acceptance, positive regard, collaboration and consensus[18] and the genuineness of the therapist.[19]

In light of this, Germer and his colleagues suggest that methods for creating a strong alliance should be taught to *at least the same extent* as theory and technique. But, they add, current training programmes generally emphasise models of treatment, perhaps because it's just easier to do that. Instruction in therapy skills, they say, is essential. But the larger challenge is to find a way to cultivate qualities associated with strong treatment relationships.[2]

We suggest that the same rationale holds true for the training of professional coaches.

Much like therapeutic training, most professional coach training tends to focus on theory and techniques, rather than more subtle aspects that impact on the coaching relationship.

How does one *teach* quality of attention, presence, empathic attunement, acceptance, unconditional positive regard, authenticity, use of self and the capacity to work with strong emotion? Developing understanding and skill in therapeutic process may be helpful, but in the presence of a certain quality of attention, clients have a huge capacity to define their particular challenges and generate options to move beyond them. No psychological techniques are required – clients simply learn, evolve and grow given the right conditions. Within this, what seems to matter most is often a skilful, conscious and plentiful supply of allowing and non-doing.

Mindfulness as advanced therapeutic training

Mindfulness training actively cultivates numerous qualities key to establishing a strong working alliance and is increasingly being incorporated into clinical training.[20]

Attention and cognitive flexibility

Mindful attention occurs naturally in everyday life, but it takes practice to maintain it. Even when we feel particularly attentive in a coaching session we are only intermittently mindful. Our minds become easily absorbed in associations and sometimes the content of our distraction is a meaningful clue to what is occurring in the room. An emotionally disengaged client might leave us distracted or bored or we might 'tune out', become restless, sleepy or partially absent if we're made anxious by the material a client brings. We can, of course, fake attention by asking probing questions but genuine interest and close attention are hard to fake. When we're alert and focused it permeates the work and both parties become fully alert to the task at hand.

Mindfulness practice is an antidote to the wandering mind. Improved attention has been highlighted as an underlying mechanism in mindfulness meditation[21] and there is significant evidence that it improves our ability to concentrate in a sustained way.[22] Neurological research suggests that mindfulness helps us engage in less self-referential thinking, especially when challenged by emotional distress[23] and can help us recover more quickly from distractions.[24] Research also indicates that mindfulness increases cognitive flexibility, our ability to 'adapt cognitive processing strategies to face new and unexpected conditions.'[25]

Presence

Mindfulness practice also seems related to *therapeutic presence*. Presence is a *way of being* in the room with a client[26] and has been described as 'an availability and openness to all aspects of the client's experience, openness to one's own experience in being with the client, and the capacity to respond to the client from this experience.'[27] Carl Rogers considered therapeutic presence to subsume empathy, unconditional positive regard and congruence and as we will see later, Dan Siegel suggests that it is the therapist's presence that leads to a client 'feeling felt.'

In a qualitative study with therapists who practice mindfulness, McCartney[28] investigated how mindfulness practice influences a therapist's ability to be present with clients. Presence was found to be enhanced by *being in the moment* with clients, an ability to pay attention in the present moment throughout the session. According to the therapists, this involved developing a still and quiet place within themselves where they felt centred and calm.

Another study of mindfulness training with counselling students found that they were more attentive and more comfortable with silence after mindfulness training.

> I am more comfortable with listening, sitting in silence, and just being present. Mindfulness is after all about being present and aware ... the course has helped me focus more on the client, instead of believing I have to 'do' something to change the client.[29]

Acceptance

Although attention regulation has received the most consideration in the psychological literature, the *quality* of mindful awareness is particularly important in any helping relationship. If a coach or client turn away from uncomfortable experience, the ability to work with that experience significantly diminishes. As we've seen, from a mindfulness perspective, acceptance refers to the ability to allow our experience to be just as it is, accepting both pleasurable and painful experiences as they arise. Acceptance is not about endorsing bad behaviour. Rather, moment to moment acceptance is a prerequisite for behavioural change. As Christensen and Jacobson note, change is the brother of acceptance, 'but it is the younger brother.'[30] And as we've seen, mindfulness orientated therapists like Brach, Germer and Neff also see *self*-acceptance as central to the process.

Interestingly, it does seem that our judgements of others arise in proportion to judgements of ourselves. A study by Henry *et al.*[31] analysed videotaped interactions between therapists and clients, rating the degree of controlling communication from the therapists. Therapists also rated themselves in terms of their own introjects during therapy. Those therapists who were less accepting of themselves were also more controlling and critical toward their clients. They concluded that therapists who were self-accepting were more likely to engage with clients in accepting and supportive ways.

Mindfulness practice is a vehicle for training acceptance, through exercising acceptance itself and by recognising when it's absent. When we learn to extend the safety of genuine acceptance to our clients, we often provide them with a uniquely safe relationship in an otherwise hostile world.

Empathy, attunement and resonance

Unsurprisingly, our own emotional awareness appears to be associated with our understanding of the emotional lives of others.[32] As we will see later, Dan Siegel suggests that our ability to become attuned to ourselves draws on the same neural circuitry that enables attunement to others. 'Attunement' describes a relationship in which one person focuses on the internal world of another in a way that the other feels understood and connected. Bruce *et al.* suggest that mindfulness is a form of self-attunement and speculate that a therapist's relationship to themselves has a direct bearing on their relationship to their clients.[33] The therapist's own mindfulness enables attunement to their clients and, consequently, supports their client's attunement to themselves.

Working with strong emotion – emotional regulation and equanimity

When we practice mindfulness, strong emotions inevitably arise and can be welcomed with the same attitude of acceptance as any other mental event. When we set aside fear and resistance we discover that no emotion is ever permanent and that we can tolerate more than we thought. Mindful tolerance represents a softening into and a befriending of experience. As such, affect tolerance or emotional regulation is likely to be a therapeutic mechanism in mindfulness meditation.[34] Because of the importance of body sensations in the experience of emotion (which is why emotions are called feelings) there is reason to believe that being more aware and accepting of bodily sensations can help regulate emotion.[35]

Affect tolerance and emotional regulation are enormously important to therapists and coaches. When we come to know directly through mindfulness practice that emotions, like all phenomena, are transitory, we are better able to invite them all in. This receptivity then extends naturally to clients and reassures them that they need not censor themselves to protect themselves – or us.

For both therapists and coaches it is often necessary to tolerate strong emotions in order to create a 'holding space'. Through regular mindfulness practice, we learn to become a vessel that can hold emotional content while maintaining equanimity. In the ancient mindfulness traditions, equanimity[36] is described as an attitude of non-discriminating, open receptivity in which all experience is welcomed. This equanimity allows us to stop trying to fix things long enough to see *what is* and this gives clients the freedom to inhabit their lives as they are or to change from a foundation of acceptance.

In a study of therapists who practice mindfulness, several described using 'witness consciousness' to observe and hold both the client's process and their experience of the client. One said 'I can feel myself, especially reaching for my witness the more dramatic it gets over there in the client's seat. It's like my witness is . . . a grounding in myself' (p. 60).[28]

In addition to creating a larger vessel, this 'holding witness' serves another important purpose – to help create boundaries. This can be necessary to prevent reactivity to what the client is generating. 'There's a trust of my awareness of what is going on in me as an indication of what is going on for them,' one of the therapists in the study recounted 'but I have to be mindful of what is going on in me in order to be able to use my organism as an instrument with them' (p. 60).[28] Developing this 'inner supervisor' allows us to mindfully manage countertransference. Familiarity with our own minds and bodies developed through mindfulness practice enables us to better see our response to a client's behaviour and to regulate this emotion, which might otherwise damage the relationship. By doing so we can be more present and accepting of clients across a range of emotionally charged situations and are more likely to maintain a strong and supportive relationship.

In two related studies, Ortner *et al.*[37] examined the effect of mindfulness on emotional reactivity. They found that experienced meditators and those trained in mindfulness were better able to perform cognitive tasks after viewing upsetting pictures compared to control groups, suggesting that mindfulness can help practitioners disengage more quickly from emotionally charged experiences.

Re-perceiving and intimate detachment

Shauna Shapiro, one of the most prolific researchers in the field of mindfulness and psychotherapy, provides a helpful perspective on the underlying mechanisms of mindfulness in supporting growth and change.

Re-perceiving – the mirror for change

For Shapiro, 're-perceiving' is a central mechanism of mindfulness. Re-perceiving is the process by which a shift in perspective occurs through dispassionately observing the content of one's consciousness. Rather than being immersed in the drama of your personal narrative, you're able to stand back and witness it. Re-perceiving is similar to 'decentering', the ability to 'step outside of one's immediate experience, thereby changing the very nature of that experience'[38] and 'detachment' which 'encompasses the interrelated processes of gaining "distance", "adopting a phenomenological attitude" and the expansion of "attentional space."'[39]

Re-perceiving describes a shift in consciousness in which what was previously 'subject' becomes 'object'. By intentionally focusing non-judgemental attention on the contents of consciousness, you're no longer completely 'fused' with that content and can observe it as if it were an object of experience. Aside from offering a new vantage point, how does re-perceiving support growth and change?

Shapiro points to self-regulation as a related mechanism whereby systems maintain stability of functioning and adaptability to change through feedback loops. According to Shapiro and Schwartz [40] intention and attention serve to enhance these feedback loops and create health:

$$\text{intention} \to \text{attention} \to \text{connection} \to \text{regulation} \to \text{order} \to \text{health}$$

Intentionally cultivating non-judgemental attention leads to connection, which leads to self-regulation and ultimately to greater order and health. By standing back and witnessing emotional states like anxiety, you're better able to free yourself from automatic behavioural patterns.

You can see how such processes might help a client where mindfulness practice has been explicitly introduced but how might re-perceiving and self-regulation work as a mechanism for change where mindfulness is only implicit in the work?

Many coaches are likely to have come across the metaphor of being like a mirror to clients,[41] but how clean or free from distortion is the mirror? We all have our own life histories and anything clients talk about is likely to trigger reactions in us. Can we be aware of these and self-manage in such a way that we simply reflect back what we are hearing?

By cultivating a capacity to dispassionately witness our own experience through mindfulness practice we become better able to extend this to clients. In this way, awareness of reactivity and self-management increases and we become better able to reflect back a client's stream of consciousness without distortion. By offering clients a new vantage point from which to see their experience they are able to exercise more choice, rather than reacting from automatic patterns of behaviour. From here the client is better able to self-regulate so that order and health follow. Put simply, it's the quality of our attention that allows clients to see themselves clearly and discern what adjustments they need to make according to their circumstances.

Intimate detachment

Anyone who has completed the Mindfulness for Coaches programme will have some first-hand personal experience of re-perceiving. Without this you might confuse re-perceiving with an attempt to detach from your experience to the point of apathy or numbness. But the actual experience of re-perceiving engenders a deep intimacy with whatever arises moment by moment.

> Re-perceiving does indeed facilitate greater distance in terms of clarity. And yet this does not translate as disconnection or dissociation ... re-perceiving simply allows one to deeply experience each event of the mind and body without identifying with or clinging to it ... re-perceiving does not create apathy or indifference but instead allows one to experience greater richness, texture, and depth, moment to moment.[42]

Again, clearly this can help a client where mindfulness practice has been explicitly introduced, but how might intimate detachment impact on outcomes where mindfulness is only implicit in the work?

Where a coach has first-hand experience of intimate detachment through mindfulness practice, they are able to extend this to clients when the client becomes the object of mindfulness awareness. Whatever arises in session can be met with this paradoxical quality of intimate detachment. This enables deep empathy and connection with the client without becoming completely immersed in their narrative, sympathising or colluding. This allows us to be intimately alongside the client and at the same time, detached enough be resourceful and maintain perspective. This is experienced by the client at a felt sense level – of feeling deeply understood, often because there are fewer introjects from us based on our own reactivity.

The mindful therapist

Dan Siegel, clinical professor of psychiatry at the UCLA, suggests that presence, the way we bring ourselves into connection with others, is the strongest predictor of outcomes in a helping relationship. He describes a neurophysiological explanation for this and ways in which mindfulness supports this.

This can be summarised as follows:

Presence → Attunement → Resonance

Being fully present with another, and open and receptive to what is arising moment by moment enables us to attune more deeply to their inner world. This

Presence

Siegel suggests that being present with others involves openness to whatever arises in reality. It means being open, now, to whatever is (p. 13).[43] Presence, he says, is a learnable skill. We can cultivate it as an enduring trait, not just as an intentionally created state.

Presence is not the same as being passive – it's an active, receptive state that depends on a sense of safety. The term 'neuroception' – coined by Stephen Porges[44] – describes the process whereby our brains continually monitor the external and internal environment for signs of danger. When danger is assessed, we activate the fight-flight-freeze response. When we see things as threatening, we leave the open state of receptive presence and enter a reactive state. If we sense danger we cannot activate what Porges calls the social engagement system. This is how we move from being receptive to being reactive. When we are reactive, presence is shut off and when we are receptive, presence can be created. This requires a tolerance for both uncertainty and vulnerability.

As coaches we can learn to monitor and modify our internal world to cultivate presence. We can learn to monitor neuroceptive signals and, when we detect a fight-flight-freeze response in our bodies, we can learn to do the internal work necessary to return to a state of presence.

Mindfulness is a state of awareness that enables us to be receptive and open and with regular practice we move toward an 'approach' state of neural firing, moving toward, rather than away from, difficult situations. In this way, it seems, regular mindfulness practice can activate the receptive state associated with the social engagement system.

'In these ways of creating receptivity and an approach state,' Siegel suggests, 'mindful awareness practices can be considered the basic training of the mind for any therapist' (p. 29).[43]

Clearly this holds true for coaches as well. In the same way that we outlined in the previous chapter, Siegel too suggests that mindfulness, presence and integration are all inter-related.

> What presence may essentially be is the ability to create an integrated state of being ... Integration is at the heart of presence ... Our work with mindfulness will always have these two sides of a focus on our own integration and focus on that of our clients.[43]
>
> pp. 31–32

Attunement

If presence is our openness to the unfolding of possibilities, attunement is the interactive dimension of being present. It's how we focus our attention on others and take their essence into our inner world.

Attunement requires presence, but more than that, it is also a process of focused attention and clear perception.

The physical side of interpersonal attunement involves the perception of signals from others that reveal their internal world. Noticing non-verbal signals such as eye contact, facial expression, tone of voice, posture, gesture and the timing and intensity of response. The subjective side of attunement is an authentic sense of connection. As Siegel suggests, 'when others sense our attunement with them, they experience 'feeling felt' by us' (p. 34).[43]

Attunement requires that our perception be as open as possible to another's signals and any corresponding incoming sensations. In this sense, moving into thoughts about the future, past or abstraction, even momentarily, signals not only a reduction in presence but also – in that moment – a reduction in the capacity for deep attunement.

Drawing on Marco Iacoboni's work on mirror neurons,[45] Siegel suggests that the first phase of attunement is the focus of attention on the signals from another. This puts into play a phase known as 'simulation' where these signals stimulate changes in our subcortical limbic brainstem and bodily areas. The second phase – interoception – involves these subcortical and bodily shifts being relayed back up into the insula and the prefrontal cortex as we have a perception of our own shifting interior.

When people have an awareness of their internal body state, which we might equate to our 'sixth sense', it's invariably the anterior insula that is activated. So, when we attune to someone else, we also need to tune into our own internal shifts.

When we attune to another person, the sequence of brain activation can go like this:

We take-in someone else's signals; shift our own subcortical states, and through the insula and medial prefrontal and anterior cingulate regions we attribute these shifts to what we've seen in the other person.

Initial perception, subcortical shifts, interoception and attribution are the key steps of attunement in Iacoboni's model. As we've previously mentioned, the skill of perceiving the interior of our body can be developed through mindfulness practices.

Studies by Sara Lazar and colleagues[46] suggest that the more we focus our attention toward bodily sensations, the more we activate and grow the insula. The more we do this through practices like the body scan, mindfulness of the breath and so on, the more capacity we'll have for internal monitoring and subsequently for attuning to others and being empathic.

A key feature that takes us away from presence and attunement is what Siegel refers to as our 'windows of tolerance'.

We all have our own triggers – issues that move us into rigidity or chaos, perhaps due to unprocessed or unresolved aspects of our own personal history. As we attempt to attune to another, knowing our window of tolerance for particular issues is crucial. Without such awareness we may project onto clients and give them the sense that they too are unable to tolerate whatever feelings or memories are emerging in the moment. In this way our own internal state of distress can influence our client's state.

Resonance

If presence enables us to be open to ourselves and others, and attunement is focusing on another person to bring their internal state into our awareness, 'resonance' is the resulting coupling of two autonomous entities into a functional whole.

As each attunes to the other, both are changed by the impact of the other. It's the neurobiology of *we*.

As we join, our nervous systems align into resonant coupling – our heart rates, breathing and non-verbal signals align. This shows up in EEG findings and when we measure heart-rate variability.

Through these mechanisms, our autonomic nervous systems – delicately balancing the brake and accelerator of our inner state by coordinating the functioning of our hearts and brains – become aligned and we resonate with each other.

Resonance can also be detected as we look to another and see that they have been impacted by our internal world. As Siegel suggests, letting our clients know that we feel their feelings enables them to 'feel felt'. 'If I am deeply moved by the recounting of some recent painful event,' he says

> I may feel the weight of that experience inside but show it outwardly by placing my hand on my heart. It's crucial not to pretend to be present and resonant in this way, but rather to be sure that your presence is communicated. Bringing the inside out is a fundamental part of our connection with another.[43]
>
> p. 57

As coaches, knowing the triggers that shut off our own resonance circuitry is essential in maintaining the presence, attunement and resonance needed for our work. Being a 'we' begins in infancy, so knowing our attachment history can be an important starting point in understanding our own capacity for attunement and resonance. Regular mindfulness practice can help us see more clearly the different aspects of ourselves playing out in day to day life and certain compassion practices also offer a systematic means to cultivate secure attachment in adulthood. This is about changing your mind from the inside out and freeing yourself to be more present, attuned and resonate with your clients. And that impacts on outcomes.

We have outlined interpersonal attunement and resonance here. But from what we have described so far it should be clear that a parallel process of mindfulness can play a key part in the intrapersonal domain. Through regular practice of being present and open to ourselves, we generate internal attunement as the observing self takes in the experiencing self with receptivity and acceptance. Attuning to ourselves within mindful states, the observing and the experiencing self come into resonance. That brings about integration.

Compassion focused therapy

Paul Gilbert, Professor of Clinical Psychology at the University of Derby, is a pioneer in the development of Compassion Focused Therapy (CFT). While developed primarily for people suffering from chronic self-criticism and shame, CFT provides key insight for the mindful coach.

Since research suggests that the attachment style of therapists impacts on the therapeutic relationship[47] similar dynamics are likely to exist in the coaching relationship. In this respect Gilbert's Compassionate Mind Training (CMT) offers coaches and therapists an opportunity to work with their early attachment patterns, influencing their attachment style and the relational safety they offer clients.

At its heart, CMT is rooted in evolutionary theory and the neuroscience of emotion regulation.

Gilbert uses the term 'multimind' to describe how our psychologies – our motives, emotions and cognitive competencies – were laid down at different times in our evolution.[48]

Our capacities for sex, hunting and gaining and defending territory, he suggests, can be traced back to reptiles over 500 million years ago.

With the evolution of mammals about 120 million years ago the psychologies for infant caring, alliance formation and play also arose.

Then, about 2 million years ago competencies for complex thinking, reflection and having a sense of self-identity began to emerge.

This variety of motives and different ways of making meaning give rise, he suggests, to the experience of a variety of possible selves. These subpersonalities can feel different things and play different parts when we are in different states of mind.

In all of this complexity, one way coherence can be achieved is through what he refers to as our ability to 'mentalize' – to reflect on and understand the contents of our own mind and those of others. He suggests that CMT creates a sense of safeness that facilitates mentalizing. Compassion enables us to explore new potentials within ourselves and integrate them into our sense of self – what Jung would have called the 'individuation process' – because it creates conditions of openness, caring, safeness and integration. 'Compassion from without and self-compassion from within facilitate acceptance ... thus creating brain patterns that make exploring and integrating different elements of our mind easier' (p. 38).[48]

Emotion regulation systems

Gilbert suggests that our brains contain at least three types of major emotion-regulation systems, each designed to do different things.

140 *Joining the dots*

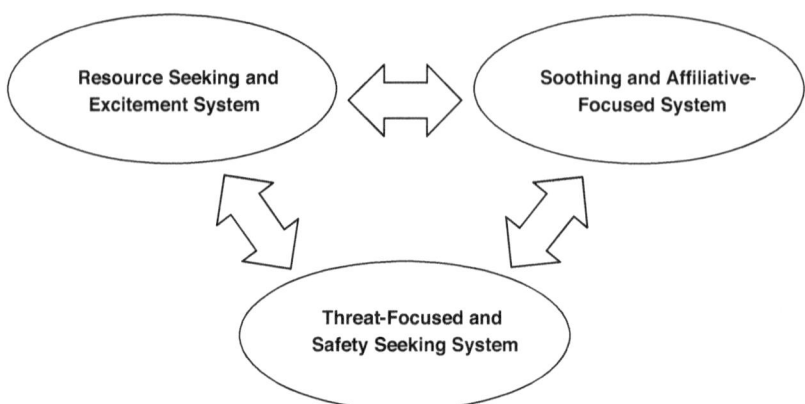

Figure 7.1 Our three major emotion-regulation systems
Adapted from Paul Gilbert, *Compassion Focused Therapy* [48]

The threat-focused and safety seeking system detects and reacts to threats quickly via the fight-flight-freeze response. It produces bursts of emotions such as anxiety, anger or disgust. Although it's a source of difficult feelings, it actually evolved as a protection system and is typically associated with the amygdala.

The resource seeking and excitement system produces positive feelings that guide, motivate and encourage us to seek out resources. We're motivated and experience pleasure by seeking out, consuming and achieving pleasing things, such as food, sex, comforts, friendships, status and recognition. When balanced with the other two systems, this system guides us towards important life goals. Gilbert describes this as a kind of 'go getting' system and it is associated with the release of dopamine.

The soothing and affiliative-focused system enables us to bring a certain soothing and peacefulness to ourselves that helps to restore balance.

When animals aren't defending themselves against threats and don't need to achieve or do anything they can settle and be content. This is a form of being happy with the way things are and feeling safe. When people practice meditation and 'slowing down' these are the feelings they report – not wanting or striving, feeling calmer inside and connected to others. These feelings of soothing and safeness, Gilbert says, are associated with endorphins and oxytocin. They enable us to be at peace with ourselves and the world, with relaxed attention and the ability to explore.

This system is also linked to warmth and kindness – so, for example, when a baby is distressed the evident love of the parent soothes and calms them.

While different types of caring impact and stimulate the soothing system, warmth is probably most associated with soothing and endorphin release.[49] From the first days of life, safeness-via-warmth is actively stimulated by caregiver signals of touch, voice tone, positive facial expressions, and mutually rewarding interchanges that form the basis of the attachment bond. These signals stimulate endorphins that give rise to feelings of safeness, connectedness and well-being, as the infant's physiological systems attune to the caregiver. As noted by both Bowlby and Porges, once soothed infants either relax, in a state of passive safeness, or they redirect attention to explore the environment in a state of active safeness.

Emotion acceptance and validation

Related to the above, researchers like Leahy[50] highlight the importance of emotion acceptance and validation in early development. Leahy outlines a useful model depicting how validation of emotions and early emotional coaching can link to different emotional strategies and relating styles. These styles will emerge in coaching and the coaching relationship.

There is increasing work showing that how a mother responds to her child's emotions and needs is crucial to the child's ability to understand and regulate his/her own mind.[51]

In the context of validating, loving relationships, we come to feel safe and able to explore our own minds, to understand our emotions, to feel soothed and contained – and in the process we become better able to understand the minds of others.

These cognitive abilities play a vital part in our metacognitive capacity to reflect on our own emotions, stand back from them and not be overwhelmed by them.

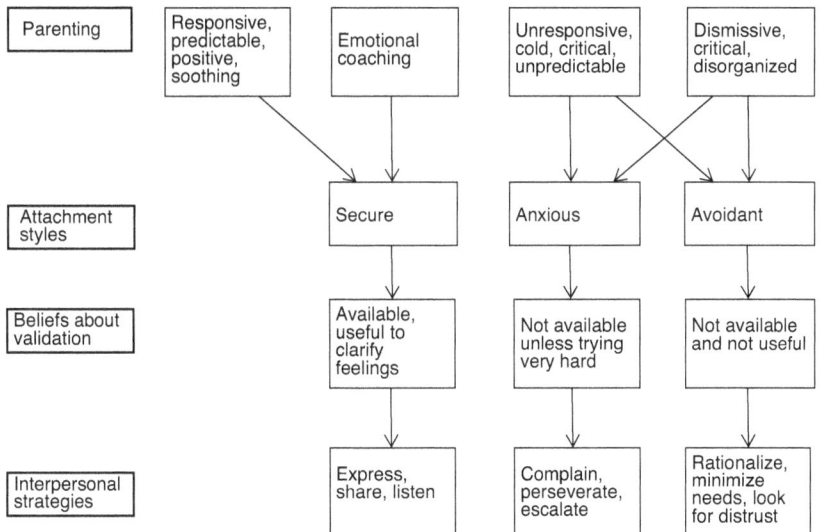

Figure 7.2 Relation of parenting, attachment styles, beliefs about validation and interpersonal strategies

Source: Reprinted with permission from Leahy, R.L. (2005)[55]

As coaches, we enter the helping relationship as a guide and in some ways an attachment figure – someone who can provide a space where the client can feel seen, safe and secure. Our job here is not to be the one who knows everything, but rather to be the one who is present, attuned, and open for resonance with whatever is arising in the client.

Compassionate mind training

Mindfulness practices, as well as the loving-kindness and compassion practices we have described, stimulate the soothing/affiliative (oxytocin/endorphin) brain systems.[52] CMT brings about physiological regulation by drawing on such practices to activate feelings of safeness and well-being and so tone down the threat system.

Aside from the practices already covered in Chapter 5, Gilbert offers others including ones that stimulate the development of the inner compassionate self.

As he suggests, we create many different patterns of brain activity in ourselves and then see these as different parts of ourselves. For example, there's the pattern that emerges with anger that we can call the angry 'part' or 'self'. We have thousands of different potential patterns within us. Developing the compassionate self can help deal with this 'multiplicity of mind' and the unpleasant, difficult or harmful patterns or 'parts of self' that arise in us. The safeness cultivated through compassion practices can help to create the neurophysiological conditions for exploration and developmental change not only in ourselves, but also our clients.

Future trends in psychotherapy

Clearly mindfulness is already having a significant impact in the field of psychotherapy, but is it simply a fad? With an eye to the future Norcross *et al.* surveyed seventy psychotherapy experts and asked them what they believed the trends in psychotherapy would be over the next 30 years. They found that 'unlike technology, the ideas that embody several of the highest rankings derive from ancient Eastern philosophies. Such modifications include mindfulness and meditation.'[53] Specifically, the experts in the study believed that the theoretical orientation that will see the most increased use will be mindfulness and mindfulness-based therapies. Perhaps due to the growing evidence base associated with MBSR and MBCT there is a feeling among the therapeutic community that this current trend is only going to grow further.

Notes

1 Passmore, J. (2014) *Mastery in Coaching*, London: Kogan Page.
2 Germer, C.K. *et al.* (2013) *Mindfulness and Psychotherapy* (2nd edn), London: Guildford Press.
3 Grepmair, L. *et al.* (2007) 'Promoting mindfulness in psychotherapists in training influences the treatment results of their patients', *Psychotherapy and Psychosomatics*, 76: 332–338.

4 McCollum, E.E. (2015) *Mindfulness for Therapists: Practice for the Heart*, New York: Routledge.
5 Beddoe, A. and Murphy, S. (2004) 'Does mindfulness decrease stress and foster empathy among nursing students?', *The Journal of Nursing Education*, 43(7): 305–312.
6 Rosenzweig, S. *et al.* (2003) 'Mindfulness based stress reduction lowers psychological distress in medical students', *Teaching and Learning in Medicine*, 15(2): 88–92.
7 Shapiro, S. *et al.* (2007) 'Teaching self-care to caregivers', *Professional Psychology*, 1(2): 105–115.
8 Shapiro, S. *et al.* (2005) 'Mindfulness based stress reduction for health care professionals', *International Journal of Stress Management*, 12(2): 164–176.
9 Cohen-Katz, J. *et al.* (2005) 'The effects of mindfulness based stress reduction on nurse stress and burnout', *Holistic Nursing Practice*, 19(2): 78–86.
10 Lutz, A. *et al.* (2009) 'Mental training enhances attentional stability', *Journal of Neuroscience*, 29: 13418–13427.
11 Brown, K. and Ryan, R. (2003) 'The benefits of being present', *Journal of Personality & Social Psychology*, 84(4): 822–848.
12 Bishop, S. *et al.* (2004) 'Mindfulness: a proposed operational definition in clinical psychology', *Science and Practice*, 11(3): 230–241.
13 Bruce, N. *et al.* (2010) 'Psychotherapist mindfulness and psychotherapy process', *Psychotherapy Theory, Research, Practice Training*, 47(1): 83–97.
14 Neff, K. (2003) 'The development and validation of a scale to measure self-compassion', *Self & Identity*, 2(3): 223–250.
15 Luborsky, L. *et al.* (2002) 'The dodo bird is alive and well – mostly', *Clinical Psychology: Science & Practice*, 9(1): 2–12.
16 Norcross, J. and Lambert, M. (2011) 'Evidence based therapy relationships', In J. Norcross (ed.) *Psychotherapy relationships that work: Therapist Contributions and Responsiveness to Patients*, New York: Oxford University Press.
17 Wampold, B. (2001) *The Great Psychotherapy Debate: Models, Methods, and Findings*, London: Routledge.
18 Norcross, J. and Wampold, B. (2011) 'Evidence-based therapy relationships', *Psychotherapy*, 48(1): 98–102.
19 Kolden, G. *et al.* (2011) 'Congruence/genuineness', *Psychotherapy*, 48(1): 65–71.
20 Aggs, C. and Bambling, M. (2010) 'Teaching mindfulness to psychotherapists in clinical practice', *Counselling and Psychotherapy Research*, 10(40): 278–286.
21 Lutz, A. *et al.* (2008) 'Attention regulation and monitoring in meditation', *Trends in Cognitive Sciences*, 12(4): 163–169.
22 Jha, A. *et al.* (2007) 'Mindfulness training modifies subsystems of attention', *Cognitive, Affective & Behavioural Neuroscience*, 7(2): 109–119.
23 Farb, N.A. *et al.* (2007) 'Attending to the present', *Social Cognitive & Affective Neuroscience*, 2(4): 313–332.
24 May, C. *et al.* (2011) 'Short term training in loving-kindness meditation produces a state, but not a trait, alteration of attention', *Mindfulness*, 2(3): 143–153.
25 Moore, A. and Malinowski, P. (2009) 'Meditation, mindfulness, and cognitive flexibility', *Consciousness and Cognition*, 18: 177.
26 Brach, T. (2012) 'Mindful presence', In C. Germer and R. Siegel (eds) *Wisdom and Compassion in Psychotherapy*, New York: Guilford Press.
27 Bugental, cited in Geller, S. and Greenberg, L. (2002) 'Therapeutic presence', *Person Centered and Experiential Psychotherapies*, 1(1–2): 72.
28 McCartney, L. (2004) 'Counsellors' perspective on how mindfulness meditation influences counsellor presence within the therapeutic relationship'. Unpublished master's thesis, University of Victoria, British Columbia, Canada.
29 Schure, M., *et al.* (2008) 'Mind-body medicine and the art of self-care', *Journal of Counselling & Development*, 86(1): 52.

30 Christensen, A. and Jacobson, N. (2000) *Reconcilable Differences*, New York: Guilford Press.
31 Henry, W. *et al.* (1990) 'Patient and therapist introject, interpersonal process, and differential psychotherapy outcome', *Journal of Consulting and Clinical Psychology*, 58: 768–774.
32 Decety, J. and Jackson, P. (2004) 'The functional architecture of human empathy', *Behavioural and Cognitive Neuroscience Reviews*, 3: 71–100.
33 Bruce, N. *et al.* (2010) 'Psychotherapist mindfulness and the psychotherapy process', *Psychotherapy Theory, Research, Practice, Training*, 47(1): 87.
34 Garland, E. *et al.* (2011) 'Positive reappraisal mediates the stress reductive effects of mindfulness', *Mindfulness*, 2(1): 59–67.
35 Bechara, A. and Naqvi, N. (2004) 'Listening to your heart', *Nature Neuroscience*, 7: 102–103.
36 The Pāli term for this from the Buddhist tradition is upekkha.
37 Ortner, C. *et al.* (2007) 'Mindfulness meditation and reduced emotional interference on a cognitive task', *Motivation and Emotion*, 31(4): 271–283.
38 Safran, J. and Segal, Z. (1990) *Interpersonal Process in Cognitive Therapy*, Basic Books.
39 Bohart, A. (1983) 'Detachment: a variable common to many psychotherapies?' Paper presented at the 63rd Annual Convention of the Western Psychological Association.
40 Shapiro, S. and Schwartz, G. (2000) 'Intentional systemic mindfulness', *Advances in Mind-Body Medicine*, 16: 128–134.
41 West, L. and Milan, M. (2001) *The Reflecting Glass*, Basingstoke, UK: Palgrave.
42 Shapiro, S. and Carlson, L. (2009) *The Art and Science of Mindfulness*, Washington DC: American Psychological Association.
43 Siegel, D. (2010) *The Mindful Therapist: A Clinicians Guide in Mindsight and Neural Integration*, New York: W.W. Norton & Co.
44 Porges, S. (2009) 'Reciprocal influences between body and brain in the perception and expression of affect', In D. Fosha *et al.* (eds) *The Healing Power of Emotion: Affective Neuroscience, Development, and Clinical Practice*, New York: W.W. Norton & Co.
45 Iacoboni, M. (2008) *Mirroring people*, New York: Farrar, Straus and Giroux.
46 Lazar, S. *et al.* (2005) 'Meditation experience is associated with increased cortical thickness', *Neuroreport*, 16: 1893–1897.
47 Liotti, G. (2007) 'Internal models of attachment in the therapeutic relationship', In P. Gilbert and R. Leahy (eds) *The Therapeutic Relationship in Cognitive Behavioural Psychotherapies*, Hove, UK: Routledge.
48 Gilbert, P. (2010) *Compassion Focused Therapy: Distinctive Features*, Hove, UK: Routledge.
49 Wang, S. (2005) 'A conceptual framework for integrating research related to the physiology of compassion and the wisdom of Buddhist teachings', In P. Gilbert (ed) *Compassion, Conceptualisations, Research and Use in Psychotherapy*, Hove, UK: Routledge.
50 Leahy, R.L. (2005) 'A social-cognitive model of validation', In P. Gilbert (ed) *Compassion, Conceptualisations, Research and Use in Psychotherapy*, Hove, UK: Routledge.
51 Cozolino, L. (2007) *The Neuroscience of Human Relationships*, New York: W.W. Norton & Co.
52 Longe, O. *et al.* (2010) 'Having a word with yourself', *NeuroImage*, 49: 1849–1856.
53 Norcross, J. *et al.* (2013) 'Psychotherapy in 2022', *Research and Practice*, 44(5): 369.

8 Mindfulness and coaching mastery

We hope the last chapter has given some insight into the world of mindfulness and psychotherapy and that you're beginning to draw your own conclusions as to what might translate into the world of coaching. Of course, we're not the first to point to a common factors rationale in the world of coaching. In *Relational Coaching* Erik de Haan also suggests that it's the common factors across different approaches that account for the greatest variance in outcome, 'To put it bluntly, research has shown conclusively that ... the specific approaches that the coach believes in most make little or no difference to the coachee ... the relational approach ... means ... rising above all of those models and philosophies.'[1] He highlights Rosenzweig's[2] conjecture that the therapeutic relationship and the presence of the therapist as a person are central, and points to more recent research and commentary on this.

Aspects that many therapists count as key to the *quality of the relationship* include:

- The therapist's empathic responding to and involvement with the client.
- The client's affectionate relationship with the therapist.
- Client and therapist agreement about the goals and tasks of the therapy.[3]

And *personal characteristics* of therapists that have been shown to make a difference to outcomes include:

- Empathy, understanding, respect, warmth and authenticity.[4]
- The therapist's own mental health.[5]
- The ability to let go of one's own system of values and to communicate within the other person's value system.[6]

In the world of coaching, de Haan suggests that the quality of the coaching relationship and the personal qualities of the coach are more important to outcomes than any particular coaching methodology.

In this chapter, we will explore coaching competencies that we believe contribute most to the quality of the coaching relationship, as well as those that imply a certain way of being on the part of the coach. We will then consider how mindfulness training might help to actively cultivate these.

Mindfulness and professional coaching standards

Over the last 20–30 years coaching has established itself as a profession of significant standing in the business world, influencing the performance and development of many of those leading the organisations that shape our society. Thanks to professional bodies including the International Coach Federation (ICF), the European Mentoring & Coaching Council (EMCC), the Association for Coaching (AC) and the Association for Professional Executive Coaching & Supervision (APECS), the field of coaching now has well established ethical and professional standards. These not only shape coaching practice but also professional coach training across the world.

Given the current dialogue within the field of psychotherapy about how mindfulness might support professional training and practice, our intention here is to stimulate a similar dialogue about how mindfulness might inform and support professional coach training and practice. Our belief is that mindfulness training has much to offer in supporting coach development and in deepening coaching relationships, thereby impacting coaching outcomes co-created at an individual, organisational and systemic level.

While the ICF, EMCC and AC have moved towards greater alignment through the formation of the Global Coaching & Mentoring Alliance (GCMA), at the time of writing there is no single unified set of competencies for the coaching profession. In the absence of this we will refer to those most widely used globally (those of the ICF) [7] and we will explore how mindfulness might support a coach's development towards coaching mastery.

Mindfulness and coaching competencies

From our experience, where mindfulness is brought implicitly into the coaching relationship by a coach who practices mindfulness, it permeates every aspect of the coaching from the way the coaching agreement is established, through to the way the coaching is ended. This was reflected in the responses of the mindful coaches we interviewed for this book. Some 29 per cent of these indicated that their mindfulness practice influenced every one of the coaching competencies referred to in our questionnaire.

> My mindfulness practice is core to who I am as a coach. By being more present and grounded in coaching sessions I am able to attend to all of the coaching competencies in a wiser and more effective way.
>
> Emma Donaldson-Feilder

> As best I can, I try to live a mindful life and therefore mindfulness impacts everything I do.
>
> Farah Govani

Of course, comments like these need to read as aspirational rather than literal. Neither Farah nor Emma are telling us that their mindfulness is so highly developed that they don't have unmindful moments. But they are suggesting something important. For those who wholeheartedly take up the practice, mindfulness isn't simply instrumental. It is, potentially at least, all-pervasive, touching every element of life. In that way, for some – including the authors – mindfulness practice impacts all aspects of coaching practice, just as it impacts all of life. But, as we will now see, some coaching competencies were highlighted more than others by our mindful coaches.

Coaching presence

100 per cent of respondents indicated that their mindfulness practice influenced their coaching presence.

Immediately this strikes us as interesting as, unlike other more process-orientated coaching competencies, coaching presence would seem to be more difficult to teach or develop through existing coach training methodologies. At one level, one can think of coaching presence as simply the capacity to be fully present from moment to moment with a client. When we talk to new participants on the Mindfulness for Coaches programme, we often hear them say something like 'I'm always fully present with my clients'. But once they practice, for example, 'mindfulness of breathing', they soon discover how the mind resists residing in the present moment. It jumps forward to the future, rewinds back into the past or slides into abstraction and conceptualisation. If you've explored this practice in Chapter 1 you'll know this for yourself.

The mind in meditation is the same mind that shows up in a coaching session. Do you ever, even just for a second, find yourself getting ahead of your client, thinking you know the solution or where they're going next? Do you ever, even just for a second, get stuck on something they said 5 seconds ago, a minute ago or even 10 minutes ago? If either are true, then at some level you're not *fully* present. Total, unwavering presence is very, very rare but it's a central contention of this book that however present you are with your clients, with mindfulness training and practice you can increase that. It's important to do this because when our minds wander, clients know at some level that we aren't fully alongside them. Our micro expressions give us away and they pick up at a subtle, felt sense level that we aren't quite with them. Coaching presence is partly about the stability of the coach's attention – their capacity to reside in the present moment with the client as each new phase of awareness emerges moment by moment.

Another common theme reported by many of our mindful coaches was how drawing on their mindfulness practice helped them *prepare* for a coaching session.

> I use it when I feel it's going to be helpful in terms of being present. I don't prepare with a meditation for every meeting . . . It depends on what's going on. I use it . . . to be in the right mental space – being able to focus.
> Prof. Jonathan Passmore

> In some companies I'll do 1:1's for an hour back to back for the day. I'm very strict about having 10 minutes gap and I'll spend 5 minutes meditating. I find that it's in between clients that it's helpful for me . . . I'm not bringing the stuff from the one before. I feel much more focused on the person that I am coaching next.
>
> Robin Kermode

Others clarified how their mindfulness practice helped them *during* coaching sessions.

> You notice . . . that your mind is wandering and you're beginning to think three questions ahead. Mindfulness offers me . . . an ability to bring attention back to what is happening in the moment.
>
> Sally Woodward

But of course coaching presence isn't just about attention – it's also about the *quality* of that attention. As Gallwey suggests, relaxed concentration seems to lead to states of flow and mental absorption in the coaching encounter – it has a certain ease to it.

True coaching presence also has other key qualities – it's warm and inviting. It invites the client to say more, to unfold more, to become more of who they already are. True coaching presence helps others access their own authentic presence. It's an attitude of acceptance, caring, allowing, openness and a welcoming of whatever arises in the field of experience of the client, the coach and in relationship. These qualities, embodied by the coach, enable the client to disclose, to open and to feel safe enough to do so.

> The only thing I'm attached to is for the client to have the best possible space in which to do their thinking and for them to feel safe, supported, and Love 2.0 – that sort of warmth, compassion and empathy. I think mindfulness allows all of that. It's just holding that space for clients because I know I can hold it for myself in my own practice.
>
> Ruth Sack

Of course presence is also often synonymous with silence. It's a silence that offers a fertile void to the client, alive with curiosity, genuine interest and possibility. Not a dull, lifeless silence or a silence working hard in the background, figuring out questions or answers to do with where the client has just been or anticipating where they might go next.

> It's about being okay with silence and understanding that really amazing work can be going on in the silences . . . if I didn't have a mindfulness practice I would find that hard.
>
> Farah Govani

Given what we know about non-verbal communication, it's interesting that we continue to place so much importance on *what* is being said in the coaching encounter, rather than what is being communicated non-verbally.

As a discovery exercise in presence[8] we invite you to watch three brief YouTube clips of three 'master coaches':

1 Leonard Bernstein conducting Haydn's 88th Symphony (4th Movement) – www.youtube.com/watch?v=oU0Ubs2KYUI;
2 Lorenzo Muti conducting Mozart's Don Giovanni overture – www.youtube.com/watch?v=qaINPnyGiPQ; and
3 Carlos Kleiber conducting Brahm's 4th Symphony – www.youtube.com/watch?v=YhPeAPK2Ih4&list=PL4A271D06748l0259.

See what you notice about what they are communicating and what they evoke in you. None are using words but each is communicating so much about their inner being and relationally, about what they are inviting. When we invite our clients to come forth in the coaching encounter, what is our presence like and what does it evoke?

As we've discussed elsewhere, our capacity to communicate without words has played an important role in our survival as a species. Our capacity to read one another, simply based on body language and micro expressions, has enabled us to transmit emotions without words. If you were at the front of a tribe and the first to spot a sabre-tooth tiger this capacity was important for survival and it remains deep in our DNA. Research conducted in the 1970s suggests that when communicating feelings and attitudes, 55 per cent is through facial expression and body language, 38 per cent is through tone, with only 7 per cent being down to the actual words used.[9] So when we sit in silence with our clients, or when we acknowledge their contributions with the occasional affirmation, what are we actually communicating at an embodied level? Do we communicate openness, curiosity, caring and acceptance of all that is arising in the client's field of experience or do our micro expressions and body language give us away when they trigger other inner states in us? Does our presence communicate a sense of warmth, openness and safety, enabling our clients to disclose and open authentically? Or does the way we are limit our clients' capacity to open?

As we saw in the last chapter, Dan Siegel describes presence as a state of open receptivity that is supported though regular mindfulness practice. Some of our mindful coaches were very specific about the state they cultivate and then bring into the coaching encounter.

> The biggest enabler [mindfulness offers] is presence – the capacity to be open, receptive and responsive. Suspending judgement and being able to offer a safe space for exploration.
>
> Jane Brendgen

> My mindfulness practice enables me to be more present more often because I am aware of both how to be present and when I am not ... I need to have put myself in a state where I am ready to be with, to receive.
>
> Lindsay Wittenberg

Of course presence isn't simply about a silent state of open receptivity. As we saw in the last chapter, therapeutic presence has been defined as 'an availability and openness to all aspects of the client's experience, openness to one's own experience in being with the client, and the capacity to respond to the client from this experience.'[10] So, coaching presence has a more *active* element to it and we will explore this later in the chapter through powerful questioning and direct communication.

Let's now look at what the ICF says about coaching presence.

At Associate Certified Coach (ACC) level while the coach is present to the client's agenda, he/she

- is attached to his/her own performance and therefore presence is diluted by the coach's own attention to self; and
- substitutes thinking and analysis for presence and responsiveness.

At Professional Certified Coach (PCC) level the coach is attending to and present to the client's agenda but

- drives the coaching and choice of tools;
- will evidence a need to have direction toward solution versus simply being in the moment with the client;
- will be choosing ways to move versus letting the client teach the coach ways to move; and
- partnership is present but mixed with coach as expert and greater than the client.

While at Master Certified Coach (MCC) level we see the shift to mastery in the following ways:

- the coach is a completely connected observer to the client;
- the connection is to the whole of who the client is, how the client learns and what the client has to teach the coach;
- the coach is ready to be touched by the client and welcomes signals that create resonance for both the coach and client;
- the coach evidences a complete curiosity that is undiluted by a need to perform; and
- the coach trusts that value is inherent in the process versus having any need to create value.

As the coach moves towards mastery, the ICF suggests, they develop an inner attitude that allows them simply to be with the client, non-judgementally, as their experience unfolds from moment to moment. On their journey to mastery, the coach has progressively dropped any sense of their own expertise or superiority and they have let go of an agenda-driven, solution-seeking approach along with their need to perform and add value. They have stopped working hard in the head to analyse the client's issues and work out 'the answer'.

The role of 'completely connected observer' here seems to resonate with what Shauna Shapiro describes as the state of 'intimate detachment' that arises through mindfulness meditation. This is the apparently paradoxical state of being intimately connected with one's moment by moment experience while having just enough detachment for clear seeing, discernment and skilful action.

Likewise, as we saw in the last chapter, the process of attunement and resonance is a subtle yet profound one. Some of our mindful coaches commented on these subtle aspects:

> Mindfulness seems to allow me to notice more . . . a wider range of things in them and myself, so I'm able to . . . attend to more information and then consider whether to bring it into the coaching conversation.
>
> Alyse Ashton

> I think it's increased my intra and interpersonal sensitivity . . . I'm much more sensitive to picking up intersubjective resonance, to feeling that in the body. To feeling in my own body what the client might be feeling. Picking up small gestures, small changes in the body but then also not projecting . . . becoming curious –'what is that?'
>
> Jane Brendgen

How might it be that a coach is open enough to pick up on (sometimes unconscious) emotions in the client and be able to mirror back a depth of empathy that enables the client to 'feel felt', often without words? This might be communicated through a nod of the head or a range of more subtle micro expressions that communicate we are seeing the world through the client's eyes. It might be something as subtle as placing a hand on the heart in response to a moving moment, communicating that we have been touched by our experience with the client and that they have been truly seen. And in doing so, we signal enough understanding, acceptance and safety for the client to continue to open to their experience. When we embody openness, warmth, acceptance and safety we create the conditions for transformational change in others. We communicate this through our presence, more often than not without words.

How does mindfulness help with this?

When we engage in regular mindfulness practice we are systematically training our capacity to pay attention, on purpose, in the present moment, non-judgementally to whatever arises in our field of experience. We're training present moment attention. Every time we notice that our mind has wandered from our intended focus – such as the breath or the body – we notice where it has gone – to the future, the past, to thinking, planning or abstraction – and we bring it back. We bring it back thousands of times. Every time we do this we are strengthening neural pathways and training our attentional muscle to reside in present moment experience.

When we extend this kind of attention to another human being and they become the object of our awareness we become mindfully absorbed in what is moving between us. We are not in our heads, analysing what the client is presenting. We don't become lost in the client's narrative and we don't become caught up in our own inner narrative. There is no sense of our needing to 'take the minutes of the meeting' or to document the client's story and there is no inner narrative compelling us to perform or 'add value' through intervention or the 'smart question'. The mind is quiet, still and at ease – it is simply open to whatever arises in the client's experience, our own experience, and that which exists between us. So there is plenty of space for the client to direct the coaching at their own pace, to set their own agenda and for the client to choose how to move. As our levels of reactivity are reduced through regular mindfulness practice, we notice less of a need to drive the coaching towards solution and find instead that we can trust in the process and trust in emergence. We come to know that both the issue and the solution will emerge naturally from the client, given the right conditions.

But mindfulness isn't simply about present moment attention. When we undertake regular practice we're also systematically cultivating a certain quality of attention – an attention that meets experience with warmth, openness, trust, curiosity, acceptance, non-judgement and a sense of allowing. The *wisdom* element of this simply allows whatever is the case to be the case and the *compassion* element meets whatever we experience with kindness.

This enables us to embrace and move towards our experience, even the unwelcome. When we systematically cultivate this kind of relationship to our own experience in formal mindfulness practices, it is only a short step to translate this into relationship with a client – for the client to become the object of mindful awareness. This creates an embodied sense of allowing in the coaching space – an allowing attitude that is supported by a reduction of ego.

This allows the client to direct the coaching at their own pace, to set their own agenda and for the client to choose how to move. As we simply allow the client's experience to be their experience from moment to moment, without judgement, we let go of the need to intervene or direct their experience toward solution. We also allow a true partnership and working alliance to emerge – one that allows the client to be the expert on their own experience. It also enables the coach to meet whatever arises with pure curiosity, undiluted by a need to perform, do anything or get anywhere. With this embodied sense of allowing in the coaching space there is an inherent trust and letting go into the process rather than a need or attachment to 'create value'.

In this space, the coach becomes the completely connected observer, intimately attuned to the client's moment to moment experience, but detached enough to mirror back what is shared in a way that allows for clear seeing, discernment, skilful action and change. Often, this enables change in well-established patterns of thinking, feeling and behaving. Sometimes these are seemingly small, but for the client who lets go of old mental models and other conditioning, the effects can be liberating and transformational, giving rise to new ways of seeing the world and new ways of being in the world: to shifts in consciousness.

> Early in my coaching education someone said if you were to boil down coaching to two things it would be being present . . . and curiosity . . . if I was to boil it down even further, it might just be presence . . . real focused attention. My mindfulness practice allows . . . my mind to come to stillness . . . that's where presence becomes really generative because it can hold this space for . . . a coachee to feel held and feel the space created from which they can come forth . . . and find those deeper truths. There's a resonance . . . where magical things happen . . . things just drop away and the true potential comes through . . . It's a place of calm . . . relaxed and alert . . . there's no forcing . . . it's just happening very naturally. So it just helps me to be in that state, to allow all of that to happen and to just be, not to allow what my mind thinks it should do but just to allow what wants to emerge . . .
>
> Julian Read

> My mindfulness practice enables me to be more present . . . And presence is, I believe, one of the greatest contributors to . . . a rich and powerful coaching relationship and coaching outcomes which are meaningful for the client . . . I'm measuring myself by different standards these days . . . much more about how I'm being, more than what I'm doing because experience has shown me that a client does the doing . . . I'm the lollipop lady on the road crossing [laughs]. That's probably the biggest influence – that my perception of my own role has changed.
>
> Lindsay Wittenberg

Establishing trust and intimacy with the client

95 per cent of respondents indicated that their mindfulness practice influenced their capacity to establish trust and intimacy with the client.

A coach's ability to establish trust and intimacy with the client is central to the change available within the coaching relationship. The ICF highlights the ability to create a safe environment and to hold the client in unconditional positive regard as key. At ACC level, the ICF suggest that the coach is still attached to his/her own performance and therefore trust and intimacy is limited. Even at PCC level, the coach is still conscious of presenting an image of a 'good coach', so is less willing to risk or not know.

At MCC level the ICF identify the shift to mastery as the coach becomes:

- connected to complete trust in new and mutual states of awareness that can only arise in the moment and out of joint conversation;
- comfortable not knowing as one of the best states to expand awareness in;
- willing to be vulnerable with the client and have the client be vulnerable with the coach; and
- confident in self, the process and the client as a full partner in the relationship.

How might a regular mindfulness practice support a coach's capacity to embody a way of being that communicates safety and unconditional positive regard, inviting, allowing and embracing vulnerability, while being completely at ease with emergence and not knowing, and cultivating greater confidence and trust in their own direct experience?

As we've seen in previous chapters, unconditional positive regard is widely referred to in both the therapeutic and coaching world. But it is one thing to know this at a conceptual level, it is another thing to consistently embody it. While both professions seem to value unconditional positive regard as central to the change process, less attention seems to be placed in their training on how to actually cultivate it. As we've seen in Chapter 5, certain mindfulness practices have something to offer in this respect.

> I think it comes down to the self-acceptance . . . and accepting our clients . . . If I don't practice loving kindness before a coaching session judgemental Farah is there.
>
> Farah Govani

Some of the ICF indicators of establishing trust and intimacy at ACC and PCC level give the impression of coaches who are bombarded by 'interference' and inner dialogue telling them to perform or perhaps even to 'get the client where they need to be'. These introjects prevent the coach from being intimately connected with the client's moment to moment experience.

> My mindfulness practice has played a part in me letting go of . . . performance anxiety . . . This has made me more relaxed and I'm probably kinder because I'm not projecting my anxiety onto my clients and thinking 'we've really got to get something sorted here'. I'm a lot more prepared to just be with them.
>
> Jane Davey

And then there's interference telling the coach to present as a 'good coach' – one who always knows what to do and who is always right. In doing so, he or she denies the possibility of spontaneously taking a creative risk in the moment or modelling vulnerability in its most powerful form – not knowing.

> If I'm coaching and I have that moment where I'm not sure what to do next, my mindfulness training has taught me that it's absolutely fine not to know. I'm now very comfortable with that and it helps me to . . . allow the silence . . . to breathe into it.
>
> Sophie Turner

> Mindfulness gives me the courage to say 'where do you want to take it?' if I don't know what to ask.
>
> Farah Govani

> The issue of taking risks I think is really significant . . . When I am present . . . I feel more ready to take a risk or experiment, or invite the client to . . . Occasionally [it] might fall flat, or they might not know what I'm talking about, but . . . more often it takes us to territory we couldn't have contemplated before the session.
>
> Lindsay Wittenberg

Mindfulness practice also brings us more directly into contact with our own vulnerability and an awareness of the shared vulnerability of the human condition. From this we become better able to hold the vulnerability or shadow of our clients with warmth, curiosity and kindness. By doing so, we offer them the opportunity to approach, explore and engage with what is difficult. Rather than avoiding it, possibilities grow for them to find new perspective or a new relationship to it.

> What I have been exploring through my mindfulness practice is to bring more coach vulnerability into coaching conversations . . . which enables and allows others to share their vulnerability.
>
> Heather Rachel Johnston

With mindfulness practice we also have the opportunity to work intimately with emergence – staying open to our experience as it arises moment by moment. When we practice in this way our ease with 'not knowing' increases and this makes it easier for us to hold a space of not knowing with and for our clients. Our experience begins to tell us that this place of not knowing is the fertile void and the jumping point to new insight.

> If possible, I sit . . . before a coaching session . . . Often during this practice, I sit with feelings of uncertainty – as a coach, I don't know what my client will bring . . . My practice helps me to acknowledge the presence of uncertainty and to turn towards it, rather than . . . try to 'fix it' / find certainties to fill the hole.
>
> Farah Govani

Another quality that emerges from mindfulness practice is a growing trust of our own direct experience. As we develop our capacity to observe the activity of our minds we become better able to recognise the doubting mind and other unhelpful inner tracks. When this narrative becomes quieter we become better able to hear the deeper wisdom of our body as emotion and intuition reveal themselves there. Developing this basic trust in ourselves enables us to let go in the coaching encounter – to trust ourselves, trust the process, and trust the client. We come to recognise that our clients are uniquely placed to not only articulate their current context, but also to find the best way in which to engage with it. By extending this trust to our clients, we help them to build the confidence to trust the power of their own wisdom and their ability to discern wisely.

Mindfulness can also play a key part in creating a safe environment for change and transformation in the coaching relationship. As we saw in the last chapter, Dan Siegel describes a process of attunement that enables us to 'feel felt' by another. Part of this process correlates with what Stephen Porges has called a 'neuroception of safety'.[11] For Porges, neuroception describes the process whereby our neural circuits, operating below the level of consciousness, distinguish whether situations or people are safe, dangerous, or life threatening. But Siegel extends this further, suggesting that during mindfulness meditation a process of *internal* attunement comes into play as we create a loving relationship with our own direct experience. Through mindfulness practice, he suggests, we become better able to meet our own experience with open receptivity and in doing so we become better able to resonate with our own authentic experience. With practice this becomes an embodied quality – a way of meeting all experience, including that of our clients.

Siegel goes on to describe how our internal attunement is also connected with our early attachment and that whatever our early attachment pattern, we all have the capacity for 'earned' security. When we are able to make sense of how our past has impacted our present, we become better able to establish secure relationships with others. For therapists and coaches in training, this sense making can happen through positive attachment relationships in therapy and through other 'self-work'. As a process of self-attunement, mindfulness meditation also represents a powerful, transformative tool helping us to see more clearly how our past shows up in our present and helping us to develop secure attachment to our self, and in turn, others.

Many of the factors highlighted by the ICF as indicators of mastery in establishing trust and intimacy are outer expressions of a deeper internal state – what Siegel might refer to as 'neural integration'. This deeper state, researchers like Porges suggest, has neurobiological correlations that lead to a softening of the facial muscles and a relaxation in vocal tone. Our internal states are often communicated more by way of body language, facial expression and tone of voice[12] than they are through our choice of words. Much of how we communicate safety and acceptance to the client takes place at an unconscious level, through facial expression and vocal tone – both of which reveal our own inner state of safety and open receptivity (or not) to what the client brings.

Through regular mindfulness practice we can develop a particular way of relating to all experience – with genuine curiosity, openness, acceptance and compassion. Siegel suggests that, with practice, this becomes embodied in our facial expression and we develop a tone of voice that reflects an inner way of being.

It only takes a momentary micro expression or a subtle change in tone on the part of the coach to communicate a subtle level of distress, anxiety or closed-ness to what the client is bringing. And, in that moment, the client holds and withholds, rather than continuing to open to their experience.

Through an embodied mindful presence, a coach communicates an open receptivity to whatever the client brings, providing enough safety to move towards and engage with what is difficult, vulnerable or perhaps part of their shadow. This affords the opportunity for the client to further explore what they're bringing and so change and transform it.

Some of our mindful coaches explicitly referenced this:

> Mindfulness has been profound in helping me regulate my anxiety . . . it helps me to stay in my window of tolerance . . . that Dan Siegel notion of how much arousal we can tolerate whilst still being functioning, thoughtful and spacious.
>
> If my client is anxious or the context is anxious or the problem is very scary to the client or to me, I have the capacity to stay regulated, to stay present . . . and that has an interpersonal regulating effect . . . It's as if I become the auxiliary cortex if the client is very agitated. Through my quality of presence, I help them to regulate down, often without saying anything . . . and that supports far better mental processing, synaptic firing, creativity and innovation.
>
> Mindfulness is the supportive quality that allows complex, stressful questions to be held and new possibilities to emerge rather than just being reacted to.
>
> Simon Cavicchia

Others, like Nancy Kline, have long known that paying attention in a particular way generates thinking in another. When we are warm, open, receptive and accepting of experience, clients pick up on this through unconscious processes and, quite literally, it helps to open their minds.

> Through being centred, grounded and present, and less likely to be reactive, there is a sense of internal safety. The client will unconsciously pick this up through the biological process of neuroception . . .
>
> [This is] cultivated through my mindfulness practice . . . there is this inter-personal base – neuro-physiological. It's in the nervous system. There

is a sense of internal safety, that I am okay with whatever arises and I'm okay with not knowing.

There is a feeling of being settled and grounded and that translates into the neuro-biology of interpersonal relationships. It enhances the client's capacity to open and to be more willing to trust and to explore and to be more curious because there's no bumping up against re-activity.

Jane Brendgen

Active listening

90 per cent of respondents indicated that their mindfulness practice influenced active listening in the coaching encounter.

For experienced mindfulness practitioners, this finding wouldn't be surprising. Every time we come to sit, it's an opportunity to practice listening deeply. One aspect of this is 'hearing' our own thoughts more clearly.

With practice, we begin to experience our thoughts as just thoughts – just our narrative. As we develop ways to exit this narrative mode and enter a more experiential mode, we gradually change our relationship to our thoughts.

Mindfulness practice also offers the opportunity to listen deeply to other aspects of our experience such as feelings, sensations, and impulses. As the mind quietens, we become better able to tune into our emotions – perhaps labelling them more clearly, or better understanding their causes. We also become more able to listen to our body-wisdom and the suppressed thoughts and emotions that show up in the body before they can be verbally expressed. We become better able to listen to our urges to do or say certain things and to discern wisely those we choose to act upon.

For any coach, this capacity to listen to oneself and to self-manage is key to the quality of the coaching relationship and the outcomes that are co-created from it.

> Most of the time, our head is so full of thoughts that we have no space to listen to ourselves or anyone else . . . Only when we have been able to open space within ourselves can we really help others. If you open the space within yourself you will find that people will want to come and be near you. You don't have to do anything, or try to teach them anything, or even say anything . . . People will feel comfortable just being around you because of the quality of your presence. If we want to help others, we need to have peace inside . . . This takes some practice . . . Take some time each day to listen with compassion . . . to the things inside that are clamouring to be heard. Then you will know how to listen to others.[13]
>
> pp. 95–101

Here is what the ICF says about active listening.

At ACC level while the coach hears what the client says, he/she

- does so at an obvious and surface level; and
- will evidence attachment to 'what's the problem', 'how do I help fix it' and 'how do I give value in fixing it'.

At PCC level the coach is focused on what the client is saying but

- more from the perspective of gathering information that fits into the coach's particular tool or discovery model;
- the coach is listening for answers, next question to ask, or looking for what to do with what they hear and will try to fit what they hear into a model they understand;
- they will often respond out of that model rather than the client's model; and
- listening tends to concentrate on content of words but will often miss key nuances.

At MCC level we see the shift to mastery in the following ways:

- the coach's listening is completely attuned as a learner and listening happens at the logical, emotional and organic level at one time; and
- the coach recognises both his/her and the client's ability of intuitive and energetic perception that is felt when the client speaks of important things, when new growth is occurring for the client and when the client is finding a more powerful sense of self.

In the movement towards mastery, there is a subtle but significant shift. At ACC level there's a lot of inner narrative on the part of the coach either trying to work out what the problem is or how to fix it and 'add value'. Even at PCC level, the coach is listening through a lens of their own mental models, a lens of looking for answers or the next question, or simply concentrating on the client's narrative at the expense of more subtle cues. At MCC level there is a shift to listening truly from the client's perspective and their mental models, not the coach's. There is also a capacity to listen well beyond the narrative – for emotions as well as at deeper intuitive and energetic levels.

How does mindfulness help with this?

Listening without an agenda

As we've seen elsewhere, mindfulness practice helps us see our inner narrative more clearly and let go of it more easily when it takes us away from presence and a state of open receptivity. When we have more spaciousness inside we're better able to simply listen without an agenda. Interestingly, the ICF defines active listening as 'listening without an agenda' but when we are coaching in an organisational context there is usually an agenda of some kind. So how do we let go of an inner narrative to work out the problem, fix it and 'add value'?

Mindfulness practice is a systematic way of listening without an agenda. While all mindfulness practice begins with a clear intention, there are no goals to be achieved, nowhere to get to and there is no state to be reached. Our only task is to pay attention, on purpose, in the present moment without judgement to whatever arises in our field of attention. That's it. The attitudinal foundations of mindfulness, discussed by Kabat-Zinn,[14] provide greater clarity about the orientation with which one pays attention:

- *Non-striving* – no goal other than to be exactly where you are. Paying attention to how you are right now – however that is.
- *Patience* – letting things unfold in their own time.
- *Beginners-mind* – seeing things as if for the first time. Being receptive to new possibilities and not getting stuck in a rut of our own expertise.
- *Non-judging* – taking the stance of an impartial witness whilst noticing the stream of judging mind. Not trying to stop it, but just being aware of it.
- *Trust* – developing a basic trust in yourself, your own intuition and feelings.
- *Acceptance* – a willingness to see things as they are.
- *Letting go* – as a way of accepting things as they are. Being willing to look at the ways we hold on shows a lot about its opposite.

Mindfulness meditation provides an opportunity to practice being with one's experience from moment to moment without judgement. By doing so, over time, our capacity to truly listen without an agenda increases.

Focus and concentration

The ICF also defines active listening as 'the ability to focus completely on what the client is saying . . .' As we've seen, mindfulness practice increases attentional control. Clearly if our mind is frequently skipping to the future or the past, to thinking, planning or abstraction, our capacity to focus completely on what the client is saying will be reduced.

Non-verbal communication and micro expressions

When it comes to active listening the ICF reference the ability to distinguish between words, tone of voice and body language and the ability to pick up on what the client is *not* saying (Level 2 and Level 3 listening).

In *Co-Active Coaching*, Kimsey-House *et al.*[15] describe these levels of listening. Level 1 listening is where we listen to the words of the other person but the focus is on what it means to us. Level 2 listening is where attention is totally focused on the other person, listening for their words, their expression, their emotion, everything they bring. Energy and information come from the client and are reflected back. Level 3 listening includes everything you can observe with your senses – what you can see, hear, smell and feel, as well as what you pick up through your intuition.

Mindfulness develops our capacity to hear the whole message from a client – not just the words but the gestures, facial expressions, tone of voice and the meaningful pauses. When we quiet our minds, we are better able to hear the heart of our clients' communication.

Building on early research into non-verbal communication, Paul Ekman has made significant advances in the field through what he refers to as 'micro expressions'. His Facial Action Coding System (FACS) describes forty-three 'action units' our faces can perform. These micro expressions can be the most important back channel in conversation because they are involuntary and reveal what isn't being said with words. Ekman maintains that attending to non-verbals is not solely for counter intelligence agents. It's a latent ability within all of us, but if we are leaning-in while our clients speak, we may miss crucial information that could reveal what might otherwise be hidden beneath the surface.

Interestingly, meditators seem to be better able to recognise these super-quick facial signals of emotion. In one study with two advanced meditators[15] Ekman found that their capacity to do this was two standard deviations above the norm – a hugely significant difference. They scored far higher than policemen, lawyers, psychiatrists, customs officials, judges and even secret service agents – the group that had previously distinguished itself as most accurate. It seems that when we bring mindful attention to others we not only pick up more of their micro expressions, we also notice asymmetries in the tone of voice and the words being said (when the words don't match the music).

> My ability to be present helps me notice my client's energy and read 'micro' reactions in their face/body, which significantly informs my active listening. This enables me to probe into areas of which the client has limited self-awareness, opening-up helpful areas of enquiry and potential shift.
>
> Jane Davey

> Yesterday I had a skype call with a client . . . she kept doing this thing with her mouth and we delved deeper and saw that it was to do with fear about this amazing goal and how she was going to make it happen. It's a very subtle thing . . . I'm more likely to pick up on it because I'm more able to pick up on it in myself.
>
> Farah Govani

Level 3 listening and intuition

Level 3 listening typically involves moving beyond the five senses and reflecting back what we're picking up through our intuition. Interestingly, neuroscience is now beginning to reveal the inner workings of this. It seems that an ancient part of the brain called the basal ganglia monitors everything we do through life to get a decision rule that 'this worked well, that didn't work well' and so on. It accumulates a kind of raw life-wisdom that is expressed to us whenever we face a decision point.

The basal ganglia have no direct connection to the verbal cortex but connect to the gut and emotional centres and tell us the answers through a kind of 'felt sense' that something feels right or doesn't feel right.

Through regular mindfulness practice we increase our capacity to tune into our own body wisdom, intuition and basic felt sense. It may be that what we are tuning into here are the basal ganglia. When we have better access to this part of our sensing system – and come to trust it – we are better able to bring this into the coaching work, offering it out lightly without attachment in service of the client.

> I'm more consistently in touch with my intuition and able to cut out the noise
>
> Karen Gervais

> Sometimes I notice quite visceral reactions to things clients say . . . I've noticed since I started mindfulness practice . . . I'm much more tuned into what might be going on in the moment . . . And so just noticing what's happening, naming it, treating it as something potentially useful – I've had some extraordinary responses to that.
>
> Sally Woodward

Dropping our mental models

When it comes to active listening, a fundamental shift towards mastery comes with the capacity to listen truly from the client's perspective and from their mental models, not our own.

It's natural that we're all likely to have our own favourite models, tools or diagnostics. The danger is we become so attached to them that we forget that they have become a filter for our experience of the client. Similarly, the way in which most coach training is currently delivered perpetuates the issue by placing an emphasis on models, techniques and 'psychological toolkits.' But, as de Haan suggests, the relational approach means rising above all of those models and philosophies. He highlights how the ability to let go of one's own system of values and to communicate within the other person's value system has been shown to have a significant impact on outcomes. [6]

> When I'm more mindful I'll be a lot more likely to follow my intuition. If I'm not grounded, I'm a lot more likely to be analytical and . . . I'll be a lot more likely to say 'I'll just use a tool'. So, I think it gives a lot more space to my intuition – which I think gives the client a lot more space.
>
> Liz Gooster

What we are proposing here is that with enough mindful presence we can become more aware when we are responding from our own mental models, rather than our clients', and choose a different response.

We can set a clear intention to reflect the raw experience of our clients back to them as best we can cleanly and undistorted by our own mental models. When we are able to do so and offer a truly open, receptive and accepting presence to our clients, we enable them to bring their mental models, their values and their meaning into conscious awareness, undistorted by ours.

In enabling them to be truly heard in this way, we trust that our clients become better able to understand themselves and in turn, make the choices they want and need to.

Even though all of this is clearly articulated within the ICF's competencies, we recognise that for many this represents a paradigm shift. One well summarised by Thich Nhat Hanh:

> We may have learned . . . in school that we have to . . . retain a lot of words, notions, and concepts; and we think that this mental stockpile is useful . . . But then when we try to have a genuine conversation with someone, we find it difficult to hear and understand the other person.[13]
>
> p. 95

> I notice that the professional bodies say that you have to be working within an accepted modality. Through Jungian supervision, I've been really supported to being in the alchemy of the relationship. Presence really supports being in the alchemical bath where base material gets transformed into something. It's not just polishing base material with somebody else's buffing protocol. It's actually transforming it into something else.
>
> Simon Cavicchia

This Zen story illustrates the importance of dropping our mental models:

> A university professor wanted to learn about Zen, so he arranged to meet with a Japanese Zen master. The master could see that the professor was already full of knowledge and wanted to impress the master with it. While the master listened patiently to the professor demonstrating his knowledge, he began pouring a cup of tea for the professor. The master filled the cup but kept pouring anyway. At some point the professor noticed the tea spilling across the table and stopped talking. He said, 'Master why do you continue to pour the tea? My cup is already full. It can't hold any more.' The master replied, 'Like this cup you are already full of your own speculations and opinions. How can I teach you Zen unless you first empty your cup?'

This story is liable to a number of different interpretations. One is quite simply that if you start drinking, you'll stop talking! Another is that if you start drinking maybe you'll learn something. Finally, if you empty your mind perhaps you'll have space for new knowledge.

Paradoxically, rather than obsessively acquiring more tools, techniques and models to intervene from, perhaps the key to mastery and offering clients an exquisite level of listening lays in 'emptying the vessel'. This is something that mindfulness training and practice can help with.

> Being fully present enables me to notice things like small facial or body movements that may be useful to bring to my client's attention . . . There's also tuning-in energetically to my client – sensing or feeling where there might be a blockage or incongruence.
>
> My presence also helps me to notice if there's anything either I or the client are not saying.
>
> Because my mind is used to coming to a place of stillness, that allows me to listen into the thoughts that are coming through from the quiet – but it also allows me to stay present to the whole. Whether it's the body, facial movements, breathing . . . it's like the eyes get de-focused and . . . I'm listening into the whole, as opposed to just words.
>
> There's a third level which is having a feeling in the body somewhere. There's a reaction that's a signal. I think because of the meditation, sometimes I will feel something not even showing up in the words . . . it's some form of energy that has information that would be valuable.
>
> Julian Read

Creating awareness

90 per cent of respondents indicated that their mindfulness practice influenced their approach to creating awareness in the coaching encounter.

Clearly, any change that arises from coaching does so as a result of new levels of awareness. Facilitating such changes is central to the aims of coaching. Chapter 6 highlights a range of different approaches to creating awareness and how these may be supported and deepened through mindfulness practice. Kabat-Zinn's definition of mindfulness, as the awareness that comes from paying attention in the present moment, on purpose and non-judgementally, reveals that mindfulness is both an awareness *practice* as well as a form of awareness *itself*. In other words, mindfulness is both a process and an outcome.

As Kabat-Zinn wrote in his foreword to the UK All-Party Parliamentary Report on Mindfulness,

> Basically, when we are talking about mindfulness, we are talking about awareness – pure awareness. It is . . . 'bigger' than thinking, because any thought, no matter how momentous . . . can be held in awareness, and thus looked at . . . in a multiplicity of ways which may provide new . . . insight and fresh perspective . . . Awareness in its purest form, or mindfulness, thus has the potential to add value . . . to living life fully and wisely and

... to making wiser and healthier ... choices ... going beyond the limitations of our presently understood models of who we are as human beings.[17]

The ICF describes '*Creating awareness*' as helping the client to gain awareness and achieve agreed upon results as well as a capacity to go beyond the immediate goal – engaging in exploration with the client.

At foundational and PCC levels, awareness is primarily generated to achieve a goal and is typically related to awareness of new techniques with limited new learning about self and who the client is.

At MCC level the ICF identify the shift to mastery in the following ways:

- the coach's invitation to exploration precedes and is significantly greater than invitation to solution;
- the coach has not concluded what the awareness should be (willing to not know);
- the coach allows the client to make the coach aware and the client's voice is more prevalent than the coach's;
- there's a lovely sense of connected observation of who the client is and what the client wants; and
- the coach does not force awareness.

In the movement towards mastery we see a subtle but significant shift from the coach narrowly developing awareness to achieve the client's particular goal to the coach enabling a much broader awareness to emerge by holding a space for the client's self-inquiry and self-discovery.

How might a regular mindfulness practice support this transition?

Through personal mindfulness practice we begin to see that the very act of paying attention in a particular way enables new awareness and insight to emerge spontaneously. The more we learn to trust this process intrapersonally, the more we are able to extend this – interpersonally – to our clients; allowing new forms of awareness to emerge simply through our way of paying attention, without having to introduce new models or techniques.

> Because I more readily feed back to the coaching client my awareness of them and what I notice about them, and invite their reflection (both in the sessions and between them), their awareness grows ... After the session ... if I put myself into a mindful state, I can quite often access things that I wasn't aware of in the session ... So I send a follow up email with 'this is what's come up for me, it might or might not resonate for you'. There are some clients who really engage with that – even the really busy ones.
> Lindsay Wittenberg

When we practice mindfulness we are also actively cultivating an 'approach' mode of mind in relation to our experience. By cultivating and embodying such an attitude, we become better able to hold a genuine sense of open exploration with our clients. And, since we cultivate awareness in an emergent way through mindfulness practice, we also become increasingly comfortable 'not knowing.'

While there's no sense of having to drive toward a solution, that's not to say that mindful coaching is unfocused. Much like personal mindfulness practice, we can establish clear intentions, and as we'll see later, there's a subtle but significant difference between this and setting goals. Mindful intentionality comes with a sense of ease, allowing for emerging issues to arise. Goals, on the other hand, without regular re-contracting, potentially remain rigidly focused on initial presenting issues.

> The more mindful I am, the more I notice; the more I notice and offer without attachment, the more possibility there is that the client might discover something about themselves that wasn't conscious but resonates . . . For me, mindfulness has become what I think of as simple awareness – a very specific orientation to noticing and observing and being with.
>
> Simon Cavicchia

When the client becomes the object of mindful attention we create plenty of space for their voice to be heard, and when our own voice finds its way in, this may simply be mirroring back what we have heard or noticed. But this witness position is not cold and disconnected. It's a place of intimate detachment – so deeply empathic that clients 'feel felt' and, at the same time, we remain detached enough to stay resourceful for the client. When we bring mindful attention to clients, the awareness that arises is not forced. We simply reflect back the awareness that is naturally arising within the client. Without attachment, we might also lightly share any awareness that may be arising within ourselves. And while we may form hypotheses about clients, we can see these for what they are – just thoughts and hypotheses. We might choose to share them lightly, or simply return to reflecting back our client's direct experience so that they can see themselves more clearly.

Ultimately, at a deeper level, mindfulness is a practice of self-inquiry and, in this respect, interpersonally, it also supports and enables self-inquiry for clients.

> I work in a vertical development context. Mindfulness is a great support in awareness raising and developing leaders' capacity to know themselves . . . If clients are at a stage in their life where . . . they are opening to a much bigger perspective of themselves . . . that can be very . . . unsettling to their self-images . . . Mindfulness, as a practice, supports them through that rocky letting-go of familiar constructs . . . shifting where to locate their sense of self. Taking the self to be more than the mental content . . .
>
> Simon Cavicchia

Jon Kabat-Zinn popularised the notion that we don't act like human beings, we act like human doings all the time, and that we should be more focused on being . . . I totally agree with that, but being suggests something that may be a little static – so I often talk about us as human 'becomings' . . . I like to get people interested in that process of becoming and how, among other things, their experience of self is a process emerging in every moment.

Arnie Kozak

Powerful questioning

76 per cent of respondents indicated that their mindfulness practice influenced powerful questioning in the coaching encounter.

As we've seen, therapeutic presence can been defined as 'an availability and openness to all aspects of the client's experience, openness to one's own experience in being with the client, and the capacity to *respond* to the client from this experience.'[10] In the same way, coaching presence has an active, responsive element to it, and this includes any questions the coach might ask.

In defining powerful questioning the ICF describes it as the ability to ask clear, direct questions that lead to new insight and move the client forward.

At ACC level:

- questions attend to the client's agenda but are generally seeking information, are formulaic and sometimes leading or have a 'correct answer' anticipated by the coach; and
- generally, questions are geared to solving issues set by the client as quickly as possible.

At PCC level:

- even powerful questions tend to focus towards solution and may be more responsive to the agenda than to the client;
- questions will tend to use coaching terminology versus using and exploring the client's language; and
- the coach will tend to ask comfortable rather than uncomfortable questions.

At MCC level the ICF identify the shift to mastery in the following ways:

- the coach asks evocative questions that are fully responsive to the client in the moment and that require significant thought by the client or take the client to a new place of thinking;
- the coach uses the client's language and learning style to craft questions;
- the coach is fully based in curiosity and does not ask questions to which the coach knows the answer;
- the questions often require the client to find deeper contact with the client's shadow and light sides and find hidden power in himself/herself; and
- the coach is not afraid of questions that will make either the coach or the client, or both, uncomfortable.

How might a regular mindfulness practice support this transition?

When the coach has a busy mind that can give rise to a high volume of questions – based perhaps on what is being stimulated in the coach's past experience or perhaps from the coach's need to understand the situation (as a pre-requisite to 'solving the problem').

Questions of this kind simply interrupt the client's flow of awareness. Similarly, when the coach's mind is pre-occupied with coaching outcomes, their questions will most likely focus on solutions and will tend to have more to do with where the coach thinks the client needs to get to, rather than where they actually are in that moment.

Regular mindfulness practice can help quieten the mind and reduce reactivity. It helps us see thoughts more clearly and allows us to have better access to our 'inner supervisor'. We may see our mind grasping for information, or notice how the client's narrative has stimulated a whole host of questions based on our past experience. Or we might spot our need to get the client somewhere. As these matters arise, we can observe the activity of the mind, let the question(s) go, and come back to being open and receptive to where the client is going next. This isn't to say that we never intervene – it's just that we get better at noticing our own reactivity and self-managing. The main outcome of this is that we ask fewer questions and create more space for the client.

> What I'm often aware of is the really good question that helps someone shift . . . 10 years ago, before I discovered mindfulness, I would have been a lot more anxious to offer something earlier on. I am now more prepared to be present and patient.
>
> Jane Davey

Regular mindfulness practice also enables clear seeing and discernment, so that when we do choose to intervene, we're often making a more conscious choice to do so and ask a question that organically flows from where the client is in that moment. That would be a question that arises from a place of deep attunement – from Level 2 or Level 3 listening. And when we ask a question from this place we shouldn't be surprised if it has a powerful resonance for the client. Through regular mindfulness practice, choices to intervene operate at a more conscious level, but this doesn't mean that things become stunted and unnatural – quite the opposite. Questions spontaneously emerge in the moment, deeply attuned to the client's language, what is noticed in their tone of voice or body language or, in the case of Level 3 listening, from deeper intuition, felt sense and the process of interoception.

> Because I'm more present and am listening with more depth and scope, my questions benefit from greater insight, better connection with who the client is and what they are communicating.
>
> Lindsay Wittenberg

In this sense, truly powerful questions are always unique to each moment and are never formulaic. Of course it's natural to see new coaches welcome standard questions to provide structure, or wanting to assemble banks of 'powerful questions'. But the reality is that truly transformational questions are never scripted and are intimately associated with present moment awareness. Through actively cultivating present moment attention, regular mindfulness practice supports the coach in asking transformational questions that are deeply attuned to the client in the moment.

> If I am orienting . . . my practice as a coach, from a place of mindfulness, everything I've said about space and allowing new forms of understanding and action to emerge applies. This includes powerful questioning. You don't just run to examples of powerful questions as written by XXX. Your questioning is informed, and it is powerful because it is steeped in a profound apprehension of the situation you are in: including the client's capacity to respond, the client's levels of psychological support and resilience, and the nature of the issue itself.
>
> Simon Cavicchia

> Ahead of a coaching session, I typically prepare a few questions that may be relevant. These come to me as I contemplate 'What is my client's deeper need?' However, they are not my starting point in the session . . . my preference is to 'Trust emergence' and see what questions appear.
>
> Farah Govani

With regular mindfulness practice we are not simply training present moment attention. We are also actively cultivating a certain quality of attention – a capacity to meet all experience with warmth, kindness, curiosity and interest. It is in this respect that we become better able to ask questions on the edge of discomfort, either for the client or the coach. As we discussed earlier, mindful attention helps to create the conditions of safety required for clients to disclose what may be vulnerable, difficult or associated with their shadow. In entering such territory, it would be a natural reaction to back-off, or move away from what is difficult, painful or uncomfortable. But by cultivating an approach mode of mind, the coach is able to meet such moments with warmth, kindness, curiosity and interest.

> I'm okay in groups where there is discomfort, tough things being said, and I'm certain that without my mindfulness practice I wouldn't be able to deal with it as easily . . . As the coach I'm the catalyst – they can say things that they wouldn't if they were in a room by themselves. They have to have confidence in me in order to feel safe enough to open up. I used to think that took a long time but actually it doesn't if you set the right atmosphere. It's just about helping people feel safe enough to share.
>
> Alan Ross

In this sense the coach becomes better able to ask powerful questions that gently invite the client to open into and engage with what is difficult or challenging. It would, however, be wrong to assume that it might only be the client who backs off from what is difficult. Even with regular mindfulness practice a coach may encounter the limits of his or her zone of tolerance through material brought by the client. But in such moments, because of their practice, a mindful coach may become aware of resistance and holding in the body and be able to soften and open to this difficulty in the moment. In doing that, they may access, and give voice to, the uncomfortable question just waiting to be asked.

Direct communication

76 per cent of respondents indicated that their mindfulness practice influenced direct communication in the coaching encounter.

As we've seen, coaching presence relates to both open receptivity to experience in the moment and the capacity to respond from that experience, often through direct communication. The ICF describe direct communication as being clear, articulate and direct in questions, observations and feedback and drawing on the client's language and interests for metaphor and learning. At ACC level, the ICF describe the coach as typically using too many words or feeling the need to 'dress up' a question or observation; questions and observations typically use the coach's language rather than the client's; and most communication occurs at a very safe level for the coach. At PCC level, the coach occasionally treats their intuitions as the truth, doesn't say what is occurring for them for fear that the client is not ready to hear it or even softens communication for fear of being wrong.

At MCC level, the ICF identify the shift to mastery in the following ways:

- the coach easily and freely shares what is so for the coach without attachment;
- the coach shares directly and simply and often incorporates the client's language; and
- the coach invites, respects and celebrates direct communication back from the client and creates sufficient space for them to have equal or more communication time than the coach.

How might a regular mindfulness practice support this transition?

At a basic level, where the mind is busy it follows that questions and observations are also likely be busy. Certainly where the coach feels the need to 'dress up' a question or observation; where they don't say what is occurring for them; or where they soften the communication, a lot of inner dialogue will be at work preventing the coach from responding more authentically in the moment. Regular mindfulness practice offers the possibility of quietening this inner dialogue, enabling the coach to share more freely, less impeded by unhelpful introjects.

> Mindfulness helps me to be in the moment and respond. You notice something more easily, and feel relaxed enough to respond – and there's a sort of rhythm to it. Often, when we're not really aware we've got too much inner dialogue going on . . . What mindfulness does for me is to say quite clearly 'Ping! Okay' I've just noticed a real misalignment or I'm feeling sceptical and I can then say it in the moment and it doesn't jolt – there's a sense of rhythm and pace.
>
> Sophie Turner

As we saw in the section on active listening, it seems that regular mindfulness practice may support our capacity to access our intuition and basic felt sense. However, developing greater trust in our own body wisdom is different to treating it as 'truth'. Through regular practice we may learn to pay more attention to this aspect of our experience and develop greater ease in giving voice to it, but we can do this lightly without attachment.

Sometimes when we share from a more intuitive place it can have deep resonance for the client. In such moments it may be that we are sensing the client's private world as if it were our own. However, because of the 'as if' element, at other times it can be more like hitting the outer edges of an archery target. If we are truly unattached to what we offer out, we enable the client to shape this in a way that can have greater meaning and resonance for them.

> What mindfulness practice really supports, in a relational way, is my not being attached. Every . . . intervention is a gesture – it's an offer purely in order to discover what if anything the client might do with it, including doing nothing, including rejecting it. I think mindfulness practice has helped me go from a conceptual understanding of non-attachment to an embodied enacting of non-attachment . . . If I'm really not attached, something usually happens that is meaningful and of value to the client.
>
> Simon Cavicchia

Apart from the matter of asking powerful questions, direct communication typically relates to how a coach offers observations and feedback to the client, either from the 'outside' or the 'inside'.

The former may relate to the tone of voice or body language of the client and, as we've seen, regular mindfulness practice supports our capacity for this kind of present moment attention, as well as our capacity to notice (and therefore feedback on) micro expressions.

Observations and feedback 'from the inside' might relate to thoughts, feelings, sensations or even impulses noticed in the coach in response to what the client shares. Most coaches seem comfortable offering feedback and observations at the level of thought, or perhaps even the mental imagery evoked through dialogue with the client. But mindfulness practice actively cultivates a capacity to drop below the level of thought and the client's narrative, enabling the coach to more readily access feelings and sensations in the body as well as their impulses. By doing so, the coach may open up a whole new vista to the client – offering in the moment feedback either at the level of emotion or perhaps even from a place of deeper body wisdom.

> I share with the coaching client my intuitions, bodily sensations, awareness and sense of what I'm picking up with greater confidence than previously. I'm more challenging and take more risks.
>
> Lindsay Wittenberg

Mindfulness practice seems to support direct communication in several others ways. Certainly, heightened levels of attunement to the client enable the coach to more readily communicate, using the client's language rather than the coach's. Similarly, by embodying an attitude of warmth, kindness, curiosity and openness, the mindful coach creates the conditions of safety for more challenging communication to take place. When held within this broader container, more challenging communication is possible right at the edges of what is comfortable – either for the client or the coach. When we can check our intentions for sharing more challenging observations and feedback, we increase the likelihood that it will be received as intended – with the care and well-being of the client in mind.

> I'm noticing how my mindfulness practice is influencing the coaching relationship. For example, holding discomfort for longer with a client who deflected a lot to avoid intimacy. I noticed when we talked about that kind of thing he crossed his legs and faced me side-on – quite often he was talking to me from that angle. He displayed a lot of deflecting and defence mechanisms. I needed to say it, so I did – and he made a joke of that as it was awkward. But I stayed with him through that, and with my discomfort in the face of his discomfort, and it really broke through.
>
> Karen Gervais

> Mindfulness gives me the courage to speak my truth with compassion. If I find myself feeling uncomfortable, knowing I need to enquire into something a client has said that could be difficult, I always come back to my feet on the floor and breath to ground myself.
>
> Farah Govani

Through regular mindfulness practice we become better able to manage our own reactivity in the coaching session and – as we cultivate the muscle of self-regulation – we increasingly create space for the client to have equal, or more communication time than the coach.

Through practice we also cultivate a particular kind of presence: a state of open receptivity. When we extend this to the client, we create the conditions for them to step forth authentically. And when we meet their direct, authentic communication with a sense of interest and allowing, we signal to them to continue to do so, again and again.

In this way we enable the client to increasingly let go of presenting what they think they *should* say, to more deeply engaging with what they *really* think, feel or want to say. In doing so, we invite the client to open more readily and more powerfully to their authentic experience.

> During a session, if I get an emotional reaction I feel that I can acknowledge it without being overtaken by it. I was in a session with a client recently and he got quite upset. He went so far as to say 'that's not coaching, I think you've just overstepped the mark'. I felt myself start to react . . . but then I thought . . . let's just stick with this and see what happens. He must have seen that it landed with me, but what he didn't get was any sort of defensive mechanism. And later he said to me 'I realise what you were doing there, I think you've tried to take it to the edge of what I was thinking and as a result you get strong insight.'
>
> Linda Feerick

Designing actions

67 per cent of respondents indicated that their mindfulness practice influenced designing actions in the coaching encounter.

The ICF define 'designing actions' as the ability to work with the client to design actions or activities outside of the coaching session to continue exploration and increase awareness and learning. At ACC level a coach tends to suggest homework they think would best handle the problem or achieve the goal. At PCC level the coach engages in some level of partnership with the client to develop actions. However, these are typically only attuned to solving the issue the client has presented, rather than broader learning that might be inherent in the situation, and forward motion tends only to be defined in terms of physical action.

At MCC level the ICF identify the shift to mastery in the following ways:

- the coach works in complete partnership with the client or lets the client lead in designing actions;
- the coach and client design actions that fit the client's goals and pace of wanted or necessary movement; and
- the coach allows action to include thinking, creating and doing and encourages informed experimentation.

How might mindfulness support this transition?

One answer lays in the attitudinal foundations of mindfulness outlined earlier in the chapter, particularly the qualities of non-striving, patience, non-judging, trust, acceptance and letting go. If the coach increasingly embodies these qualities through regular mindfulness practice, how might this show up in designing actions? And given what we know about self-directed change, how might this support change from the inside out?

Non-striving

When a coach is striving for a result, it's likely that they will have some pre-conceived idea as to where they think they need to get the client to and they might feel the need to direct them in setting homework. When the coach does this, their anxiety to get the client somewhere can bypass the possibility that the client has great thinking of their own. A non-striving approach simply invites the client to share what new awareness or actions they are taking away from the session. When we do this, we invite the client more deeply into the process of self-directed change.

Patience

While part of being a coach involves helping our clients see new possibilities for themselves, at times our appetite and vision for change for our clients may be greater than theirs. But if it remains predominantly our vision for our clients, rather than their own, it won't prompt sustainable change. The quality of patience, cultivated in mindfulness practice, helps us see that lasting transformation always happens organically in its own time. When we embody patience with our clients, we invite and allow them to design their own actions at their pace, not ours.

Non-judging

When we invite our clients to design their own actions it's likely that judgement may arise. When this happens, we might simply notice the stream of our judging mind – labelling things as good, bad, or neutral. Simply becoming more aware that we are judging allows us more choice and freedom in the moment. We might choose to accept our client's actions as they are, knowing that because they are their actions not ours, they are more likely to follow through on them. Or we might choose to stretch their thinking with a few suggestions of our own. But if our suggestions are not welcomed, or turn into a form of attached coercion, then the likelihood increases that the client will resist following through on them.

Trust

When we invite clients to design their own actions, we are enabling them to develop a basic trust in themselves, their own authority, intuition, feelings and wisdom. If we can't extend such trust to our clients how can we expect them to trust themselves and their own ability to change? They uniquely know best how they might adapt and experiment based on new awareness that has arisen in the coaching session. But of course, this kind of trust is based on the trust we have cultivated towards ourselves and our own experience within our own personal practice. When we have practiced this intrapersonally it makes it much easier to extend to others interpersonally.

Acceptance and letting go

When we invite our clients to design their own actions we practice acceptance and letting go. Acceptance of things as they actually are, rather than how we would like them to be; and a letting go of our need to somehow change and transform the client. Our capacity to bring acceptance and a sense of letting go into relationship is directly related to our capacity to cultivate this intrapersonally in our own mindfulness practice. As we know from the Paradoxical Theory of Change, as we learn to accept ourselves as we are, rather than how we would like to be, and as we let go of our need to change and transform ourselves, meaningful change becomes more possible.

> I don't feel as driven as I used to feel about getting somewhere, even when the client has a hope that they will get somewhere and even when they are frustrated that they're not getting to where they want to get to ... That capacity to be with, to have faith in the process ... the more you do that ... the richer will be the experience of the client and what they take away from the session and how they use it between now and the next session ... I think that letting go is important.
>
> Lindsay Wittenberg

Planning and goal setting

57 per cent of respondents indicated that their mindfulness practice influenced planning and goal setting in their coaching practice.

The ICF define 'planning and goal setting' as the ability to develop and maintain an effective coaching plan with the client, paying particular attention to SMART goals and successes that are important to the client. At ACC level the coach tends to adopt goals suggested by the client at their most obvious level with the coach sometimes substituting his/her expertise for the client's. At PCC level the coach engages in some partnership with the client to develop goals and plans but actions tend to focus on solving the situational issue the client has presented rather than looking for broader learning that might be inherent in the situation. The coach also tends to edit plans presented by the client.

At MCC level the ICF identify the shift to mastery in the following ways:

- the coach lets the client lead in designing goals and planning;
- the coach engages the client in relating goals and plans to other aspects of what the client wants, broadening the scope of learning and growth; and
- the coach and client agree goals and plans that fit the client's pace of wanted or necessary movement.

Much like 'designing actions' the more a coach embodies the core attitudinal qualities cultivated through regular mindfulness practice, the more this will show up in the way they approach planning and goal setting with the client. Through *non-striving*, the coach is better able to let go of the need to change the client as well as any pre-conceived ideas about where they think they need to get the client to.

> Mindfulness is part of what keeps me clean in the work. It enables me to remain interested without being attached to outcomes.
>
> Ruth Sack

The mindful coach becomes better able to *trust* the client to set their own goals and have the *patience* to proceed at their client's pace. *Non-judging* and *acceptance* support the mindful coach in letting go of judgements about their client's goals. But this doesn't mean that they blindly accept them at face value. The 'approach' mode of mind – cultivated through mindfulness practice – naturally brings deep curiosity to the goal-setting phase, probing well beyond what is obvious or situational. Through deeper levels of empathy the mindful coach more naturally attunes to what is most meaningful and important to the client, enabling the emergence of goals and plans that broaden the scope of learning and help the client grow.

> I believe I may be transferring to the client a greater depth of awareness on my part which translates into a journey towards more meaningful goals – and the meaning of their goals.
>
> Lindsay Wittenberg

By bringing a more mindful presence into the planning and goal setting phase, the mindful coach is better able to leave his or her own ego at the door. There is less need to substitute his or her expertise for the client's or to edit their plans and goals. Once an initial coaching plan is agreed, the mindful coach is comfortable with allowing for emergence. Experienced coaches are aware of the difference between the presenting issues shared early in a coaching encounter and the deeper issues that often emerge as trust and disclosure increase. Mindfulness practice increases a coach's capacity to work skilfully with both – to establish clear intentionality at the outset and to work in a truly emergent way. This allows the client to be with things as they are, rather than how they would like them to be. Paradoxically, from this place there is more opportunity for grounded action, adaptation and movement on the part of the client.

> What I have been exploring through my mindfulness practice is to try and get beneath the striving and goal setting. I think it allows me to be less outcome and more process driven, trusting the client has the resources to resolve their issues and helping them find them.
>
> Heather Rachel Johnston

Managing progress and accountability

52 per cent of respondents indicated that their mindfulness practice influenced managing progress and accountability in the coaching encounter.

The ICF define 'Managing progress and accountability' as the ability to hold attention on what is important for the client and to leave responsibility with the client to take action. At ACC level the coach tends to suggest forms of accountability that may feel a bit parental in nature. At PCC level the coach develops methods of accountability in some partnership with the client, but these methods are often reflective of coach training tools.

At MCC level the ICF identify the shift to mastery in the following ways:

- the coach has the client determine their own methods of accountability and offers support to those methods; and
- the coach trusts the client to be accountable to themselves and lovingly calls the client to discussion if agreed upon forward movement does not occur.

As we saw in Chapter 1, regular mindfulness practice actively cultivates metacognitive skills related to attentional control. We've also seen how mindfulness practice supports greater empathy and attunement to others. In these respects, mindfulness practice would seem to support a mindful coach to not only identify what is most important to the client, but also to hold attention on it with non-judgemental curiosity. Skills learned intrapersonally through personal mindfulness practice start to find their way into interpersonal mindfulness where the client and their coaching agenda become the object of awareness. When the client's attention wanders from the focus of their coaching or the actions they committed to, the coach simply acknowledges where the client's attention has gone to and non-judgementally brings the focus back.

> I model embracing mind wandering and non-judgementally returning to intent. I work for 2 hours with a client, and in that period their mind will wander. I'm able to compassionately let the wandering happen and then invite and see if we can gently come back to the focus. There's an understanding of this wandering, this returning, this wandering, this returning.
>
> Sue Cruse

The attitudinal quality of non-judgement cultivated through mindfulness practice also enables an adult dialogue of genuine curiosity with the client if agreed upon forward movement does not occur. There is no sense of a controlling/critical parent judging what has or hasn't happened – just genuine curiosity as to what may have stopped the client from doing what they said they wanted to do.

Similarly, through cultivating the attitudinal qualities of *non-striving* and *letting go*, the mindful coach is better able to leave responsibility with the client to take action. There is no sense of trying to change the client. The coach simply helps them to identify what is most important and then holds attention on it. Even if well meaning, any coach offering methods of accountability based on their own coach training is still seeking to control progress and accountability in their own terms rather than the client's. Through cultivating the attitudinal quality of *trust*, the mindful coach invites and allows clients to determine their own methods of accountability in their own way and in their own language.

When we trust our clients to be accountable to themselves we are enabling them to develop a basic trust in themselves. If we cannot extend such trust to our clients, how can we expect them to trust themselves and their own ability to change?

> I don't manage progress and accountability. That's not my business as a coach informed by mindfulness. My business is to trust that the client will, through the process, become what it is that they can become and in their becoming they will do whatever is optimal and take responsibility for progress. If a 'manual' says 'send the coachee an email asking them if they've acted on their commitment' you can't know if that's going to be experienced as supportive, infantilising, patronising, prying or disrespectful.
>
> Simon Cavicchia

That isn't to say that a mindful coach simply ignores the issue when agreed upon forward movement does not occur. It's just that such dialogues take place with love, kindness and a sense of acceptance. This isn't the kind of acceptance that breeds complacency – instead, it's an acceptance that has both a wisdom and a compassion element to it. The wisdom to allow whatever is the case to be the case enables clear seeing of things as they actually are, while the compassion element simply enables us to meet all experience with kindness.

This enables coaches and clients to approach and move towards all their human experience – their aversion to the 'unpleasant' and unwanted and their attachment to and craving for the 'pleasant'.

Summary

In this chapter, we have looked to make more explicit links between mindfulness and coaching professional competencies, specifically those associated with coaching mastery. What seems apparent from our survey and interviews with mindful coaches is that when mindfulness is brought implicitly into the coaching relationship through the embodied presence of a mindful coach it has the potential to permeate every aspect of the coaching. In this way, mindfulness is not so much something you 'do', by bringing it explicitly into the coaching relationship, rather, it is an embodied way of being with the client.

Most, if not all, of our mindful coaches shared how mindfulness practice influenced coaching presence, their ability to establish trust and intimacy with the client, active listening and their way of creating awareness in the coaching encounter. Interestingly, they also shared how less obvious coaching competencies are influenced by mindfulness practice – from powerful questioning and direct communication through to establishing the coaching agreement, planning and goal setting, designing actions and managing progress and accountability.

At a level of mastery, coaching is less about doing and more about a way of being. But this non-doing isn't passive – it's a way of paying attention, on purpose in the present moment, non-judgementally. It's a dynamic and creative state of open receptivity. By systematically cultivating this type of attention, mindfulness practice enables the coach to bring this into the relationship with the client as the object of awareness. That enables the coach to become the completely connected observer to the client's present moment experience. Open receptivity enables the coach to intimately attune to the client's experience moment by moment and enables deeper levels of listening at an intuitive level. When the client 'feels felt' in this way, deeper levels of safety and trust enable the client to open and disclose more and more in service of their growth and learning. In such places of deep attunement, transformational resonance is created with the client.

This type of generative attention may well be sufficient in and of itself to enable new levels of awareness to arise. However, as we have seen, a broader definition of presence includes not only an open receptivity to present moment experience, but also the capacity to respond from it. In this way, powerful questions and direct communication attuned to present moment awareness also offer an opportunity to deepen levels of attunement, resonance and awareness with the client.

Even where coaching competencies may appear to be more active or action orientated, such as establishing the coaching agreement, planning and goal setting, designing actions and managing progress and accountability, by drawing on the attitudinal foundations of mindfulness, the mindful coach is better able to get out of the client's way, enabling the client to do more of this for themselves at their own pace and in their own way.

Our intention in making more explicit links between mindfulness and coaching mastery has been to illustrate how mindfulness might inform and support professional coach training and practice. At present, most professional coach training tends to focus on imparting theory and techniques rather than the subtler, but no less important aspects that impact on the coaching relationship. In our view, mindfulness training has much to offer in supporting coach development and in deepening coaching relationships, thereby impacting on coaching outcomes co-created at an individual, organisational and systemic level.

Notes

1 de Haan, E. (2008) *Relational Coaching: Journeys Towards Mastering One to One Learning*, Chichester: John Wiley & Sons.
2 Rosenzweig, S. (1936) 'Some implicit common factors in diverse methods of psychotherapy', *American Journal of Orthopsychiatry*, 6: 412–415.
3 Wampold, B. (2001) *The Great Psychotherapy Debate: Models, Methods, and Findings*, London: Routledge.
4 Lambert, M. and Bergin, A. (1994) 'The effectiveness of psychotherapy', In S. Garfield and A. Bergin (eds) *Handbook of Psychotherapy and Behaviour Change* (4th edn), Hoboken, NJ: John Wiley & Sons.
5 Beutler, L. *et al.* (1986) 'Therapist variables in psychotherapy process and outcome', In S. Garfield and A. Bergin (eds) *Handbook of Psychotherapy and Behaviour Change* (3rd edn), Hoboken, NJ: John Wiley & Sons.
6 Norcross, J. (1993) 'Tailoring relationship stances to client needs', *Psychotherapy: Theory, Research and Practice*, 30: 402–403.
7 International Coach Federation (n.d.) 'ICF core competencies rating levels', http://coachfederation.org/files/IndCred/ICFCompetenciesLevelsTable.pdf.
8 Thanks go to Clive Lafferty at www.tandemconsult.com.
9 Mehrabian, A. (1972) *Nonverbal Communication*, PLACE: Walter De Gruyter.
10 Bugental, cited in Geller, S. and Greenberg, L. (2002) 'Therapeutic presence', *Person Centered and Experiential Psychotherapies*, 1(1–2): 72.
11 Porges, S. (2011) *The Polyvagal Theory: Neurophysical Foundations of Emotions, Attachment, Communication, and Self-Regulation*, New York: W.W. Norton & Co.
12 Ekman, P. (2001) *Telling Lies*, New York: W.W. Norton & Co.
13 Nhat Hanh, T. (2015) *Silence: The Power of Quiet in a World Full of Noise*, London: Rider.
14 Kabat-Zinn, J. (2004) Full Catastrophe Living, London: Piatkus.
15 Kimsey-House, H. *et al.* (2011) *Co-Active Coaching*, Boston, MA: Nicholas Brealey.
16 Goleman, D. (2003) *Destructive Emotions*, London: Bloomsbury.
17 The Mindfulness All-Party Parliamentary Group (2015) 'Mindful nation UK', www.themindfulnessinitiative.org.uk/images/reports/Mindfulness-APPGReport_Mindful-Nation-UK_Oct2015.pdf.

9 Mindfulness, leadership and organisation development

While this book is predominantly aimed at professional coaches, much of what is discussed here applies just as much to leaders. Mindfulness, or its absence, impacts on the way we relate to ourselves and others in any context and it is increasingly being thought of as a significant leadership competency.

The context in which leaders are called upon to operate today is hugely demanding. Political and economic instability, constant market disruption, climate change, ever more rapidly increasing globalisation, the proliferation of data and communications media and the sheer overwhelm of input – all of that before even considering the other more functional aspects of the leadership task.

Trying to navigate these contexts, leaders sometimes find themselves in circumstances that can be described as paradoxical,[1] sometimes called upon to institute strategies that can appear to be intrinsically conflicted. For example, in 2010 the CEO of Unilever, Paul Polman, launched the Unilever Sustainable Living Plan. The plan aimed at doubling the size of the business by 2020 while simultaneously improving the health and well-being of more than a billion people *and* cutting the company's environmental impact in half. Those aims seems to conflict with one another. Polman's intention might seem to be paradoxical. But he argues that over the longer term, investments that are socially and environmentally beneficial lead to greater profits, whereas a single focus on short-term profits can fuel decisions that harm society as well as the environment. That may seem persuasive to many readers, but Polman has faced continuous challenge in executing this apparently paradoxical plan. Its inherent uncertainty and ambiguity have caused senior team leaders to feel high levels of anxiety and to fight amongst themselves over resource allocation.[2]

As well as often needing to contend with paradox, leaders today are frequently embedded in an unprecedentedly diverse range of relational networks[3] – often spread over multiple locations and time zones. The capacity to communicate and to work well with diverse others has never been greater. Not only that, as organisations grow larger and change happens faster, leaders increasingly find themselves working within systems that are deeply and inherently complex rather than 'simply' complicated.[4]

182 *Joining the dots*

Under such circumstances, leaders today are called on to develop the capacities for relating to and working well with others and coping – indeed thriving – in situations where they lack the capacity to engineer or control outcomes. To do all of this, they need to be personally resilient, able to collaborate, and capable of navigating and making decisions in conditions of high complexity.

Mindfulness training, we have found, can really help. In fact, we'd say, it should be considered an essential element in any programme of leadership development.

To assess the value of mindfulness training in leadership development, in 2015/16 Michael, along with Megan Reitz and other colleagues at Ashridge Executive Education at Hult International Business School, undertook a research project looking into the effects of an eight-week Mindful Leader training programme conducted with senior business leaders.[5]

The project explored how mindfulness practice supports the development of key leadership capacities required for the 21st century. Specifically, the team set out to examine how eight weeks of mindfulness training, in a form not unlike that outlined in the first four chapters of this book, would impact leaders' capacities for collaboration, resilience and deciding in complexity. Crucially, whereas the Mindfulness for Coaches course focuses on the impact of mindfulness on the coaching context – as well as the coaches' life – the Mindful Leader programme focused on the context of leadership today. Michael brought an expertise in teaching mindfulness to senior executives to the programme, Megan brought her many years' experience of leadership development – as well her personal mindfulness practice.

A cohort of 57 senior leaders was recruited and divided into two groups: an experiment group and a control group. Both groups attended the eight-week Mindful Leader programme at Ashridge. Before the training began, both groups – all 57 participants – were measured using a range of psychometric and other tests. Then the experiment group was given the training. Once that had happened, both groups were measured again. The experiment group's results were now available to compare with the control group's results – before the control group received the training. That gave the researchers an insight into some of the measurable effects of the training.

By way of those measurements, participants undertook a customised Mindful Leader 360 – a diagnostic report that lets people compare their perception of themselves with that of their boss, their peers and people who report to them. In this case, the 360 focused on the leaders' apparent capacities for collaboration, resilience, care and concern for self and others, perspective taking and agility in complexity.

The participants also completed a set of psychometric measures designed to assess their empathic tendencies;[6] their levels of anxiety;[7] their personal resilience;[8] their working memory capacity;[9] and their overall mindfulness.[10]

Besides these 'quantitative' measures, the researchers gathered a large amount of 'qualitative' data. Whenever the course participants met in small groups during the training, to discuss among themselves aspects of the course and their personal practice, they were given voice-recorders. The final small group conference calls were also recorded. In this way the researchers gathered 27 hours of data which were transcribed and then meticulously coded and analysed to get a sense of the participants' experiences of the course and of the outcomes they were finding in their own lives.

The training took place at Ashridge Business School and participants attended 3 half-days and a full-day session held at fortnightly intervals. They also took part in small-group conference-calls with one of the teachers at week eight.

Leaders typically come to a business school like Ashridge in search of more effective cognitive tools and skills. They are smart, high-achieving people who expect to be taught something, to grasp it intellectually, challenge it or accept it, and then – if they agree with it – quickly put it into practice. That works well with some of the tools and models they would typically learn at a business school. But mindfulness training isn't like that. It's not something you can simply hear, grasp and apply. It's a skill that needs to be cultivated over time. It takes persistent and patient training.

Several key challenges stood out for Michael and Megan as they tried to cajole the busy executives to confront, observe and befriend the contents of their own minds. In particular, they had to try to overcome some of the deeply ingrained myths and misunderstandings around mindfulness that pervade our culture today.

Identifying mindfulness with meditation – as many people do these days – several of the leaders came along expecting that by learning to meditate they would somehow be able to stop or empty their minds – at least for a time. But as mindfulness practitioners know, that's not likely to happen.

Very, very occasionally, unusually gifted novice meditators find they can still their minds to the point where thinking drops away for sustained periods while they're meditating. But that is very rare. More importantly, it is also not the intention of the practice. With mindfulness meditation, the intention is to help people to discover the nature of their minds and to see something of how their habitual mental processes shape their perceptions and their actions.

The aim of a mindfulness course isn't to completely silence the mind. Rather, it's intended to help people come into a warmer and more resourceful relationship with their own minds, with others and with the world around them. It aims to help them to develop greater choicefulness in how they respond to what they find.

It takes much patient repetition, deep enquiry and a constant inventiveness with metaphor to get these points across to time-poor, hard-pressed executives who constantly think they're failing because they find that their minds are so busy when they sit and meditate.

Mindfulness, as any attentive reader will know by now, isn't the same as meditation. It's a state of mind that meditation can help to cultivate. But that issue takes a while to settle on a course. It can take a while for participants to experience mindfulness as a quality of awareness that can arise amid daily activity if they prepare the ground for it by meditating.

And of course, mindfulness isn't about getting skilled in following your breath. As Michael found himself repeating often in the class, that is an uninteresting skill. 'I went to a top-flight business school for 20 hours over 4 sessions and I learned how to follow my breath really closely . . .' In and of itself, that wouldn't be a particularly interesting outcome. But becoming better at managing your mind and your mental states, better at handling your personal and working relationships, and better able to make clear decisions in the turmoil of complexity – that's worth investing in.

Time and again – especially in the earlier part of the course – Michael and Megan found themselves having to gently shepherd the participants back to a kinder and more allowing attitude towards their own experience, as they judged themselves to be failing in their efforts to master the workings of their own minds.

The participants were asked to do 20 minutes of home practice for each day that the course ran and to log their practice daily. The researchers collected these practice logs and correlated the amount of time people spent practicing with the changes that showed up in the quantitative measures described above.

The research suggests that the programme was in fact effective in developing the leaders' capacities for resilience, collaboration and deciding in complexity. Crucially, the data shows that this effect was reliant on the extent of home practice undertaken. Simply attending the programme, not accounting for levels of home practice, significantly enhanced self-report assessments of resilience – as measured by both the 360 and the Ashridge Resilience Questionnaire. It also improved the element in the overall mindfulness inventory that measured participants' ability to describe their internal experiences, as well as the total score on that inventory. Similarly, mindfulness training alone – again, without accounting for mindfulness practice – did not impact any of the measures of empathy.

However, when the researchers accounted for the level of formal meditation practice, the data told a different story.

The real benefits of the Mindful Leader programme depended on the amount of formal mindfulness practice that participants undertook over the eight-week period.

The more mindfulness practice an individual undertook, the greater the improvement in their scores on many of the measures including:

- resilience as measured by both the self-report 360 and the Ashridge Resilience Questionnaire;
- collaboration as measured by the self-report 360;
- agility in complexity as measured by the self-report 360;
- all characteristics of mindfulness as measured by the mindfulness inventory; and

- the empathic tendencies of 'fantasy' (the ability to transpose oneself imaginatively into the feelings of others) and 'perspective taking' (the ability to adopt the psychological viewpoint of others). The more the leaders practiced, the more likely they were to experience a reduction in personal distress in the presence of another's suffering, as measured by the empathy index used in the study.

Although mindfulness practice predicted changes to four of the five resilience scales used, it did *not* predict changes in empathic concern, as the researchers had expected. Nor were there significant impacts on others' perceptions in the 360. Unexpectedly, neither mindfulness training nor practice impacted working memory, as measured by the OSPAN. Nor did they impact anxiety. There is much that can be said about these few unexpected outcomes, and they will be discussed at greater length in a paper that the team has yet to publish.

For now, though, we will focus on the positive outcomes that were discovered and, crucially, on the fact that those who reported that they undertook the assigned formal mindfulness practices for 10 minutes or more per day, showed significant increases in some of the key measures in comparison to those who practiced less than 10 minutes.

There is some benefit, it seems, in simply attending an eight-week Mindful Leader programme. It can, the data suggests, increase one's self-perception of resilience. But once people practice for more than 10 minutes a day several other desirable factors improve – and the more people practice, the more they improve.

The qualitative data supports this. Here, the most widely reported impact was also on personal resilience.

Participants frequently reported an increased capacity for self-awareness and self-management, especially around emotional regulation, perspective taking and the ability to 'reframe' potentially difficult or stressful situations both at home and at work.

They reported enhanced sleep, reduced stress levels and improved work-life balance, as well as increased confidence in the face of difficult situations.

They reported an increased ability to focus, to remain calm under pressure and an enhanced adaptability/agility through a decreased attachment to positions or views. All of that seemed to enable better decision making. 'I find it easier to evaluate the different options more rationally and calmly', one of the participants reported, 'and I probably base fewer decisions on prejudice and prior experience.'

When it came to the impact on collaboration, participants frequently referred to increased empathy through a deeper appreciation of others' state and position.

'I tend to talk at a thousand miles an hour', one of them said.

> I have an agenda that is thirty points long, and I have been *exhausting* to be around when we've got a lot to do. And I've made a conscious effort

to slow down, and take the time to, not so much just focus on the task, but recognise there's a person in front of me, and they're having their own experience of this stuff.

When it comes to leading in conditions of complexity, participants described an increased ability to focus, to remain calm under pressure and an enhanced adaptability, or agility, through a decreased attachment to positions or views.

'It's helped me with clarity: I get rid of the other stuff in my mind that's going on or that's there and I can focus more and make better decisions.'

Some participants related their improved ability to deal with complex and dynamic circumstances to their enhanced resilience, which shows how these themes are intertwined.

Data from the 12 week follow up survey suggested that these impacts last. When asked the extent to which the programme had developed their capacity to some, a great or a very great extent, 93 per cent of participants recognised they had experienced impacts in relation to their resilience and 85 per cent spoke of impacts in terms of leading in complexity, and the same for collaboration.

Based on what they learned from exploring the qualitative data in depth, the research team formulated a theory of mindful leadership (see Figure 9.1).

This highlights three higher order 'meta-capacities' developed by participants through regular mindfulness practice:

- metacognition – the ability, at crucial times, to step out of the fast-flowing steam of their experience and come away from the 'automatic pilot' of familiar, habitual reactions;
- curiosity – towards their own experience, others and the world around them including a movement *towards*, rather than away from difficulty; and
- allowing – the non-judgemental aspect of mindfulness. Allowing what is the case to be the case and meeting all experience with warmth and kindness.

Between them, these three capacities create space for mindful leaders to respond, rather than react, to events. This space, in turn, enables a range of cognitive and emotional skills which are vital for successful leadership today:

- focus – participants reported greater focus and clarity of thought which helped with making better decisions and being fully present during key activities;
- emotional regulation – making a more conscious choice about how to respond to a situation rather than allowing emotions to dictate an automatic reaction;
- perspective taking – participants explained how the space created through the meta-capacities enabled them to see a situation from multiple angles or views, which in turn enhanced the quality of decision making;

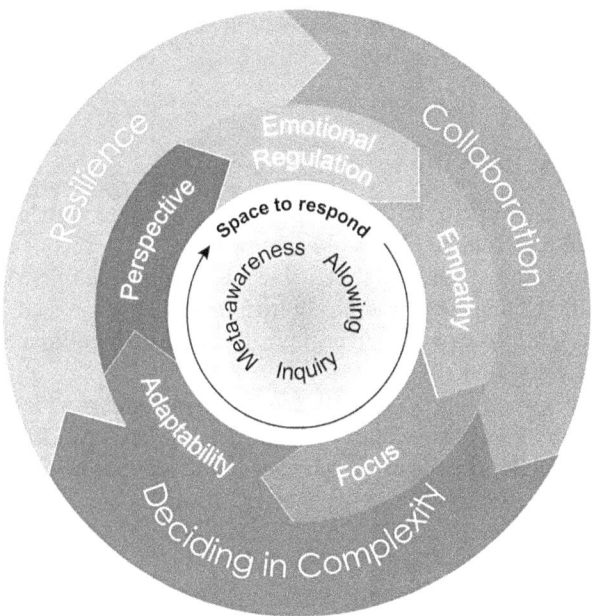

Figure 9.1 A theory of mindful leadership
From *The Mindful Leader*[5]

- empathy – participants reported an improvement in their ability to consider other peoples' experience and a desire to focus more on others; and
- adaptability – participants spoke of adapting to difficult situations and changing their automatic response to a situation.

These enhanced cognitive and emotional skills in turn result in improved resilience, collaboration and the capacity to decide in complexity.

One thing that became clear from the small-group recordings, however, is the fact that finding even 10 minutes to practice every day was often experienced as challenging by the busy senior executives.

We live in a world where many people want, and often expect, instant results. But no new skill or capacity is ever developed without application and practice. What this research reminds us of is that mindfulness is not a 'quick fix' or an intellectual exercise – it requires practice over a sustained period for the benefits to be fully realised.

But, in as little as eight weeks, tangible and meaningful change is possible. As one participant summed up,

> Mindfulness is not a 'silver bullet' solution as many books and courses would have one believe. Seen in context, as a gradual increase in awareness of these aspects in one's life, it is however essential and a great help in

188 *Joining the dots*

interacting with collaborators, managing a team, decision making and putting things in perspective.[5]

p. 26

Mindfulness and emotional intelligence

For Mark, the route into mindfulness started back in 2002 with leadership and organisation development. Having been employed to enable a cultural transformation programme in a large retail business, one of his first tasks was to define the culture and behaviours required from the organisation's top 250 leaders. That led him to a consideration of emotional intelligence (EQ) and the work of Daniel Goleman.[11]

It's now common knowledge that IQ is not enough for outstanding individual, team or organisational performance and growth. But while this is known conceptually, the means to develop EQ in an accelerated and tangible way has remained relatively elusive. It's not uncommon to see organisations, with intellectually bright leadership teams, constructing stellar strategies but lacking the EQ to engage large numbers of people to deliver those strategies effectively. In organisation systems terms, this is the equivalent of an individual having a great idea in their head but being unable to put it into action through their body. And even where their body is mobilised, it is often done in a way that pays little attention to the long term well-being or sustainability of that body. We often hear about strategies falling short because they fail to 'engage hearts and minds', but when so much emphasis continues to be placed on intellect alone, it's hardly surprising that hearts, and the discretionary effort that goes with them, remain untapped.

There are different models of EQ and employee engagement but one from the Hay Group that has significantly shaped organisational life globally can be represented as follows:

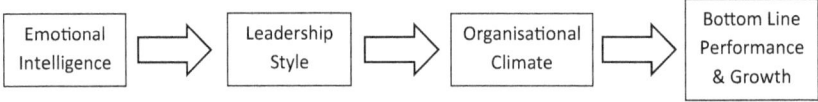

EQ impacts the way leaders lead and the climate they create for others to be at their best. This, and levels of discretionary effort, then have a significant impact on bottom line performance. Happy and engaged employees create happy and engaged customers who become advocates for the business and support its growth through repeat business and advocacy. This of course leads to happy shareholders. We can simplify the model as follows:

Mindfulness, leadership & organisations 189

In *Working with Emotional Intelligence*,[11] Goleman cites a variety of evidence in support of his assertion that higher levels of EQ in leaders and organisations leads to higher levels of performance and growth. If one accepts the assertion, then the really crucial question is – 'how do we tangibly and systematically increase levels of EQ in leaders and organisations?'

Back in 2004 this was a question Mark was asking. Having designed a leadership model based on EQ and begun an organisational dialogue about moving that from an aspirational model to it being embodied in the organisation, something significant happened. A failed IT transformation programme wiped millions off the bottom line, budgets were slashed and suddenly the organisation agenda changed.

At this point another question arose for Mark – 'If I'm really interested in the question of how to transform organisations shouldn't I start with transforming myself?'

This question arose from his reading of Goleman's *Destructive Emotions*,[12] which outlined early neuroscientific research using brain imaging technology with Tibetan Buddhist monks. The research implied that, at will, these

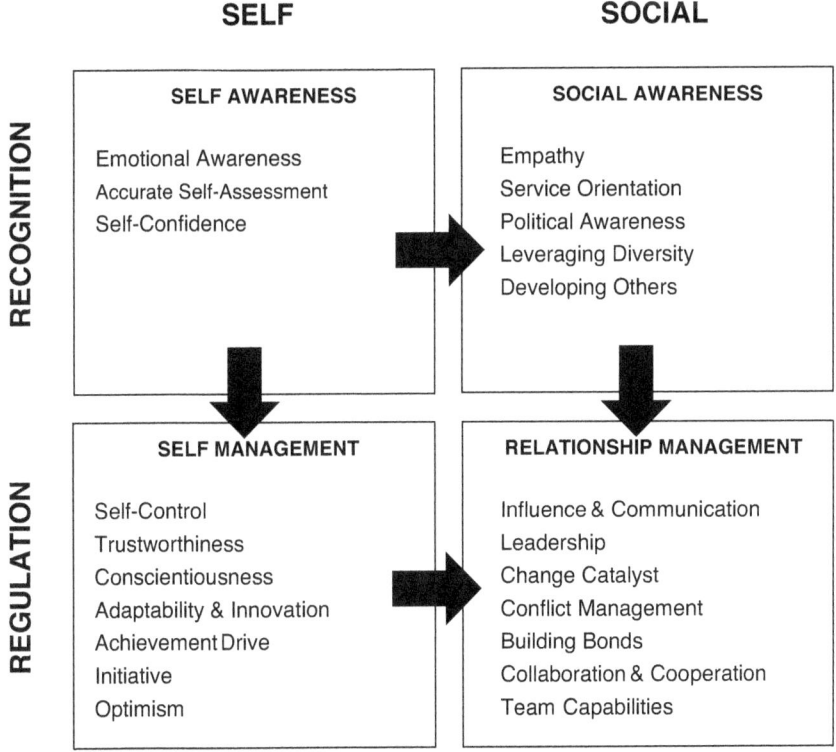

Figure 9.2 Goleman's model of emotional intelligence
Adapted from Daniel Goleman, *Working with Emotional Intelligence*[11]

Joining the dots

advanced meditators could access and affect the emotional control centres of their brains. To understand why this was significant let's take a closer look at EQ.

Prior to Goleman's work, most leadership competency models predominantly focused on social awareness and relationship management competencies – externally observable behaviours in the social domain of organisational life. In some cases there may even have been acknowledgement of some aspects of self-management, typically achievement drive. Goleman's model gave greater significance to the 'inner' domains and their impact on the 'outer'/social domains. In particular, the causal arrows tell a very compelling story. In order to reliably demonstrate social intelligences (bottom right quadrant) one must have social awareness and the capacity to self-manage.

Goleman's model also drew attention to the top left quadrant. It suggested that we cannot really understand others if we don't first understand ourselves. And we cannot hope to manage ourselves effectively if we don't first understand ourselves.

So the key to EQ seems to lie in self awareness, and specifically emotional awareness – the ability to know the emotions that are arising within us moment by moment. What seemed apparent from *Destructive Emotions* was that if you want to accelerate self awareness and understand yourself and your inner emotional landscape better, one of the best ways to learn that might be to meditate.

With this hunch and a working hypothesis, summarised in the following model, in 2005 Mark began a 12 month experiment in Dharamsala, India – using himself as a laboratory.

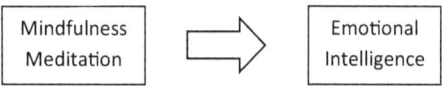

What Mark found were many of the mindfulness practices outlined in Chapters 1–4. Like most new mindfulness practitioners, he began to discover for himself that simply paying attention in a particular way enabled new levels of self-awareness to arise naturally. With practice it became possible to develop a quality of attention that enabled a capacity to see thoughts, feelings, sensations and impulses more clearly. By developing these new metacognitive skills and greater *emotional awareness* it allowed more space for creative, adaptive response rather than unconscious, automatic reaction – it enabled better *self-management*. In addition, by practicing the attitudinal qualities of mindfulness in daily practice, Mark also began to discover a more *empathic* way of relating to experience – both his own and others – and through practices like LKM and 'Just like me', other methods for developing *empathy* and attunement to others arose. In this way Mark found the answer to his question about how to tangibly and systematically increase levels of EQ in leaders and organisations.

There is now data that highlights the potential impact of mindfulness on levels of EQ[13] and we can complete a simple yet powerful model that is beginning to shape the business world:

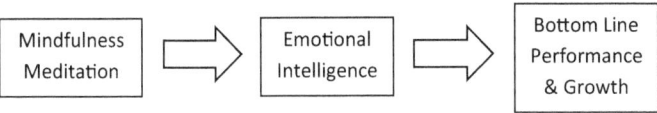

Organisations have broadly come to accept the second half of the equation and many build this into their organisation development strategy by measuring EQ to guide recruitment and internal progression. However, most have singularly failed to identify a systematic way to increase levels of EQ to a meaningful degree in their existing leadership populations. That's not to say that experiential learning has no impact on emotional competencies or that coaches can't help leaders develop EQ. But how do you train empathy and service orientation? You can teach empathic listening and customer service skills, but how do you train an *inner* orientation to attune deeply to others or to want to serve other people? Organisations often recruit for it but how do you develop it? Similarly, how do you develop initiative and adaptability? And most importantly, how do you develop emotional awareness and self-management? In this respect the limitations of most traditional learning are revealed in Figure 9.3.

Most traditional training and development takes place well above the water line – simply adding new knowledge and skills. This can be referred to as horizontal development. There's nothing inherently wrong with it but it only really engages a fraction of our potential. Robust experiential learning and coaching often takes the learner below the water line – surfacing and then working with pre-conscious material and, given the right conditions of safety, unconscious material well below the surface of awareness. In surfacing and then examining unconscious material, deeper transformational change can occur. But this type of vertical development depends on the presence of a coach or facilitator for the learning to occur.

Mindfulness is different. With regular practice, the mindfulness practitioner develops their own method and ability to access and work with material below the immediate surface of awareness. When we sit with ourselves we can become familiar with the habitual patterns of thought and emotion that drive our behaviour – and the results these bring. We can also touch deeper truths: our values and what we hold most dear. That enables us to act more in alignment with our values and to live and work with greater authenticity, ease and flow.

This isn't to say that mindfulness training requires no guidance – quite the opposite. People often learn about these matters from observing their embodiment in the teachers they learn from. But through their guidance, mindfulness teachers equip practitioners with the skills to navigate their own

192 *Joining the dots*

Figure 9.3 The behavioural iceberg
Adapted from Selfridge and Sokolik [14] and French and Bell [15]

minds and they empower them to guide transformational change in themselves. This is change 'from the inside out'.

Mindfulness and vertical development

Nick Petrie, author of *The How-To of Vertical Leadership Development*, suggests that there are few practices that produce as many benefits as mindfulness.

From a vertical perspective, the regular practice of turning inward and observing one's own thoughts helps leaders observe the constant process of their own meaning-making. Stick with it long enough and you start to notice that who you think 'you' are is mainly just a story you are constructing and reconstructing moment to moment.[16]

For the last 60 years, much of leadership development has focused on what happens in a leader's head, he says. Commentators like Dan Siegel, he adds, tell us that the mind is 'embodied', not just 'enskulled', and the implication of this for leadership development is that if we want to help adults develop and evolve, the most direct path may be through the body, not the head.

Mindfulness is not simply about training the mind in the obvious sense of the word. Certainly it can increase awareness of cognition, but it also increases awareness at an embodied level, enabling practitioners to access aspects of themselves of which they were previously unaware. As Kabat-Zinn clarifies,

> In Asian languages, the word for mind and the word for heart are the same word. So when we hear the word mindfulness, we have to inwardly also hear heartfulness in order to grasp it even as a concept, and especially as a way of being.[17]

So mindfulness is also heartfulness. It has a tonal quality of warmth, openness, and whole-heartedness and it reminds us that, as a quality of presence and a way of being, mindfulness comes from lower down in our body, not something purely in our head.

Vertical development for a VUCA world

'A new type of thinking is essential if mankind is to survive and move toward higher levels.'[18]

It's now 70 years since Einstein made this appeal and it's as true today as it was then. As he also said: 'You cannot solve a problem from the same consciousness that created it. You must learn to see the world anew'.

Today we face unprecedented global challenges – exponential growth in population, declining resources, climate change, species extinction, global pandemics and major economic disruptions. At the same time unprecedented opportunities are also emerging – the accelerating rate of technological progress and knowledge access, an energy revolution, nanotechnology, biotechnology, an increasing rate of interdependence and conscious capitalism (more on that later).

And where are leaders in all of this? Increasingly we experience living and working in a VUCA world: one that is volatile, uncertain, complex, and ambiguous. Everything is inter-connected and no one can predict what big changes are coming next. Leaders who are equal to the task are those who can deal with ambiguity, notice key patterns, and look at the world through multiple stakeholder perspectives.

How can we future-proof leadership capability to work in this way? Eigel and Kuhnert make the following suggestion:

'The future of our organisations depends on successfully identifying and developing all leaders to higher [developmental levels] – to a place of greater authenticity – so that they can respond effectively to the increasingly complex demands of our times.'[19]

In the 1950s, Jean Piaget showed that as children grow, the way they think advances through predictable stages. At each higher stage they can think in more sophisticated ways and deal with increasingly difficult problems. But developmental stages do not stop at childhood. In the 1960s, psychologists like Loevinger and Graves began to focus on how adults develop from the baby's narrow, self-centred view of the world to the mature wisdom and powerful action of exemplary adults. They showed that we can identify several different ways of adult meaning-making. Each world view or stage is more comprehensive, differentiated and effective in dealing with the complexities of life than its predecessors.

Researchers like Torbert, Kegan, Cook-Greuter and Joiner have since been instrumental in bringing this into the world of work and leadership. They make a distinction between vertical and horizontal development. Horizontal development is the accumulation of new knowledge, skills and competencies. Vertical development, on the other hand, involves a complete transformation in the individual's overall view of reality that transforms what they think, feel and do.

As Petrie puts it, 'If horizontal development is about transferring information to the leader, vertical development is about transformation of the leader.'[20] Rather than just adding software into a leader's existing 'operating system', vertical development is an inside out transformation that upgrades the operating system itself. As we upgrade, or mature, vertically we expand our capacity for understanding ourselves and our experiences – we see the world with different eyes.

Vertical development is often described in terms of stages, waves, levels of development or 'action-logics'.

In Torbert's framework[21] there are eight action-logics that represent how people organise and interpret reality (see Figure 9.4). These include what we see as the purpose of life, what needs we act upon, what ends we move toward, our emotions and our experience of being, and how we think about ourselves and the world. Each involves the reorganisation of meaning making, perspective, self-identity, and our overall way of knowing.

In Kegan's model of adult development[22] those at stage 3, 'The Socialised Mind', shape their thinking and actions based on what they believe is expected by others – they could be described as followers. At stage 4, 'The Self-Authoring Mind', people use their own inner belief system as a compass to decide what is right or wrong and how to act – they could be described as self-directed leaders. Those at stage 5, 'The Self Transforming Mind', can look at their own beliefs and see them as limited or partial, can hold more contradictions in their mind and no longer feel the need to gravitate toward polarised thinking. Clearly someone at stage 4 will have a greater ability to lead in unknown environments where there are less certain answers or no one to ask for direction than someone at stage 3. Likewise, someone at stage 5 can handle even more complex and ambiguous environments.

Using a climbing metaphor, Cook-Greuter describes how vertical development is like having a higher vantage point on a mountain,

> At each turn of the path up the mountain I can see more of the territory I have already traversed ... The closer I get to the summit, the easier it becomes to see behind to the shadow side and uncover formerly hidden aspects of the territory. Finally at the top, I can see beyond my particular mountain to other ranges and further horizons. The more I can see, the wiser, more timely, more systematic and informed my actions and decisions are likely to be.[23]

Each stage represents a centre of gravity from which the individual sees the world. What they think, how they feel, and what actions they take are influenced by this. With each new vertical transformation, what the individual was once subject to and could not see can now be seen as object and therefore worked with. At the next stage the previous assumptions, beliefs, attitudes and self-images come into view.

As Brown[24] points out, later action-logics have been shown to correlate with increased leadership effectiveness. Leaders with post conventional action-logics tend to think more strategically, collaborate more, seek out feedback more often, resolve conflicts better, make greater efforts to develop others, and are more likely to redefine challenges so as to capitalise on connections across them. This increased leadership effectiveness comes from new capacities that arise as individuals develop into post-conventional meaning-making. These include increased cognitive functioning, strengthened personal and interpersonal awareness, increased understanding of emotions, and more accurate empathy.

> At these very complex stages of development, many meta-cognitive and meta-emotional capacities arise ... These include the ability to take a systems view and even a unitive view on reality; simultaneously hold and manage conflicting frames, perspectives and emotions; and deeply accept oneself, others, and the moment, without judgment. Such individuals also report deep access to intuition and perceive their rational mind as a tool, not as the principal way to understand reality. They appear to heavily tolerate uncertainty and even collaboratively engage with ambiguity to create. Finally, they experience frequent 'flow' and 'witnessing' states of consciousness.[24]

Figure 9.4 Torbert's framework of action logics

Adapted from Rooke and Torbert.[25] Percentages of the adult population for each stage from Cook-Greuter.[25,26] Material on the Ironist drawn from Cook-Greuter.[23,26] and Torbert[27]

	Action logic	Main focus	Characteristics	Strengths	% Adult pop	Effect as leaders
Pre-conv	1 Opportunist	Own immediate needs, opportunity, self-protection	Self-oriented so will win at all costs.	Sales or emergencies	4.3	Significantly less effective at implementing organizational strategies.
Conventional stages of consciousness	2 Diplomat	Socially-expected behaviour, approval	Wants to belong so avoids conflict. Won't give tough feedback or make difficult decisions.	Team player	11.3	
	3 Expert	Expertise, procedure, and efficiency	Operates from expertise and seeks efficiency. Influences through facts but lacks emotional intelligence	Specialist	36.5	
	4 Achiever	Delivery of results, effectiveness, goals, success within system	Achieves strategic goals through teams but may inhibit innovation	Management	29.7	Effective manager. Action and goal oriented.

5 Individualist	Self in relationship to system; interaction with system	Creates new structures to address gaps between strategy and performance. Unconventional / ignores rules so may irritate others.	Consulting roles	11.3	Consistent capacity to innovate and transform organizations.
6 Strategist	Linking theory and principles with practice; dynamic systems interactions	Generates organizational and personal transformations. Challenges existing norms, highly collaborative, combines vision with pragmatism	Transformational leader	4.9	
7 Alchemist	Interplay of awareness, thought, action, and effects; transforming self and others	Generates social transformations. Reinvents organizations in historically significant ways	Leading society-wide transformations	1.5	
8 Ironist	Being; experience moment to moment arising of consciousness	Institutionalizes developmental processes through "liberating disciplines." True visionary	Catalysing deep development of individuals and collectives	0.5	

Rows 5–6: Postconventional: general systems stages of consciousness
Rows 7–8: Postconventional: unitive stages of consciousness

And this is vital, because leaders who have access to post-conventional meaning-making systems are better able to respond to complex, ambiguous, and sophisticated challenges. As leaders and organisations wrestle with being competitive in a VUCA world, more and more leaders need to be agile enough to deliver transformation and change in complex and ambiguous environments.

Given the small proportion of leaders at post-conventional stages (about 15 per cent as Torbert suggests), how best can we support leaders in developing beyond conventional stages of meaning making? As Cooke-Greuter notes,

> Development in its deepest meaning refers to transformations of consciousness. Because acquisition of knowledge is part of horizontal growth, learning about developmental theories is not sufficient to help people to transform. Only specific long-term practices, self-reflection, action inquiry, and dialogue, as well as living in the company of others further along on the developmental path has been shown to be effective.[23]

As one of our mindful coaches observed:

> If I work with people in the Individualist stage they are very successful – accountants, lawyers, engineers . . . they easily run large outlets of about one hundred thousand people . . . then suddenly their disciplines, mindsets and linear, empirical thinking runs into its limit . . . and they say 'how do I get to Strategist or Magician?' . . . Well mindfulness is a pretty good practice . . . If people don't have a centre and know the centre in themselves where they can go to contain the anxiety from running very large outlets with multinational and very difficult situations, if they allow the anxiety and the system to influence their processes, it takes them out and they don't last long. But if they know their centre, they've got a place, a refuge if you like, or a secure place that is reliable in terms of its contribution, they do brilliantly. It's very practical in that sense – it's a combination of developmental stages and mindfulness.
>
> Sol Davidson

Following his survey of experts in this field Petrie recommends the following practices in support of vertical development:

1 Heat experiences:
   - Give assignments to the least qualified person.
   - Create 'heat seeking leaders'.
   - Create a culture of developmental risk taking.
   - Uncover your immunity to change.
   - Manufacture heat in the classroom.

2 Colliding perspectives:
   - Replace 'bad' action learning with peer coaching.
   - Frame-breaking experiences: spend a day in your customer's rice paddy.

- Develop a systems perspective: the organisational workshop.
- Step into another worldview: deep listening.
- Hold two opposing ideas in your mind: polarity thinking.

3 Elevated sense making:
- Learn from the gurus: use stage maps.
- Coach with a vertical lens.
- Make sense with a late-stage mentor.
- Facilitate vertical development for the executive team.
- Copy Google and Buddha: teach mindfulness and meditation.

And 'most thought provoking': change your body, re-pattern your mind.[14]

Further research exploring the explicit links between mindfulness and vertical development is needed. However, you may already have noticed that many of the capacities associated with post-conventional development stages have been highlighted elsewhere in the book as being actively cultivated through mindfulness practice. These include metacognitive skills, personal and interpersonal awareness, increased understanding of emotions, empathy, the capacity to deeply accept oneself, others, and the moment without judgement, deep access to intuition, the capacity to tolerate uncertainty, to experience frequent states of 'flow' and 'witness consciousness.' The Mindful Leader programme that Michael and Megan Reitz created, taught and researched alongside colleagues at Ashridge Business School showed these kinds of outcomes.

If we go back to core definitions, we remember that mindfulness is an *outcome* as well as a process – it's the conscious awareness that arises from paying attention in a particular way. If, as Cooke-Greuter suggests, 'Development in its deepest meaning refers to transformations of consciousness' then mindfulness practice certainly offers a potent means for doing so.

A number of commentators suggest that vertical development is fast becoming one of the most important trends in leadership development. As McGuire and Rhodes suggest,

> Organisations have grown skilled at developing individual leader competencies, but have mostly ignored the challenge of transforming their leader's mind-set from one level to the next. Today's horizontal development within a mind-set must give way to the vertical development of bigger minds.[28]

What's clear is that coaches continue to have a significant part to play in this by 'coaching through a vertical lens'. But if we wish to support leaders to develop and grow vertically, it isn't enough to know about developmental stages theoretically – we need to understand it experientially. In this respect, mindfulness offers much to both leaders and coaches alike.

Conscious capitalism

Leaders at later stages of development have always had the capacity to create systems that serve a pro-social purpose. Given the challenges we face today we should perhaps not be surprised that new business models are emerging that operate from this perspective. One such model is *Conscious Capitalism*[29], offered as an alternative to traditional capitalism and as a blueprint for the future. John Mackey, CEO of Whole Foods Market and Raj Sisodia propose an organisational model based on four core tenets: higher purpose, stakeholder integration, conscious leadership and conscious culture. But this isn't a model simply for 'nice' business – it's based on sustainable high performance. Their research suggests that conscious businesses out-perform the overall stock market by a ratio of 10:1 over a 15 year period.

Higher purpose

The first tenet of conscious capitalism is that business has the potential to have a higher purpose than merely maximising profits. Every conscious business has a higher purpose which addresses questions like: Why is the world better because we are here? This acts as a magnet to attract the right team members, customers, suppliers, and investors and aligns the ecosystem, getting everybody pointing in the same direction and moving together in harmony.

Once purpose and values have been articulated, it's important that leaders embody them and talk about them with customers, team members, suppliers and investors. They must also be integrated into processes like recruitment, appraisal, research and development and strategic planning, and be at the forefront of decision making. When purpose and values are clear, leadership teams can be highly responsive to opportunities, making quicker and bolder decisions rather than knee-jerk reactions to changes in the competitive environment.

Stakeholder integration

The second tenet is based on the awareness of an interdependent stakeholder eco-system, and the intention to create value for all stakeholders. Traditional business models often treat stakeholders other than investors as the means to maximising profit. But without consistent customer satisfaction, team member happiness and supplier and community support, short term profits are unsustainable. The best way to maximise long term profits is to create value for the entire interdependent system.

> Management's responsibility is to hire the right people, train them well, and ensure that those team members flourish ... The team member's job is to satisfy and delight customers ... Management helps the team

members experience happiness, team members help the customers achieve happiness, the customers help the investors achieve happiness, and when ... profits ... are re-invested ... you get a virtuous circle.[29]

p. 72

Conscious culture

Mackey and Sisodia suggest that conscious cultures have seven core characteristics:

1. *Trust* – high levels internally and externally.
2. *Accountability* – team members are truly accountable to each other and customers.
3. *Caring* – genuine care for all stakeholders.
4. *Transparency* – strategic plans and financial information are widely discussed.
5. *Integrity* – strict adherence to doing what is ethically right.
6. *Loyalty* – stakeholders are more understanding with each other about short term blips.
7. *Egalitarianism* – no class system to separate leaders from team members.

They also point to a particular kind of management approach that fosters *intrinsic* motivation (autonomy, mastery and purpose) in team members, as well as promoting decentralisation, empowerment and innovation.

Conscious leadership

Conscious leaders are perhaps the most important element in the equation as they create and shape conscious businesses,

> Conscious leaders abundantly display many of the qualities we most admire in exemplary human beings. They usually find great joy and beauty in their work and in the opportunity to serve, lead and help shape a better future ... Conscious leaders commonly have high ... emotional, spiritual and systems intelligence. They also have an orientation toward servant leadership, high integrity, and a great capacity for love and care ... They are keenly self-aware and recognise their own deepest motivations and convictions.[29]

p. 183

But how can leaders develop themselves to become more conscious? A simple answer is regular mindfulness practice but let's explore that in more detail.

Following higher purpose

For Mackey and Sosidia the starting point is setting an intention to become a conscious leader and inquiring into your life purpose. 'Your inner heart knows' they say,

> it is whispering to you right now ... Quiet your mind, listen attentively to your inner heart and follow its guidance. Our inner heart will always be our best guide in life if we can develop enough self-awareness to be able to hear it and the courage to follow it.[29]
>
> p. 196

Regular mindfulness practice helps with both these things. It helps us grow our self-awareness so we know when we are following our hearts and when we've lost our way. It also helps us learn how to deal with fear. 'Contemplative practices that teach us how to quiet our minds' the authors suggest 'can also help us overcome fear' (p. 197).[29]

Developing emotional intelligence

As we've previously seen, through regular mindfulness practice we can create a more intentional life in accordance with our feelings, values, aspirations and ideals, rather than simply reacting to things and following impulses and desires.

Becoming more aware of our emotions, Mackey and Sosidia suggest, we begin to realise that many of them, such as envy, resentment, greed, bitterness, malice, anger, and hatred, are life stultifying, Whereas emotions such as love, generosity, gratitude, compassion and forgiveness are expansive and life-enhancing. 'We need to consciously cultivate life-enhancing emotions and learn to neutralise life-stultifying emotions when we become aware of their presence', they say, 'this is the essence of personal mastery and emotional intelligence' (p. 201).[29]

Developing systems intelligence (SYQ)

Conscious leaders see more clearly the larger systems of which they are a part. They can feel the system as they go, sensing misalignment in a way that anticipates issues, sometimes before these have even had a chance to take hold. Leaders can develop SYQ by practicing thinking in terms of the stakeholder system but as Mackey and Sisodia note,

> The exercises that develop EQ ... can also help develop our SYQ. Slowing our minds down is essential ... the less speedy but attentive mind is more capable of being in the here and now, noticing things and the relationship between them, and seeing the larger system.[29]
>
> p. 203

Mackey and Sisodia are explicit about the role of meditation practice in developing conscious leaders and point to Buddhist insight meditation as a way to integrate this into regular working lives,

> Contemplative practices such as meditation ... are very valuable in helping an individual develop into a more conscious leader. They require setting time aside to be by ourselves, which is critical for self-awareness, as well as for helping us to centre ourselves, become aware of our feelings, and slow down the mind ... The most important thing we can do is practice regularly. We can't just have a theoretical understanding of meditation – it's the practice that makes the difference.[29]
>
> p. 212

Resonant leadership

Resonant leadership is a term first coined by Richard Boyatzis, professor of organisational behaviour at the Weatherhead School of Management and Annie McKee, former Global Director of Management Development for The Hay Group. It describes the way in which great leaders attune to themselves, and then in turn to their people, in order to draw out and amplify what is best in themselves and others. As we saw in Chapter 7, Dan Siegel suggests that the neural integration[30] that arises from mindfulness training significantly increases our capacity for this.

For Boyatzis and McKee, mindfulness is a key leadership competency. They describe it as 'the capacity to be fully aware of all that one experiences *inside the self* – body, mind, heart, spirit – and to pay full attention to what is happening *around us* – people, the natural world, our surroundings and events'.[31] For them, it all starts with self awareness. This enables you to choose how best to respond to people and situations and allows you to be authentic and consistent. We trust and follow people whose behaviour, beliefs and values are aligned. Mindfulness enables us to make better choices because our perceptions are clearer, we notice things that would normally pass us by and we gain access to deeper insight and wisdom.

In *Becoming a Resonant Leader*[32], McKee *et al.* outline three contemporary myths about leadership. The first is that 'smart is good enough'. As we've seen, leaders with higher emotional and social intelligence are more effective because they manage themselves more effectively in the face of stress and ambiguity and are better at inspiring others by being more attuned to them. Key to this is emotional self awareness – the ability to recognise emotions as they happen and understand their effects on oneself and others. Interestingly, a neurobiological study published by Creswell *et al.* showed evidence that mindfulness training increased levels of emotional self awareness and the ability to manage negative feelings.[33] People who frequently lose their temper don't make good leaders – nor do those who freeze under pressure. Leaders are constantly being watched by their people so it's important they're able to monitor and manage their own emotional states.

This leads us to the second myth that 'mood doesn't matter'. Leader's emotions are contagious – we're wired to constantly tune into the emotional state of those around us and that affects what we think, feel and do. The way people perceive their leaders' states has a direct impact on them. In a study by Wager et al.[34] they found that employees who worked under unfavourably perceived supervisors exhibited markedly higher blood pressure and other physical signs of distress. When people are fearful, anxious or angry it arouses their sympathetic nervous system and they shut-down, fight back or want to run away. Often they feel frazzled and don't perform at their best. By contrast, when they are optimistic, energised and excited they think more clearly and creatively, are more resilient and perform better.

The third myth is that 'great leaders can thrive on constant pressure'. Unending responsibilities, constant pressure and 24/7 availability can often lead to what McKee et al. call 'power stress', and causes leaders to fall into 'sacrifice syndrome' – a vicious cycle of stress and sacrifice that can result in mental and physical distress, diminished effectiveness and burnout. That then spreads through emotional contagion as stressed leaders spread dissonance throughout their teams and organisations. To counter this McKee et al. suggest that leaders need to understand the crucial role that *renewal* plays in sustaining effectiveness. They suggest that through mindfulness practice, leaders can counteract sacrifice syndrome and actively cultivate renewal. They also point to research linking mindfulness practice to increased cognitive flexibility, creativity and problem solving skills.[35]

Mindful leadership – what's in a name?

When we refer to an emotionally intelligent leader, a resonant leader, a conscious leader, a post-conventional leader or even an adaptive leader we're describing leadership phenomena that are very similar – leaders with differentiated capabilities that enable them to operate at higher levels of performance in a world that is constantly changing.

Of course there are specific nuances to each, but essentially we are describing leaders who are deeply attuned to themselves and the world around them, in a way that enables them to accurately read and respond to subtle changes in their internal and external environment. As a species, this capacity to adapt to our changing environment has always been central to our survival and at its best, to our growth and ability to flourish. Our suggestion is that in today's VUCA world, our ability to actively cultivate these capacities is central to flourishing at an individual and organisational level. If leaders or organisations wish to optimise the way they function and gain long term advantage, these leadership qualities will become a necessity. As mindfulness increasingly moves into the mainstream we offer the following description of a mindful leader:

A mindful leader consciously engages in regular formal mindfulness practice as a systematic way to cultivate emotional and systems intelligence. Mindful leaders understand themselves and others at a deeper level and operate from this awareness. They operate in a more conscious and purposeful way; are better able to see, feel and transform the systems of which they are a part; and they seek to enable others to do the same. They engage in development to post-conventional stages and are adaptive to the changing environment around them, rather than simply reacting to it.

Through regular mindfulness practice, mindful leaders actively cultivate the meta-capacities of metacognition, curiosity and allow and create greater space for adaptive responses. These meta-capacities enable focus, emotional regulation, perspective taking, empathy and adaptability, which in turn result in improved resilience, collaboration and the capacity to lead in complexity. By actively cultivating their mind and their way of being, mindful leaders create the conditions for growth and flourishing to arise in themselves and those around them.

The mindful organisation and a mindful nation

In 2015, the UK Government's Mindfulness All-Party Parliamentary Group (MAPPG) concluded in its Mindful Nation UK report that while there is still much research to be done, mindfulness is already a promising innovation in the workplace context with an early but rapidly evolving evidence base.

In 2016, the Mindfulness Initiative, secretariat to the MAPPG, set up a working group from a range of private sector organisations including EY, GE, HSBC and Jaguar Landrover, supported by a panel of leading mindfulness trainers and academics. In its recent report [36] the Mindfulness Initiative confirm that there are a number of potential organisational benefits to mindfulness training including:

- well-being and resilience;
- relationships and collaboration; and
- performance (including leadership, creativity and innovation).

Since the leading cause of sickness absence in the UK is mental ill health, accounting for 70 million sick days every year,[37] it's perhaps not surprising that the most obvious organisational benefit relates to well-being and resilience. Since a number of randomised controlled trials of workplace mindfulness-based training courses have found positive effects on burnout, well-being and stress,[38] this represents a significant organisational opportunity.

But a focus on addressing dis-ease, whilst important, potentially under-estimates the benefits mindfulness training offers in supporting organisational performance, growth and flow. In terms of relationships and collaboration, 45 workplace mindfulness research studies have linked mindfulness to improved relationships at work, supporting collaboration and improving employees' resilience in the face of challenges.[39,40]

In terms of leadership, Michael and Megan's research at Ashridge Business School points to the future in equipping leaders for a VUCA world, while other research has found that leaders' mindfulness improved staff engagement and job performance.[41] In terms of creativity and innovation, recent research suggests that there is a 'direct relation between mindfulness and creativity'[42] likely to be supported through improved focus, idea generation and flexible thinking.

Another aspect outlined by the Mindfulness Initiative is 'organisational mindfulness' a form of organisational transformation that comes about by way of collective mindfulness.

> Workplace mindfulness is possible not only for individuals, but within and across teams of people ... When mindfulness becomes a shared social practice in an organisation, and permeates routines, processes and practices between people and across teams, then the organisation as a whole becomes more resilient and performs more sustainably.[43]

In line with the original Mindful Nation UK report, the Mindfulness Initiative continue to highlight the importance of identifying suitably qualified mindfulness training providers and measuring outcomes in order to build a solid evidence base. They also make helpful recommendations in terms of embedding mindfulness at an organisational level, with case studies from a variety of organisations including Capital One, GSK and EY.

We feel sure that with a focus on these three things the idea of the mindful workplace will increasingly become a reality amongst progressive employers. And as the Mindfulness All-Party Parliamentary Group continue to make recommendations for the criminal justice, healthcare and education sectors we feel sure that the idea of a Mindful Nation will also move closer to becoming a reality in the UK.

Given what we know about mindfulness and its capacity to support growth and flourishing that has to be a good thing for us all.

Notes

1 Lavine, M. (2014) 'Paradoxical leadership and the competing values framework', *Journal of Applied Behavioral Science*, 50(2): 189–205.
2 Smith, W.K. *et al.* (2016) '"Both/And" Leadership', *Harvard Business Review*, (May).
3 Marion, R. and Uhl-Bien, M. (2001) 'Leadership in complex organizations', *The Leadership Quarterly*, 12(4): 389–418.
4 Snowden, D. and Boone, M. (2007) 'A leader's framework for decision making', *Harvard Business Review*, 85(11): 68–76, 149.
5 Reitz, M. *et al.* (2016) 'The mindful leader: developing the capacity for resilience and collaboration in complex times through mindfulness practice' http://ashridge.org.uk/Media-Library/Ashridge/PDFs/Publications/Ashridge-Mindful-Leader-for-web-low-res.pdf.

6 Davis, M.H. (1980) 'A multidimensional approach to individual differences in empathy', *JSAS Catalog of Selected Documents in Psychology*, 10: 85.
7 Beck, A. *et al.* (1988) 'An inventory for measuring clinical anxiety: psychometric properties', *Journal of Consulting and Clinical Psychology*, 56: 893–897.
8 Davda, A. (2011) 'Measuring resilience: a pilot study', *Assessment & Development Matters*, Autumn: 11–14.
9 Turner, M. and Engle, R. (1989) 'Is working memory capacity task dependent?', *Journal of Memory and Language*, 28: 127–154.
10 Baer, R *et al.* (2006) 'Using self-report assessment methods to explore facets of mindfulness', Assessment, 13: 27–45.
11 Goleman, D. (1998) *Working with Emotional Intelligence*, London: Bloomsbury.
12 Goleman, D. (2003) *Destructive Emotions*, London: Bloomsbury.
13 Chu, L. (2010) 'The benefits of meditation vis-à-vis emotional intelligence, perceived stress and negative mental health', *Stress and Health*, 26: 169–180.
14 Selfridge, R. and Sokolik, S. (1975) 'A comprehensive view of organizational management', *MSU Business Topics*, 23(1): 46–61.
15 French, W. and Bell, C (1998) *Organization Development*, London: Pearson.
16 Petrie, N. (2015) 'The how-to of vertical leadership development – part 2', *Center for Creative Leadership*, www.ccl.org/wp-content/uploads/2015/04/vertical LeadersPart2.pdf.
17 Kabat-Zinn, J. (2005) *Coming To Our Senses*, London: Piatkus.
18 *New York Times* (1946) 'Atomic education urged by Einstein', 25 May (Column 6): p. 13.
19 Eigel, K. and Kuhnert, K. (2005) 'Authentic development', In W. Gardner *et al.* (eds) *Authentic Leadership Theory and Practice*, Bingley, UK: JAI Press.
20 Petrie, N. (2014) 'Vertical leadership development – part 1', *Center for Creative Leadership*, www.nicholaspetrie.com/wp-content/uploads/2013/11/Vertical Develop ment-Part-12.pdf.
21 Torbert, B. *et al.* (2004) *Action Inquiry: The Secret of Timely and Transforming Leadership*, San Francisco, CA: Berrett-Koehler.
22 Kegan, R. (1994) *In Over Our Heads*, Cambridge, MA: Harvard University Press.
23 Cook-Greuter, S. (2004) 'Making the case for a developmental perspective', *Industrial and Commercial Training*, 36 (7).
24 Brown, B. (2012) 'Leading complex change with post-conventional consciousness', *Journal of Organizational Change Management*, 25(4): 560–575.
25 Rooke, D. and Torbert, W. (2005) 'The seven transformations of leadership', *Harvard Business Review*, 83: 66.
26 Cook-Greuter, S. (1999) 'Postautonomous ego development', *Dissertation Abstracts International*, 60 06B(UMI No. 993312).
27 Torbert, W. (1987) *Managing the Corporate Dream: Restructuring for Long-Term Success*, New York: McGraw-Hill.
28 McGuire, J. and Rhodes, G. (2009) *Transforming Your Leadership Culture*, Wiley, p. 12.
29 Mackey, J. and Sisodia, R. (2013) *Conscious Capitalism*, Boston, MA: Harvard Business Review Press.
30 Siegel, D. (2007) *The Mindful Brain*, New York: W.W. Norton & Co.
31 Boyatzis, R. and McKee, A. (2005) *Resonant Leadership*, Boston, MA: Harvard Business School Press.
32 McKee, A. *et al.* (2008) *Becoming a Resonant Leader*, Boston, MA: Harvard Business School Press.
33 Creswell, J. *et al.* (2007) 'Neural correlates of dispositional mindfulness during affect labelling', *Psychosomatic Medicine*, 69(6): 550–565.
34 Wager, N. *et al.* (2003) 'The effect on ambulatory blood pressure of working under favourably and unfavourably perceived supervisors, *Occupational Environmental Medicine*, 60(7): 468–474.

35 Ashby, F.G. *et al.* (1999) 'A neurophysiological theory of positive affect and its influence on contagion', *Psychological Review*, 106(3): 529–550.
36 The Mindfulness Initiative (2016) 'Building the case for mindfulness in the workplace', http://themindfulnessinitiative.org.uk/images/reports/MI_Building-the-Case_v1.1_Oct16.pdf.
37 Davies S.C. (2013) *Annual Report of the Chief Medical Officer 2013, Public Mental Health Priorities: Investing in the Evidence*, London: Department of Health.
38 Chiesa, A. and Serretti, A. (2009) 'Mindfulness-based stress reduction for stress management in healthy people', *Journal of Alternative Complementary Medicine*, 15: 593–600.

  Pidgeon A. *et al.* (2014) 'Evaluating the effectiveness of enhancing resilience in human service professionals using a retreat-based mindfulness with Metta Training Program', *Psychology, Health and Medicine*, 19: 355–364.
39 Mindfulnet.org (2016) 'Gathering the evidence base for mindfulness at work: scientifically evaluated and academic research', www.mindfulnet.org/page18.htm.
40 Glomb, T. *et al.* (2011) 'Mindfulness at work' *Personnel and HR Management*, 30: 115–157.
41 Reb, J. *et al.* (2012) 'Leading mindfully', *Mindfulness*, 5(1): 36–45.
42 Ostafin, B. and Kassman, K. (2012) 'Stepping out of history: mindfulness improves insight problem solving', *Consciousness and Cognition*, 21(2): 1031–1036.
43 Weick, K. and Sutcliffe, K. (2006) 'Mindfulness and the quality of organisational attention', *Organisation Science*, 17(4): 514–526.

Appendix A
Research methodology

Twenty four mindful coaches were invited to contribute to the inquiry process. Firstly they were invited to complete a questionnaire. They were then invited to be interviewed, exploring just four key questions.

Questionnaire

A   How frequent is your mindfulness practice?

B   Roughly how many hours of mindfulness practice do you engage in on a monthly basis?

C   What beneficial effects has your mindfulness practice had on you personally, if any?

D   Please indicate below if you feel your mindfulness practice influences any of the following areas of your coaching practice:

Ethics & Standards	Yes ☐	No ☐
Establishing The Coaching Agreement	Yes ☐	No ☐
Establishing Trust & Intimacy With The Client	Yes ☐	No ☐
Coaching Presence	Yes ☐	No ☐
Active Listening	Yes ☐	No ☐
Powerful Questioning	Yes ☐	No ☐
Direct Communication	Yes ☐	No ☐
Creating Awareness	Yes ☐	No ☐
Designing Actions	Yes ☐	No ☐
Planning & Goal Setting	Yes ☐	No ☐
Managing Progress & Accountability	Yes ☐	No ☐

If yes to any of the above please say how.

What more do you think, feel or want to say about how your mindfulness practice influences your coaching practice?

E. Please indicate below which, if any, inform your coaching approach:

Person Centred Approach	Yes ☐	No ☐
Gestalt	Yes ☐	No ☐
Cognitive Behavioural	Yes ☐	No ☐
Psychodynamic	Yes ☐	No ☐
Somatic	Yes ☐	No ☐
Solutions Focused	Yes ☐	No ☐
Time to Think (Nancy Kline)	Yes ☐	No ☐
Transactional Analysis	Yes ☐	No ☐
Other – please state	Yes ☐	No ☐

Does your mindfulness practice deepen or support any of these approaches in any way? If so, please say how.

F. Do you feel your mindfulness practice impacts on the coaching relationship with your clients in any way? If yes, please say how.

G. Do you feel your mindfulness practice impacts on the coaching outcomes you co-create with your clients in any way? If yes, please say how.

Interview

1. How has your mindfulness practice impacted on you personally?
2. How does your mindfulness practice influence your coaching practice?
3. What, if any, coaching models inform your coaching approach and how does your mindfulness practice deepen or support these?
4. How does your mindfulness practice impact on the coaching relationship you create with your clients and the outcomes you co-create with them?

Appendix B
Our mindful coaches

Alyse Ashton
Alyse@eye2eyedev.com

Jane Brendgen
Jane.brendgen@yahoo.com

Wendy Briner
Wendyabriner@gmail.com

Simon Cavicchia
Simon@simoncavicchia.co.uk

Sue Cruse
Susanmcruse@gmail.com

Jane Davey
Janekdavey@gmail.com

Sol Davidson
Sol.davidson@tiscali.co.uk

Emma Donaldson-Feilder
Emma@affinityhealthatwork.com

Elizabeth English
Elizabeth@lifeatwork.co.uk

Linda Feerick
Linda.Feerick@alliancecoaching.co.uk

Angus Fisher
Angus.fisher@rflca.com

Karen Gervais
Karengervais@turquoisesky.co.uk

Liz Gooster
Liz.Gooster@alliancecoaching.co.uk

Farah Govani
Farah@govanicoaching.com

Heather Rachel Johnson
www.mindtrip.co.uk

Robin Kermode
Robin@zone2.co.uk

Arnie Kozak
arnie@vitalleadershipcoaching.com

Prof. Jonathan Passmore
Jonathancpassmore@yahoo.co.uk

Julian Read
Julian.read@easyrevolution.com

Alan Ross
Alan@arkassociates.com

Ruth Sack
Ruth.sack@alliancecoaching.co.uk

Sophie Turner
Sophie.Turner@pinsentmasons.com

Lindsay Wittenberg
lw@lindsaywittenberg.co.uk

Sally Woodward
sally@sallywoodward.co.uk

Appendix C
Good practice guidelines for teaching mindfulness-based courses

Published by the UK Network of Mindfulness Teacher Training Organisations (April 2015).

A teacher of mindfulness-based approaches should have the following:

A. Mindfulness-Based Teacher Training

1. Familiarity through personal participation with the mindfulness-based course curriculum that they will be learning to teach, with particular in-depth personal experience of all the core meditation practices of this mindfulness-based programme.
2. Completion of an in-depth, rigorous mindfulness-based teacher training programme or supervised pathway over a minimum duration of 12 months.

B. Training or background required in addition to mindfulness-based teacher training

1. A professional qualification in mental or physical health care, education or social care, or equivalent life experience, recognised by the organisation or context within which the teaching will take place.
2. Knowledge and experience of the populations that the mindfulness-based course will be delivered to, including experience of teaching, therapeutic or other care provision with groups and/or individuals, unless such knowledge and experience is provided to an adequate level by the mindfulness-based teacher training itself. An exception to this can be when teaching with the help of a colleague who knows well the population to whom the course will be delivered and has a relevant qualification. They would also need to have an understanding of mindfulness-based approaches.
3. If delivering MBCT, knowledge of relevant underlying psychological processes, associated research and evidence-based practice, unless these are provided to an adequate level by the mindfulness teacher training programme.

4   If delivering MBCT or other mindfulness-based course with a clinical population, an appropriate professional clinical training

C. Ongoing Good Practice Requirements

1. Commitment to a personal mindfulness practice through: daily formal and informal practice participation in annual residential teacher-led mindfulness meditation retreats
2. Engagement in processes which continue to develop mindfulness-based teaching practice: ongoing contacts with other mindfulness practitioners and teachers, built and maintained as a means to share experiences and learn collaboratively and regular supervision with an experienced mindfulness-based teacher including:
   i   opportunity to reflect on/inquire into personal process in relation to personal mindfulness practice and mindfulness-based teaching practice
   ii receiving periodic feedback on teaching through video recordings, supervisor sitting in on teaching sessions or co-teaching with reciprocal feedback.
3. A commitment to ongoing development as a teacher through further training, keeping up to date with the evidence base, recording and reflecting on teaching sessions, participation in web forums etc.
4. Adherence to the ethical framework appropriate to the teacher's professional background and working context.

Further reading

Mindfulness

Begley, S. (2007) *Train Your Mind, Change Your Brain: How a New Science Reveals Our Extraordinary Potential to Transform Ourselves*, Ballantine Books.
Chaskalson, M. (2014) *Mindfulness in Eight Weeks*, Harper Collins.
Germer, C. (2009) *The Mindful Path to Self-Compassion*, Guildford Press.
Gilbert, P. (2010) *The Compassionate Mind*, Constable.
Hanson, R., and Mendius, R. (2009) *Buddha's Brain: The Practical Neuroscience of Happiness*, New Harbinger Publications.
Hanh, T.N. (1991) *The Miracle of Mindfulness*, Rider & Co.
Kabat-Zinn, J. (2005) *Coming to Our Senses: Healing Ourselves and the World through Mindfulness*, Piatkus.
Kabat-Zinn, J. (2013) *Full Catastrophe Living: How to Cope with Stress, Pain and Illness Using Mindfulness Meditation*, 2nd edn, Piatkus.
Kabat-Zinn, J. (1994) *Wherever You Go, There You Are: Mindfulness Meditation in Everyday Life*, Hyperion.
Kramer, G. (2007) *Insight Dialogue: The Interpersonal Path to Freedom*, Shambhala.
McCowan, D., Reibel, D., and Micozzi, M. (2011) *Teaching Mindfulness: A Practical Guide for Clinicians and Educators*, Springer.
Neff, K. (2011) *Self Compassion*, Hodder & Stroughton.
Williams, M., and Penman, D. (2011) *Mindfulness: A Practical Guide to Finding Peace in a Frantic World*, Piatkus.

Mindfulness and psychotherapy

Crane, R. (2008) *Mindfulness-Based Cognitive Therapy*, Routledge.
Germer, C.K., Siegel, R.D., and Fulton, P.R. (2013) *Mindfulness and Psychotherapy*, 2nd edn, Guildford.
Gilbert, P. (2010) *Compassion Focused Therapy*, Routledge.
Hick, S.F., and Bien, T. (eds.) (2008) *Mindfulness and the Therapeutic Relationship*, Guildford Press.
McCollum, E. E. (2015) *Mindfulness for Therapists: Practice for The Heart*, Routledge.
Segal, Z.V., Williams, J.M.G, and Teasdale, J.D. (2012) *Mindfulness-Based Cognitive Therapy for Depression: A New Approach to Preventing Relapse*, 2nd edn, Guildford Press.
Shapiro, S.L., and Carlson, L.E. (2009) *The Art and Science of Mindfulness: Integrating Mindfulness into Psychology and the Helping Professions*, American Psychological Association.

Siegel, D. J. (2007) *The Mindful Brain: Reflection and Attunement in the Cultivation of Well-Being*, W.W. Norton.
Siegel, D. J. (2010) *The Mindful Therapist: A Clinician's Guide to Mindsight and Neural Integration*, W.W. Norton.

Psychology / psychotherapy

Fredrickson, B. (2010) *Positivity: Ground-breaking Research to Release Your Inner Optimist and Thrive*, Oneworld.
Fredrickson, B. (2013) *Love 2.0: How Our Supreme Emotion Affects Everything we Feel, Think, Do and Become*, Hudson Street Press.
Gendlin, E. T. (2003) *Focusing: How To Gain Direct Access to Your Body's Knowledge*, 25th Anniversary edn, Rider.
Goleman, D. (2004) *Destructive Emotions: How Can We Overcome Them? A Scientific Dialogue with the Dalai Lama*, Bloomsbury.
Parfitt, W. (2003) *Psychosynthesis: The Elements and Beyond*, PS Avalon.
Rogers, C. R. (1980) *A Way of Being*, Houghton Mifflin.

Coaching

de Haan, E. (2008) *Relational Coaching: Journeys Towards Mastering One-To-One Learning*, John Wiley & Sons.
Gallwey, T. (2000) *The Inner Game of Work: Overcoming Mental Obstacles for Maximum Performance*, Orion Business Books.
Kline, N. (1999) *Time to Think: Listening to Ignite The Human Mind*, Cassell.
Strozzi-Heckler, R. (2014) *The Art of Somatic Coaching: Embodying Skillful Action, Wisdom, and Compassion*, North Atlantic Books.

Leadership and organisation development

Boyatzis, R., and McKee, A. (2005) *Resonant Leadership*, Harvard Business School Press.
Chaskalson, M. (2011) *The Mindful Workplace: Developing Resilient Individuals and Resonant Organisations with MBSR*, Wiley-Blackwell.
Goleman, D. (1998) *Working with Emotional Intelligence*, Bloomsbury.
McKee, A., Boyatzis, R., and Johnston, F. (2008) *Becoming a Resonant Leader*, Harvard Business School Press.
Mackey, J., Sisodia, R. (2013) *Conscious Capitalism*, Harvard Business School Press.

UK Government reports

Mindfulness All-Party Parliamentary Group (2015) *A Mindful Nation UK*, http://themindfulnessinitiative.org.uk/images/reports/Mindfulness-APPG-Report_Mindful-Nation-UK_Oct2015.pdf
The Mindfulness Initiative (2016) *Building the Case for Mindfulness in the Workplace*, http://themindfulnessinitiative.org.uk/images/reports/MI_Building-the-Case_v1.1_Oct16.pdf

Further resources and downloads

There is a website dedicated to this book, www.mindfulnessforcoaches.co.uk, which contains links and further information for those who want to explore further. Details of how to book on a Mindfulness for Coaches programme can be found there.

The following guided practices for the programme can be downloaded from Michael's website: www.mbsr.co.uk/mp31.php

Track	Title	Minutes
1	The Raisin Exercise	10
3	The Body Scan (Shorter Version)	15
4	Mindfulness of Breathing (10 Minutes)	10
5	Mindfulness of Breathing (5 Minutes)	5
7	Mindful Movement (Shorter Version)	15
8	Three-Step Breathing Space	3
9	Walking Meditation	10
10	Mindfulness of the Breath and Body	10
11	Mindfulness of Sounds and Thoughts	10
13	Sitting With The Difficult	10
16	20 Minute Sitting Meditation	20

Anyone wishing to deliver mindfulness training in the workplace should first of all be trained themselves, both in mindfulness and in mindfulness instruction (see below). They should keep up their own practice and follow the 'Good Practice Guidelines for Teaching Mindfulness-Based Courses' laid out in Appendix C.

If you wish to find an eight-week MBSR course in the UK the website www.bemindful.co.uk is a good place to look for one local to you.

In the USA, the Centre for Mindfulness in Medicine, Health Care, and Society is where it all started: www.umassmed.edu/cfm/ . They offer a range of programmes and their website offers links to a host of local practitioners in the USA and elsewhere. As they note, however, they don't vouch for the quality of these.

Google may also help to locate a course for you if you search for 'MBSR'. But beware – not everyone offering MBSR these days is qualified to do so. Check credentials carefully. If in doubt, phone the instructor and have a chat.

There are mindfulness teacher-training courses available in different parts of the world and a web search in your own location will be more up to date than this list could be. Details of mindfulness teacher-training providers in the UK can be found at www.mindfulnessteachersuk.org.uk.

The Centre for Mindfulness Research and Practice, which is part of the School of Psychology at Bangor University, is where we both trained. They offer a master's degree in mindfulness-based approaches and hold regular seven-day teacher-training retreats for those who have an established mindfulness practice. See www.bangor.ac.uk/mindfulness.

At the time of writing there is a masterclass series at the Oxford Mindfulness Centre that offers workplace-specific sessions. This is being carried out in conjunction with the Centre for Mindfulness Research and Practice at Bangor University and is intended to be a precursor to a training pathway for those interested in teaching in workplace settings. For more information, visit: http://oxfordmindfulness.org/business-homepage/events/omc-masterclasses/

Index

Note: Page numbers in *italic* refer to figures

acceptance 9, 90, 97, 100–101, 131–132, 160, 175, 176, 178; mindfulness practice 109, 132
action logics 194, 195, *196–197*
active listening 158–162, 164, 179
'allowing' attitude 37, 38, 61, 63, 111, 152–153
amygdala 4, 87, 140
anger 33, 102, 124, 140, 142
antidepressants 5, 6
anxiety 9, 39, 40, 113, 134, 140, 157
'approaching' attitude 37, 38, 40, 61, 63, 165
approach systems 39, 40
Åsberg, M. 74
Ashton, A. 88, 110, 114, 117, 151
Assagioli, R. 124
Association for Coaching (AC) 146
Association for Professional Executive Coaching & Supervision (APECS) 146
attending empathically to the felt sense of a conversation 73
attention 17, 30, 56, 113, 152–153; paying attention 6–8, 18, 19, 20, 25–26, 152, 157–158, 165, 190; wandering mind 7–8, 13, 16, 17–19, 20, 21, 34, 131, 177–178
attitude 17, 18–19, 108, 111, 133, 149; 'allowing' 37, 38, 61, 63, 111, 152–153; 'approaching' 37, 38, 40, 61, 63, 165
attunement 71, 72, 86, 110, 132, 135, 136–139, 151, 156
automatic routines 13–15
autonomy 121
avoidance systems 39, 40

Bartley, T. 31
behavioural activation system (BAS) 40
behavioural iceberg *192*
Berne, E. 120, 121
biotech company (example) 39
Bluckert, P. 68, 69
bodily awareness 30, 31–32, 33
body language 115, 149, 156, 160, 168, 171
body scan meditation 23–25, 26, 27, 35, 46, 101, 115
body sensations 31, 32, 55, 123, 124, 132–133, 137
Boyatzis, R. 203, 204
brain 4, 19, 38–39, 40, 61, 72, 86, 87, 142
breath 15–16; Three Step Breathing Space 32, 42–44, 49, 66, 90
breathing meditation 15, 16, 17–19, 21, 27, 35, 46, 48, 49, 61
Brendgen, J. 91–92, 95, 107, 109, 122, 149, 151, 158
Briner, W. 95
Broaden and Build theory 83, *84*, 84–85
Brown, B. 195
Buddha 3, 6
burnout 74, 96, 129, 204, 205

cancer survivor (example) 58, *59*, 60
Carlson, L. E. 96
Cavicchia, S. 114, 116, 157, 163, 166, 169, 171, 178
Chaskalson, M. 69–70, 75, 76, 182–183, 184, 199, 206
chronic pain 4
coaches 6, 7, 10, 68, 73, 76, 92–94; emotional regulation 133; mindfulness practice 10, 11; mindfulness training 61; positivity resonance 87–88; secondary traumatic stress 101, 102; self-compassion 102, 104

Index

coaching approaches 107, 126; cognitive behavioural therapy 5, 117–118; Focusing 123–124; Gestalt 115–117; Inner Game 118–120; person-centred approach 107–110, 113; psychodynamic approach 121–122; Psychosynthesis 124–125; Relational Coaching 113–114; somatic coaching 122–123; Time to Think approach 110–113; Transactional Analysis 120–121
coaching competencies 145, 146–147, 153–157, 179–180
coaching exercises: attending empathically to the felt sense of a conversation 73; focusing attention within 47–48; noticing judgements 65
coaching mastery 146, 150–151, 153–154, 159, 162–164, 165, 167, 170–173, 176, 177, 179–180
coaching profession 92, 110, 128, 146
coaching relationship 61, 68–69, 91, 95–96, 104, 113–114, 122, 126–127, 142, 145–147, 152–155, 179–180
coaching standards 146
coach training 111–112, 128, 130, 146, 180
cognitive behaviour therapy (CBT) 5, 117–118; Mindfulness-Based Cognitive Therapy 5–6, 93, 117–118
Cohen-Katz, J. *et al.* 129
compassion 8–9, 14, 90, 97, 99, 103, 139, 142, 152, 178–179
Compassionate Mind Training (CMT) 139, 142
compassion fatigue 95–96, 103, 104, 129
Compassion Focused Therapy (CFT) 139
congruence 61, 68–69, 108, 109
conscious capitalism 193, 200–201
conscious cultures 201
conscious leadership 201, 202, 203
Consumer Insights 30
contemplations 90
Cook-Greuter, S. 194, 195, 198, 199
countertransference 90, 91, 122, 133
Cruse, S. 124, 178

Davidson, R. J. 38–39, 40
Davidson, S. 198
Davey, J. 154, 161, 168
decentering 5, 58, 60, 134
de Haan, E. 68, 113, 145
delusion 42
depression 4–5, 6, 9, 40
designing actions 173–174, 179–180

difficult emotions 101–102, 104
digital devices 30–31
direct communication 170–172, 179–180
discomforts 16, 37–38
dis-identification 124, 125
Donaldson-Feilder, E. 94, 146
Downey, M. 118, 119

eating meditation 11–13
edge of our comfort zone 36–38
ego states 120, 121
Ekman, P. 33, 86, 115, 161
emotion acceptance 141
emotional awareness 132, 190, 203
emotional intelligence (EQ) 188–189, *189*, 190–191, 202
emotional reactivity 98, 133, 134, 135, 152, 168, 172–173
emotional regulation 132–133
emotional states 31, 33, 134, 203–204
emotion-regulation systems 139–141, *140*
empathy 60, 68–70, 71, 91, 109–110, 129
English, E. 123
EQ *see* emotional intelligence
equanimity 15, 90, 91, 133
eudaimonic well-being 57, 58
European Mentoring & Coaching Council (EMCC) 146
events diary 27, 48–49
evolution 30
exhaustion funnel 74, *74*
experiential mode 34, 35, 54, 55, 56, 118
eye contact 86, 87

Facial Action Coding System (FACS) 161
facial expressions 33, 86, 112, 115, 149, 156, 157, 161
Farb, N. A. 34–35, 55, 56–57, 58
feelings 20, 21–22
Feerick, L. 173
Fisher, A. 94
Five Factor Mindfulness Questionnaire (FFMQ) 69–70
Focusing 123–124
focusing attention within 47–48
forget and remember: attitude 18–19; intention 18, 19; meditation 17–20; paying attention 18, 19
formal mindfulness practice 45–46, 56, 76, 77, 184
frames of mind 52–53
Fredrickson, B. L. 56–57, 58, 83, 84, 85–86, 87, 88, 89, 111
Fulton, P. R. 93, 128, 130

Gallwey, W. T. 118, 119, 120, 148
Garland, E. L. 56–57, 58
Gendlin, E. T. 123–124
generative attention 110, 112, 113, 179
Germer, C. K. 93, 97, 99, 102–103, 105, 128, 130
Gervais, K. 162, 172
Gestalt 115–117
Gilbert, D. T. 7–8
Gilbert, P. 105, 139, 140, 142
Gillie, M. 115, 116
Giving and Receiving Compassion 102
Global Coaching & Mentoring Alliance (GCMA) 146
Goldin, P. R. 56–57, 58
Goleman, D. 188, 189, 190
Good Practice Guidelines for Teaching Mindfulness-Based Courses 93, 213–214
Gooster, L. 107, 110, 162
Govani, F. 101, 113, 146, 148, 154, 155, 161, 169, 172
Grepmair, L. *et al.* 129
guidelines (meditation instructions) 89–90, 91

happiness 4, 8, 15, 39, 100, 103
Hasson, U. 86
health benefits 9–10, 76–77, 94–95, 129
hedonic well-being 57
Henry, W. *et al.* 132
home exercises 26–27, 48–49, 65–66, 77–78
horizontal development 191, 194, 199
human beings 13, 16, 30, 71–72, 100
human body 16, 30, 31, 72

ICF *see* International Coach Federation
impulses 20, 21–22
informal mindfulness practice 45, 46, 76
inner climate 31, 32, 33
Inner Game 118–120
Insight Dialogue (ID) 89–92
intention 17
interference 119, 154–155
International Coach Federation (ICF) 146, 150–151, 153–154, 156, 158–159, 160, 165, 167, 170, 173, 175–176, 177
interpersonal meditation 89
interpersonal mindfulness 83, 89
Interpersonal Mindfulness Program (IMP) 89–92, 109
Interpersonal Reactivity Index (IRI) 69–71
interpretation 52–53
intimate detachment 135, 151, 166

Johnston, F. 203, 204
Johnston, H. R. 118, 155, 177
just like me practice 72–73, 190

Kabat-Zinn, J. 3–4, 5–6, 39, 117, 166; mindfulness 6–7, 8, 164, 193
Kegan, R. 194–195
Kermode, R. 148
key cognitive skills 20, 56, 186–187
Killingsworth, M. A. 7–8
Kimsey-House, H. 160–161
kindness 9, 37, 69, 88–89, 90, 98
Kline, N. 25, 110–112, 113, 157
Kozak, A. 95, 118, 167
Kramer, G. 89, 90, 91, 109

Lambert, M. 130
leaders 181–182, 183, 186–187, 188, 189, 193–194, 195, 198, 203–204, 206; conscious leadership 201, 202, 203; mindful leaders 204–205
leadership development 182–183, 184–186, 190, 191, 193, 195, 199, 200
Leahy, R. L. 141
letting go 160, 175, 176, 178
LKM *see* loving-kindness meditation
London Underground (example) 21–22
love 85
Love 2.0 (Fredrickson, 2013) 85
loving-kindness 15, 88, 99, 142
loving-kindness meditation (LKM) 88–89, 190
lying meditation 46; body scan meditation 23–25, 26, 27, 35, 46, 101, 115

Mackey, J. 200, 201, 202, 203
McCartney, L. 131
McCollum, E. E. 129
McKee, A. 203, 204
McMordie, M. 188, 189, 190
'Managing Progress & Accountability' 177–180
MBCT *see* Mindfulness-Based Cognitive Therapy
MBSR *see* Mindfulness-Based Stress Reduction
meditation 3, 10, 15, 17–20, 45–47, 61, 65–66, 183; body scan meditation 23–25, 26, 27, 35, 46, 101, 115; breathing meditation 15, 16, 17–19, 21, 27, 35, 46, 48, 49, 61; decentring 5, 58, 60, 134; eating meditation 11–13; 'mindfulness of breath and body' meditation 44–45, 46, 61
meditation instructions 89–90, 91

meditation practices 10, 15
meditators, experienced 39, 133
mental models 153, 159, 162–163
meta-capacities 186, 205
metacognition 56–57, 58, 60, 124, 190
micro expressions 33, 86, 115, 149, 151, 156–157, 161, 171
mindful attention 22, 64, 113, 114, 116, 119–120, 130–131, 161, 166, 169
mindful awareness 71, 98, 109, 116, 131–132, 136, 164–166
Mindful Leader programme 182–183, 184–186, 187–188, 199
mindful leaders 186, 204–205
mindful leadership, theory of 186, *187*
mindful-movement stretches 35–36, 37–38, 46
Mindful Nation UK report (2015) 205, 206
mindfulness 3–4, 5–11, 14–15, 21, 97, 98, 183–184, 191, 193, 199, 203
Mindfulness-Based Cognitive Therapy (MBCT) 5–6, 93, 117–118
Mindfulness-Based Stress Reduction (MBSR) 4, 103, 129
Mindfulness Initiative (2016) 205, 206
'mindfulness of breath and body' meditation 44–45, 46, 61
'mindfulness of breathing' meditation 15, 16, 17–19, 21, 27, 35, 46, 48, 49, 61
mindfulness practice 10–11, 17, 21, 61, 76–77, 83, 109–110, 122, 126, 191–193; acceptance 109, 132; breath 16; health benefits 9–10, 76–77, 94–95, 129; presence 131; unconditional positive regard 107; wandering mind 131
Mindfulness Report (UK, 2010) 9–10
mindfulness teaching 77, 92–93
mindfulness-to-meaning theory *57*, 57–58, *59*
mindfulness training 5, 6, 8, 9, 15, 20, 92, 93, 130–133; amygdala 4; bodily awareness 33; body sensations 31; health benefits 9–10; MBSR 4
Mindful Self Compassion (MSC) programme 99, 105
mindful stretching 35–36, 37–38, 46
mind modes 34–35, 39, 54, 55
monkeys (example) 32

narrative mode 34, 35, 54, 55, 56, 118
Neff, K. 98, 99, 101, 105
negative emotions 84, 102, 103

nervous systems 4
neural coupling 86, 87
neural systems 71, 72, 156
neuroception 136, 156
NICE (National Institute for Health and Clinical Excellence, UK) 6
non-judgmental approach 8–9, 114, 174, 176, 177, 178, 179
non-striving approach 160, 174, 178
non-verbal communication 160–161
Norcross, J. 130
Norcross, J. *et al.* 142
noticing judgements 65

openness 69, 85, 88–89
organisations 181, 188–189, 191, 198, 205–206
Ortner, C. *et al.* 133
oxytocin 86–87

Passmore, J. 147
patience 160, 174, 176
patients 3, 4, 129; *see also* therapeutic relationship
paying attention 6–8, 18, 19, 20, 25–26, 152, 157–158, 165, 190
person-centred approach 107–110, 113
Petrie, N. 192–193, 194, 198–199
physical barometer 31–32
Piaget, J. 194
planning and goal setting 175–177, 179–180
pleasant-events diary 27
Polman, P. 181
Porges, S. 136, 141, 156
positive emotions 40, 57, 58, 60, 83–85, 88–89
positive reappraisal 40, 57, 58, 60
positivity resonance 85–88, 89
posture 16
powerful questioning 167–170, 179–180
practising therapists 61, 94, 108, 127, 128, 145; acceptance 132; attunement 132; compassion fatigue 103; emotional regulation 133; meditation 129; presence 131; secondary traumatic stress 95; self-compassion 97, 98, 104; therapeutic relationship 128, 129, 130
prefrontal cortex 4, 38–39, 40, 72
presence 34, 35, 113, 131, 135–136, 147–151, 167
pressure-performance curve *41*, 41–42
psychodynamic approach 121–122
Psychosynthesis 124–125
psychotherapy 94, 104, 128, 142

Radical Acceptance 100, 104
raisin exercise 11–13
reaction 61, 63, 66
Read, J. 153, 164
reading others 32–33, 72
Reitz, M. 76, 182–183, 184, 199, 206
relapsing depression 4, 5, 6
Relational Coaching 113–114
relaxed concentration 119, 120, 148
re-perceiving 134–135
resilience 57, 71, 129, 184, 185, 205
resonance 136, 138–139, 151, 171
resonant leadership 203
response 61, 63, 66
Rogers, C. R. 60, 61, 68, 107, 108–109, 110, 113, 127, 131
Ross, A. 169
routine activities 26, 27

Sack, R. 148, 176
Sandahl, P. 160–161
sati-sampajañña 6
Schermuly, C. C. 96
Schwartz, G. 134
secondary traumatic stress 95–96, 101, 102, 103
Segal, Z. V. 4, 5–6, 93
self-awareness 69, 109, 124–125, 190, 203
self-care 96–97
self-compassion 83, 97–99, 100, 102–103, 104, 105
self-kindness 98
self-regulation 121, 134–135, 172–173
sensations 20, 21–22, 23–25, 31, 34, 55
senses 21, 34
Shapiro, S. L. 96–97, 133, 134, 151
Shapiro, S. L. *et al.* 129
Siegel, D. J. 34, 93, 138, 157, 203; attunement 71, 110, 132, 137, 156; presence 131, 135, 136, 149
Siegel, R. D. 128, 130
sitting meditation 16, 45–46
'sitting with the difficult' meditation 61–63
smiles 86, 87
Soften, Soothe and Allow 101–102
somatic coaching 122–123
Sosidia, R. 200, 201, 202, 203
sounds and thoughts meditation 63–65
stakeholders 200–201
standing meditation 46
stress 4, 40–42, 66, 90, 95–96, 103, 204, 205

stress signatures 42
suffering 98, 99, 100, 101
supervision 101, 103
Systems Intelligence (SYQ) 202–203

TA *see* Transactional Analysis
taking care of ourselves 73–76
taxi drivers, London 19
Teasdale, J. D. 4, 5–6, 93
therapeutic relationship 68, 69, 117, 128, 129–130
thoughts 20, 21–22, 52–53, 55–56
three step breathing space 32, 42–44, 49, 66, 90
Time to Think approach *25*, 110–113
Torbert, W. 194
Transactional Analysis (TA) 120–121
transference 104, 122
trust 86, 153–154, 156, 160, 175, 178, 179
Turner, S. 155, 171

uncomfortable emotions 101–102
unconditional positive regard 60, 68–69, 83, 104, 109, 153, 154
Unilever Sustainable Living Plan 181
unpleasant-events diary 48–49
US Marines (case study) 4, 10

vagal tone 87, 88
vagus nerve 86, 87
validation 141
vertical development 191, 193–195, 198–199
VUCA (volatile, uncertain, complex, ambiguous) world 193, 198, 204, 206

walking meditation 46–47
wandering mind 7–8, 13, 16, 17–19, 20, 21, 34, 131, 177–178; *see also* paying attention
well-being 4, 9–10, 75–76, 129, 205
Whitworth, L. 160–161
Williams, J. M. G. 4, 5–6, 93
wisdom 8, 9, 103, 178, 203
witness consciousness 104, 124, 125, 126, 133, 199
Wittenberg, L. 94, 110, 114, 116–117, 150, 153, 155, 165, 168, 172, 175, 176
Woodward, S. 95, 148, 162
working-memory capacity 4, 10
working relationally with present moment attention 25–26
World Health Organization 5

Taylor & Francis eBooks

Helping you to choose the right eBooks for your Library

Add Routledge titles to your library's digital collection today. Taylor and Francis ebooks contains over 50,000 titles in the Humanities, Social Sciences, Behavioural Sciences, Built Environment and Law.

Choose from a range of subject packages or create your own!

Benefits for you
- Free MARC records
- COUNTER-compliant usage statistics
- Flexible purchase and pricing options
- All titles DRM-free.

Benefits for your user
- Off-site, anytime access via Athens or referring URL
- Print or copy pages or chapters
- Full content search
- Bookmark, highlight and annotate text
- Access to thousands of pages of quality research at the click of a button.

REQUEST YOUR FREE INSTITUTIONAL TRIAL TODAY
Free Trials Available
We offer free trials to qualifying academic, corporate and government customers.

eCollections – Choose from over 30 subject eCollections, including:

Archaeology	Language Learning
Architecture	Law
Asian Studies	Literature
Business & Management	Media & Communication
Classical Studies	Middle East Studies
Construction	Music
Creative & Media Arts	Philosophy
Criminology & Criminal Justice	Planning
Economics	Politics
Education	Psychology & Mental Health
Energy	Religion
Engineering	Security
English Language & Linguistics	Social Work
Environment & Sustainability	Sociology
Geography	Sport
Health Studies	Theatre & Performance
History	Tourism, Hospitality & Events

For more information, pricing enquiries or to order a free trial, please contact your local sales team:
www.tandfebooks.com/page/sales

 Routledge — Taylor & Francis Group The home of Routledge books

www.tandfebooks.com

For Product Safety Concerns and Information please contact our EU
representative GPSR@taylorandfrancis.com
Taylor & Francis Verlag GmbH, Kaufingerstraße 24, 80331 München, Germany

www.ingramcontent.com/pod-product-compliance
Lightning Source LLC
Chambersburg PA
CBHW050532300426

44113CB00012B/2057